Media semiotics

D0416143

MANCHESTER
UNIVERSITY PRESS

Jonathan Bignell

Media semiotics

AN INTRODUCTION

Second edition

Manchester University Press

Manchester and New York

distributed exclusively in the USA by Palgrave

Copyright © Jonathan Bignell 1997, 2002

The right of Jonathan Bignell to be identified as the author of this work has been asserted by him in accordance with the Copyright, Designs and Patents Act 1988

First edition published by Manchester University Press
Reprinted 1998, 1999, 2001

This edition published 2002
by Manchester University Press
Oxford Road, Manchester M13 9NR, UK
and Room 400, 175 Fifth Avenue, New York, NY 10010, USA
www.manchesteruniversitypress.co.uk

Distributed exclusively in the USA
by Palgrave, 175 Fifth Avenue, New York,
NY 10010, USA

Distributed exclusively in Canada
by UBC Press, University of British Columbia, 2029 West Mall,
Vancouver, BC, Canada V6T 1Z2

British Library Cataloguing-in-Publication Data
A catalogue record is available from the British Library

Library of Congress Cataloging-in-Publication Data applied for

ISBN 0 7190 6205 5 paperback

This edition first published 2002

10 09 08 07 06 05   10 9 8 7 6 5 4 3

ST HELENS
COLLEGE

302.23
BIG

137404

June 2019

LIBRARY

Typeset in Photina
by Northern Phototypesetting Co Ltd, Bolton
Printed in Great Britain
by Bell & Bain Ltd, Glasgow

To Victor and Janet Bignell

Contents

List of illustrations

Preface and acknowledgements

The first edition of this book was published in 1997, and arose from my experience of teaching a course called 'Media Semiotics'. Each year a group of undergraduates explored semiotic theories in relation to words, still images and moving images in a range of contemporary media. At least one person always asked whether there was one really useful book that I could recommend. Such a book would introduce the key theoretical issues, demonstrate how they can be applied, discuss the various problems which media material presents to semiotic theories, and outline the shortcomings of semiotic analysis as well as its strengths. The book would work as a course text, with progression from topic to topic, and would also be an aid to revision and further work after the end of the course. *Media Semiotics: An Introduction* aims to achieve these objectives, and the first edition has been widely used by students studying media. Since 1997 I have received many useful comments from tutors and students about the book, and the new edition incorporates revised and extended sections which take account of this feedback. The media landscape has changed since 1997, especially in the growing importance of 'new media' (the Internet, interactive software, mobile communications, etc.). This new edition of *Media Semiotics* includes revisions to all the chapters to bring them up to date, and also includes new sections on recent media developments.

I would like to repeat the acknowledgements to people who helped directly or indirectly with the first edition of this book: to tutors who inspired my work, including Stephen Heath and Stuart Laing; to supportive colleagues in my former post at the University of Reading; to former postgraduate students whose ideas influenced my own, including Tania Christidis and Ian Stewart; and to all those students who have taken my course in Media Semiotics and road-tested the ideas in this book. The work on the second edition has been made easier by the supportive environment of the Department of Media Arts at Royal Holloway,

University of London, and I would like to pay tribute to the staff and students I work with there. In particular, conversations with students working with semiotic methods have helped me to think through some of the material in this edition, and I am grateful to Andrew O'Day, Dee Amy-Chin, Georgina Massie, Helen Quinney, and many others.

Illustrations are an important but sometimes problematic aspect of books about the media, and I would like to thank those people who helped me to obtain the illustrations in this edition, especially the staff of BBC Picture Archives, and David Sutcliffe for photographing three of the illustrated items. For copyright permissions, I gratefully acknowledge TBWA for the Wonderbra advertisement, DMP DDB Needham for the VW Golf Estate advertisement photographed by Malcolm Venville, and BBC Picture Archive for the stills from BBC programmes.

I am grateful to Mike Cormack for his helpful comments on the original proposal for the book, and to Sean Cubitt for his careful reading of the manuscript of the first edition. Manchester University Press has enthusiastically supported the second edition, and I am grateful to its staff for their encouragement and close involvement in this and other projects. Louise Allen provided valuable help in suggesting ways of making the second edition more useful in teaching, and I am also grateful to the other tutors who have provided feedback. Lib Taylor has been there throughout the evolution of the book, and I thank her once again for her support, encouragement and love.

Introduction

Every day we encounter and make use of a huge variety of media. Some of them fall into the category habitually referred to as 'the media', like newspapers, magazines, television, cinema or radio. All of these are obviously communications media, which make available a wide range of messages and meanings. But the term 'media' refers more widely to all those things which are channels for communicating something. If we widen the term 'media' to include anything which is used as a channel for communicating meanings, a large part of our experience of the world involves interactions with media. Walking down the street, all kinds of messages are being generated for us by, for instance, shop signs, posters, and traffic lights. Even the people passing by are generating meanings by virtue of the kind of clothes they are wearing, or their hairstyles. Meanings are being made everywhere, through a huge variety of different channels of communication, a huge variety of media. Since media in this broad sense are so important to the experience of living in society, it is clearly both useful and interesting to find a way of understanding how these media are meaningful to us.

In recent times, one of the most powerful and influential ways of thinking about media has been the approach known as semiotics (or semiology). The names semiotics and semiology derive from the ancient Greek word *semeion*, which means 'sign'. Semiotics or semiology is a way of analysing meanings by looking at the signs (like words, for instance, but also pictures, symbols etc.) which communicate meanings. Because society is so pervaded by media messages, semiotics can contribute to far more than our understanding of 'the media' in the narrow sense of mass media products like those discussed in the following pages. The power of the semiotic approach lies partly in its applicability to the much wider field of meaning-making which includes, for instance, fashion, theatre, dance, literature, and architecture. But this book has been written primarily for students of the media, for use as part of courses in Media Studies,

Cultural Studies, or Communications Studies for instance. Therefore this book deals with the semiotic approach partly by conducting critical analyses of recent material in 'the media' of advertising, magazines, newspapers, television, cinema, and the 'new media' of mobile communications, interactive television, the Internet and computer games. The analyses of these different kinds of written and audio-visual media are used to introduce, discuss and evaluate semiotic methods, and to show how this method can be extended or challenged by other approaches.

My primary focus is on how semiotics can be used in the study of the media, because of the assumption that meanings in the media are communicated by signs, and semiotics is concerned with the question of how signs work. Semiotics was first developed as a way of understanding how language works, and language is the medium which we use most often. We use language to communicate by speaking and by writing, and much of 'the media' uses language either as the primary medium of communication, or to support other media of communication like pictures, for instance. Semiotic analysis has been extended to the analysis of non-linguistic media of communication, and chapter 1 takes up the initial linguistic focus of semiotics by explaining its approach to language and then to visual signs. The chapters which follow build on these foundations and explore how semiotics can be used in the study of advertising, magazines, newspapers, television, cinema, and 'interactive media'. Like every analytical method, semiotics makes use of some technical language, has drawn on insights which come from other related disciplines, and has evolved and changed over time. In this book, some of the terminology of semiotics is explained, some ideas which it has borrowed from other disciplines are discussed, and some developments of semiotics in response to new challenges and difficulties are assessed.

This book assumes no prior knowledge about semiotics. It does assume a basic familiarity with the kinds of media found in British and American culture. It will be enough to have noticed some advertisements, to have read some newspapers, read some magazines, watched some television, been to the cinema, and used a personal computer, for instance. As I have already hinted, this book is not just an introduction to media semiotics, it is a critical introduction. Key ideas from semiotic approaches to the media are discussed in the chapters which follow, but these ideas are also tested out, modified, and their limitations explored. There is no perfect analytical method for studying the media since different theoretical approaches define their tasks, the objects they study, or the questions they ask in different ways. For instance, at one extreme it could be argued that meanings in the media can be understood by doing a very detailed analysis of media texts (like newspapers or television programmes). At the other extreme, it could be argued that meanings in the media can be understood by asking individuals how they interact personally with media in their own lives. These two positions are oversimplified caricatures of, respectively, a very rigid kind of semiotic analysis known as structuralism, and a recently developed kind of media research known as ethnography. Clearly, each of them takes a quite different approach to what appears to be the same issue.

This book takes a position somewhere between those two extremes. These are the five basic assumptions which underlie my approach to meanings in the media. First, the patterns and structures of signs in media texts condition the meanings which can be communicated and understood. Second, the signs in media texts are understood in relation to other signs and other texts in a social and cultural context. Third, each medium has features specific to it and features which are shared with other media. Fourth, texts and media position their audiences in particular ways, and audiences understand and enjoy the media in different and diverse ways. Fifth, studying the negotiation of meanings between media and audiences is important in understanding the ways that we think about ourselves and our culture. These assumptions form the basis of the issues which are explored and discussed in the chapters which follow, though the weight given to each of them varies. This often reflects the different emphases of academic approaches to the different media, because the study of the media is not a homogenous subject, though there are overlaps between currents of critical thinking as well as relatively discrete areas. In writing this book, I have aimed to maintain a consistent focus on semiotic analysis, while at the same time acknowledging other ways of studying the media to some extent. Some of these different academic approaches (like psychoanalytic criticism) add weight to semiotics, while others (like ethnographic research) are virtually opposed to it.

There are alternative ways in which this book could have been organised, around theoretical issues for instance, or by following the history of developments in a particular field of study. I have chosen the present structure because it seems the clearest for a teaching and learning context. The order and emphases of each chapter should enable the reader to gain an understanding of critical discourses developed in semiotics for each medium and to pick up the common conceptual strands which link the study of these media together. In a similar way, challenges to semiotics are gradually posed as the book proceeds, and are exemplified in relation to particular examples and cases in the various media which my chapters discuss. Each chapter has a section at the end called *Sources and further reading*, which notes important and accessible works for the reader who wishes to follow up semiotic studies of the relevant medium, and also cites works which are critical of semiotics. For greater clarity and ease of use, I have collected the majority of references together in these sections, rather than citing a mass of books in the text itself. A section called *Suggestions for further work* also appears at the end of each chapter, with seven tasks and questions which encourage readers actively to make use of semiotics and other approaches to the media which are relevant to the issues raised in the chapter.

1

Signs and myths

The semiotic point of view

Semiotics originates mainly in the work of two people, Ferdinand de Saussure, and Charles Peirce. Their ideas are quite closely related, but exhibit some differences, so I am going to explain some of their major insights separately in this chapter, and then indicate the kind of synthesis between them which is referred to as simply 'semiotics' in this book. Saussure was an academic who taught linguistics at the University of Geneva in the early twentieth century. His *Course in General Linguistics* was published in French in 1915, three years after his death. Saussure's book is a reconstruction of a series of lectures that he gave on language, assembled from the notes taken by his students and jottings discovered by his colleagues. The book explains his groundbreaking view of language, and was a major contribution to the discipline of linguistics. But Saussure viewed linguistics as only one part (though a privileged part) of a much broader science which he predicted would one day exist, a science which he called semiology. Both semiology and semiotics get their names from the Greek word *semeion*, which means sign, and they both refer to the study of how signs communicate meanings. Semiotics is now the more common name for this kind of study. Saussure showed that language is made up of signs (like words) which communicate meanings, and he expected that all kinds of other things which communicate meanings could potentially be studied in the same way as linguistic signs, using the same methods of analysis.

Semiotics or semiology, then, is the study of signs in society, and while the study of linguistic signs is one branch of it, it encompasses every use of a system where something (the sign) carries a meaning for someone. Much of this book is concerned with the semiotic analysis of language, but much of it is also concerned with non-linguistic things (like photographs, for instance) which carry meanings for someone. The same semiotic approach can be used to discuss language-based media and image-based media, because in either case we find signs which carry meanings. Since language is the most fundamental and pervasive medium for human communication, semiotics takes the way that language works as the model for all other media of communication, all other sign systems. That is the way in which this book proceeds; explaining some of semiotics' insights into how language works, and expanding this semiotic method to other media in society.

It is usual to assume that words and other kinds of sign are secondary to our perception and understanding of reality. It seems that reality is out there all around us, and language usefully names real things and the relationships between them. So, for example, the world contains lots of very young people, and language provides the word 'children' to identify them. But by contrast, Saussure proposed that our perception and understanding of reality is constructed by the words and other signs which we use. From Saussure's semiotic perspective, the sign 'children' enables us to think of these very young people as a group who are distinct from 'adults', and who share common features. But different social groups, at different places around the world, at different times in history, have used the distinction between 'children' and 'adults' in different ways. Being referred to as a 'child' might have to do with age, legal status, religious status, physical ability, or many other things. Culture and society decide what the sign 'child' means, rather than nature or biology. What makes the sign 'child' meaningful to us is the distinction between 'child' and 'adult', according to the conventions which are normal in our culture.

At the same time as language and sign systems shape our reality, they are also media in which to communicate about this reality. A system of signs which works in this way has to be thought of as a medium in a more extended sense than the way that a medium is conventionally thought of. A medium is conventionally something which acts as a channel, passing something from one place to another. For example, sound is passed to our ears through the medium of air, and electricity travels to our homes though the medium of electrical cable. But if language and other sign systems are not simply channels, if they give form and meaning to thought and experience instead of just naming what was already there, then there is nothing which exists before signs and media communicate thought and experience. [Rather than thinking of signs and media as channels which translate pre-existing thought and reality into communicable form, signs and media are the only means of access to thought or reality which we have.]

This is one reason why Saussure's work is so important. Although Saussure never made this leap, his semiotic method, showing how we are surrounded by and shaped by sign systems, leads to the realisation that consciousness and experience are built out of language and the other sign systems circulating in society that have existed before we take them up and use them. Language was already there before we were born, and all of our lives are lived through the signs which language gives us to think, speak, and write with. All of our thought and experience, our very sense of our own identity, depends on the systems of signs already existing in society which give form and meaning to consciousness and reality. Semiotics reminds us, for example, that it is language which enables us to refer uniquely to ourselves by giving us the sign 'I', and that language gives us the words which divide up our reality in meaningful ways.

We shall be returning to these complex ideas about the self and reality later in this book, and testing them out in relation to some concrete examples. But perhaps it is already evident at this stage that thinking about signs, media and meaning in semiotic terms will have large implications for the ways in which the self, identity, reality, and society are understood. Before getting too carried away by the general thrust of these ideas, we need to be specific about how Saussure's view of language works. In doing this, some of the recurring semiotic terminology used later in this book can be explained, and we can also move from thinking mainly about language to considering visual signs with the help of some ideas developed by the American philosopher Charles Peirce.

Sign systems

Saussure's first move was to set limits to the variety of tasks which his study of language might involve. Instead of considering language from a psychological, sociological, or physiological point of view, he decided to focus on a clearly defined object of study: the linguistic sign. He showed that the linguistic sign is arbitrary. The linguistic sign 'cat' is arbitrary in that it has no connection either in its sound, or its visual shape, with what cats are really like. In another language, the sign for cat will be different from the linguistic sign in English (e.g. French uses *chat*). Clearly, there must be a kind of agreement among the users of our language that the sign 'cat' shall refer to a particular group of furry four-legged animals. But this agreement about signs is not consciously entered into, since we learn how to use language so early in our lives that there can be no deliberate choice available to us. Language has always been there before we arrived on the scene. Even if I perversely decided to adopt another sign for what we call a cat, like 'yarup' for instance, this sign would be entirely useless since no-one else would understand me. The capacity of linguistic signs to be meaningful depends on their existence in a social context, and on their conventionally accepted use in that social context.

Each linguistic sign has a place in the whole system of language (in Saussure's original French, *langue*), and any example of actual speech or writing (in French, *parole*) uses some particular elements from the system. This distinction is the same as that between, for instance, the system of rules and conventions called chess, and the particular moves made in an actual game of chess. Each individual move in chess is selected from the whole system of possible chess moves. So we could call the system of possible chess moves the *langue* of chess. Any individual move in a game of chess would be *parole*, the selection of a move from the whole set of possible moves allowed in the *langue* of chess.

The same distinction can be made about language. In English, there is a huge range of meaningful utterances which a speaker (or writer) can make. In order for an utterance to be meaningful, it has to conform to the system of rules in the English language. The whole system of rules governing which utterances are possible is the *langue* of English, and any utterance that is actually made is an example of *parole*. *Langue* is the structure of rules which can be partially glimpsed in any concrete example of *parole*. The linguistic signs of *parole* are only meaningful if they are used in accordance with the rules of *langue*. The first two important ideas from Saussure then are that first, linguistic signs are arbitrary and agreed by convention, and second that language is a system governed by rules, where each instance of speech or writing involves selecting signs and using them according to these rules.

Each sign in *langue* acquires its value by virtue of its difference from all the other signs in *langue*, the language system. We recognise the sign 'cat' by its difference in sound and in written letters from 'bat' or 'cap' or 'cot' or 'top', for example. Saussure described language as a system which has no positive terms, and by this he meant that signs have no special right to mean something in particular and not something else. Instead, signs acquire their potential meaningfulness by contrasting themselves with what they are not. 'Cat' is not 'bat' or 'cot'. So language is a system of differences between one sign and all others, where the difference between one sign and the others allows distinctions of meaning to be made. At any point in time it is the difference of one sign from all other existing signs which allows that sign to work. So no sign can have meaning except inasmuch as it is differentiated from the other signs in *langue*. 'Cat' works as a sign by being different from 'bat', rather than by any internal property of the sign 'cat' itself.

Written or spoken languages are only one example of what Saussure believed to be the feature which characterises the human animal: that we make use of structures of signs which communicate meanings for us. Just as language can be investigated to discover how *langue* is structured as a system, allowing us to communicate with linguistic signs, the same kind of investigation can be carried out on any medium in which meanings are generated by a system of signs. Saussure's linguistics shows the way in which semiotics operates, by seeking to understand the system of *langue* which underlies all the particular instances of *parole* in a signifying system. Semioticians search for the systems which underlie the ability of signs like words, images, items of clothing, foods, cars, or whatever to carry certain meanings in society.

The systems in which signs are organised into groups are called codes. This is a familiar term, for instance in the phrase 'dress codes'. In our society, the dress code that governs what men should wear when going to a formal wedding includes items like a top hat and a tail jacket. These items of clothing are signs which can be selected from the almost infinite *langue* of male clothing, from the code of male formal dress, and they communicate a coded message of 'formality'. By contrast, a man might select jogging shorts, training shoes and a baseball cap to go to the local gym. These clothing signs belong to a different dress code, and communicate a message of 'informality'. In the case of dress codes, it is possible to select the clothing signs which we use in order to communicate particular messages about ourselves. Even when clothes perform practical functions (like the loose and light clothes worn to play sports) codes still give social meanings to our choices, like codes of fashionableness and codes governing what men may wear versus what women may wear. In the same way, there are linguistic codes within the whole system of *langue*, which divide language up just as clothes are divided up into coded sets of signs. There are linguistic codes appropriate for talking to babies, talking to royalty, writing job applications, or writing love poems.

The message conveyed by linguistic signs often has much to do with how they can be used as part of coded ways of speaking or writing. Similarly, a television sequence of a newsreader behind a desk is a message which gains its authority by drawing on recognisable codes, while different codes constrain the way we might interpret a sequence showing cowboys shooting at each other on the main street of a western town. As we begin to address different kinds of sign in different media, the concept of a code becomes very useful in dividing signs into groups, and working out how the meaning of signs depends on their membership of codes. Individual signs become meaningful because of their difference from all other signs. But the role of signs as members of code groupings means that many signs are heavily loaded with a significance which comes from the code in which they are used.

Components of the sign

Saussure drew a distinction between the evolution of linguistic signs through time, called 'diachronic' linguistics, and the study of signs existing at a given point in time, called 'synchronic' linguistics. From a diachronic point of view, we might investigate the way that a particular sign like 'thou' used to be used in ordinary language but is now used only in religious contexts. But from a synchronic point of view, it is the place of 'thou' in our own historical moment that is of interest, not how it has gained its current role in our language. The linguists who preceded Saussure had concentrated on diachrony, the development of language over time, and Saussure argued that this approach was useless for giving us an understanding of how language works for the people who actually use it. For a community of language users, it is the system and structure of the current language, *langue*, which makes articulation meaningful, and not the history of how signs have come to take the form they have now. His emphasis on synchrony enabled him to show how signs work as part of a structure that is in place at a given point in time. The same emphasis on synchronic analysis works for any other communication method where signs contrast one with another. For instance, denim jeans used to be work-clothes, and were clothing signs in a code of clothes for manual labour. Today, jeans are a sign whose meaning is 'casual style' or 'youthfulness', signs belonging to a style code of everyday dress in contrast to suit trousers, which signify 'formality' and belong to a different dress code. The coded meaning of jeans depends much more on their relationship with, and difference from, other coded signs in the clothing system today, rather than their meaning depending on the history of jeans. Synchronic analysis reveals more about the contemporary meaning of jeans than diachronic analysis.

In his analysis of linguistic signs, Saussure showed that there are two components to every sign. One is the vehicle which expresses the sign, like a pattern of sound which makes up a word, or the marks on paper which we read as words, or the pattern of shapes and colours which photographs use to represent an object or person. This vehicle which exists in the material world is called the 'signifier'. The other part of the sign is called the 'signified'. The signified is the concept which the signifier calls forth when we perceive it. So when you perceive the sign 'cat' written on this page, you perceive a group of marks, the letters c, a, and t, which are the signifier. This signifier is the vehicle which immediately calls up the signified or concept of cat in your mind. The sign is the inseparable unity of the signifier with the signified, since in fact we never have one without the other.

This stage of the explanation of the sign says nothing about any real cat out there in reality: the sign cat is made up of two entities, signifier and signified, which are joined together in the minds of language users. The sign cat does not refer to any particular cat, but to a mental concept. It is perfectly possible to use a sign, like 'God', which does not relate to any observable thing out there in the real world. Many linguistic signs, like nouns, clearly relate to actual things, like cats, which could be observed in reality. The actual things which signs refer to are called 'referents', so the referent of the sign 'cat' which I speak when talking to my own cat has my particular cat as its referent. If I write a note to my neighbours when I leave for a holiday, saying 'Please feed cat', it is clear from the context that my cat is the referent of the sign, but the sign 'cat' could refer to any cat. And just as the English language arbitrarily connects the signifier 'c, a, t' with the signified 'cat' in our minds, so too the language arbitrarily connects the whole sign 'cat' with a particular sort of living creature, the real cats which can be referents of this sign.

Once Saussure had divided the sign into signifier and signified, it became possible to describe how language divides up the world of thought, creating the concepts which shape our actual experience. This can be illustrated by a simple comparison between signs in different languages. In English, the signifier 'sheep' is joined to a particular signified, the concept of a certain type of animal, and the signifier 'mutton' is joined to the signified of the meat of this animal. In French, the signifier *mouton* draws no distinction between the signified animal and its meat. So the meaning of 'mutton' in English is sustained only by its difference from 'sheep'. Meaning is only generated by the relationships between signifiers, and the signified is shaped by the signifier (not the other way around). The signifieds or concepts in our minds are shaped by the signifiers that our language provides for us to think and talk with. In English we have only one signifier for the signified colour white, so the signified concept of whiteness is indivisible, one single thing. But we can conceive of a language where there are several words subdividing whiteness into several distinct colours. For speakers of such a language our signified white would not be one colour but several different and separate colours, just as for us redness is divided into the distinctly different colours scarlet, crimson, vermilion etc. The systems which structure our language also structure our experience of reality, as indicated at the beginning of this chapter. This surprising reversal of common sense comes logically from Saussure's thinking about the components of the linguistic sign.

Sequences of linguistic signs

One of the distinctions between linguistic signs and other kinds of sign is that language is always dependent on time. In a written or spoken articulation, one sign must come before the next, and the articulation is spread out over time. In photographs, paintings, or an outfit of clothes, each sign is present at the same time as the others: the signs are distributed across space rather than time. In film or television for example, both space and time are involved, since the shapes on the screen are next to other shapes in the same space, while the image changes over time as the film progresses. When signs are spread out in a sequence over time, or have an order in their spatial arrangement, their order is obviously important. In a sentence like 'The dog bites the man', meaning unfolds from left to right along the line of the sentence, as we read the words in sequence one after another. This horizontal movement is called the 'syntagmatic' aspect of the sentence. If we reverse the order into 'The man bites the dog', the meaning is obviously different. Each linguistic sign in the syntagm could also be replaced by another sign which is related to it, having perhaps the same grammatical function, a similar sound, or relating to a similar signified. It is as if there are vertical lists of signs intersecting the horizontal line of the sentence, where our sentence has used one of the signs in each vertical list.

These lists of signs are called 'paradigms'. We could replace 'dog' with 'cat' or 'tiger', and replace 'bites' with 'licks' or 'kicks' or 'chews'. Each different selection from these paradigms would alter the meaning of the syntagm, our horizontal sentence of words.

So an important aspect of how language makes meaning must be that each linguistic sign is surrounded by paradigms of associated signs that are not present. Explaining the meaning of an instance of *parole* must involve noting the way that the syntagmatic ordering of signs affects meaning, and the way that the signs not selected from a particular paradigm shape the meaning of the sign that has been selected. As a general principle, every sign that is present must be considered in relation to other signs present in the structure of the articulation, and every sign present has meaning by virtue of the other signs which have been excluded and are not present in the text.

Visual signs

Most of the account of linguistic signs above comes directly from Saussure, but some of the principles and terms which we shall need in the chapters that follow derive from the semiotic work of the American philosopher Charles S. Peirce (1958). In particular, the semiotic analysis of images and other non-verbal signs is made much more effective by some of Peirce's distinctions. Although language is the most striking form of human sign production, the whole of our social world is pervaded by messages which contain visual as well as linguistic signs, or which are exclusively visual. Gestures, dress codes, traffic signs, advertising images, newspapers, television programmes and so on are all kinds of media which use visual signs. The same principles underlie the semiotic study of visual signs and linguistic signs. In each case, there is a material signifier, which expresses the sign, and a mental concept, a signified, which immediately accompanies it. Visual signs also belong to codes, are arranged in syntagms, and selected from paradigms. In the last few pages, I have used some examples of visual signs along with linguistic ones, to suggest that they can be approached in similar ways.

We have already seen how linguistic signs are arbitrary, since there is no necessary connection between the signifier 'cat' on this page and the signified concept of cat in our minds, and nor is there any connection except a conventional one for English speakers between the whole sign 'cat' and its referent, the kind of furry four-legged animal which is sitting next to my desk. The relationship of signifier to signified, and of sign to referent, is entirely a matter of the conventions established by *langue* in general, and in this case by the English language in particular. This type of sign, characterised by arbitrariness, Peirce calls the 'symbolic' sign.

But a photograph of a cat looks recognisably like a specific cat. The arrangement of shape and colour in the photograph, the signifier which expresses the signified 'cat', has a close resemblance to its referent, the real cat which the photograph represents. In a photograph, the signifier is the colour and shape on the flat surface of the picture. The signified is the concept of a cat which this signifier immediately calls up. The referent is the cat which was photographed. Just as my cat is white with some black and orange patches, so a photograph of my cat will faithfully record these different shapes and colours. This kind of sign, where the signifier resembles the referent, Peirce calls an 'iconic' sign. We shall encounter iconic signs in our exploration of the semiotics of various visual media. Unlike the case of linguistic signs, iconic signs have the property of merging the signifier, signified and referent together. It is much more difficult to realise that the two components of the photographic sign plus their referent are three different things. It is for this reason that photographic media seem to be more realistic than linguistic media, and we shall be exploring this issue in greater depth later.

When a cat is hungry and miaows to gain our attention, the sound made by the cat is pointing to its presence nearby, asking us to notice it, and this kind of sign Peirce calls 'indexical'. Indexical signs have a concrete and often causal relationship to their signified. The shadow cast on a sundial tells us the time, it is an indexical sign which is directly caused by the position of the sun, and similarly smoke is an index of fire, a sign caused by the thing which it signifies. Certain signs have mixed symbolic, indexical and iconic features. For instance, a traffic light showing red has both indexical and symbolic components. It is an indexical sign pointing to a traffic situation (that cars here must wait), and using an arbitrary symbolic system to do this (red arbitrarily signifies danger and prohibition in this context).

Connotation and myth

The rest of this chapter deals with semiotic ideas which are found in the work of the French critic Roland Barthes. His ideas build on the foundations outlined so far, and take us closer to the semiotic analysis of contemporary media. Because we use signs to describe and interpret the world, it often seems that their function is simply to 'denote' something, to label it. The linguistic sign 'Rolls-Royce' denotes a particular make of car, or a photographic sign showing Buckingham Palace denotes a building in London. But along with the denotative, or labelling function of these signs to communicate a fact, come some extra associations which are called 'connotations'. Because Rolls-Royce cars are expensive and luxurious, they can be used to connote signifieds of wealth and luxury. The linguistic sign 'Rolls-Royce' is no longer simply denoting a particular type of car, but generating a whole set of connotations which come from our social experience. The photograph of Buckingham Palace not only denotes a particular building, but also connotes signifieds of royalty, tradition, wealth and power.

When we consider advertising, news, and TV or film texts, it will become clear that linguistic, visual, and other kinds of sign are used not simply to denote something, but also to trigger a range of connotations attached to the sign. Barthes calls this social phenomenon, the bringing-together of signs and their connotations to shape a particular message, the making of 'myth'. Myth here does not refer to mythology in the usual sense of traditional stories, but to ways of thinking about people, products, places, or ideas which are structured to send particular messages to the reader or viewer of the text. So an advertisement for shoes which contains a photograph of someone stepping out of a Rolls-Royce is not only denoting the shoes and a car, but attaching the connotations of luxury which are available through the sign 'Rolls-Royce' to the shoes, suggesting a mythic meaning in which the shoes are part of a privileged way of life.

Media texts often connect one signified idea with another, or one signifier with another, in order to attach connotations to people and things and endow them with mythic meanings. There are two ways in which these associations work. One is called 'metaphor' and works by making one signified appear similar to another different signified. The other is called 'metonymy' and works by replacing one signified with another related signified. For example we can imagine that Rolls-Royce might launch a fast new car, using the advertising slogan 'The new Rolls-Royce eats up the tarmac'. In this syntagm of linguistic signs, both metaphor and metonymy have been used. The sign 'eat up' has nothing to do with driving cars. But the slogan asks us to realise how a fast car might 'consume' distance in a similar way to gobbling down food. In a metaphorical sense, a fast car might eat up the road as it rushes along. Metonymy is also used in the slogan. The sign 'tarmac' clearly has a relationship with roads, since roads are made of tarmac. In the advertising slogan the sign 'road' has been replaced metonymically by the sign 'tarmac' which takes its place. Returning to the imaginary shoe advertisement denoting a person's foot stepping out of a Rolls-Royce, the shoe and the Rolls-Royce have been made to appear similar to each other because they are both luxurious, so this is a metaphorical relationship. But since we see only a foot stepping out of the car, the foot is a metonym which stands for the whole person attached to it. Our imaginary shoe advertisement is combining signs in complex ways to endow denoted objects with mythic meanings.

Myth takes hold of an existing sign, and makes it function as a signifier on another level. The sign 'Rolls-Royce' becomes the signifier attached to the signified 'luxury', for example. It is as if myth were a special form of language, which takes up existing signs and makes a new sign system out of them. As we shall see, myth is not an innocent language, but one that picks up existing signs and their connotations, and orders them purposefully to play a particular social role.

selling products

Mythologies of wrestling

In 1957 the French lecturer and critic Roland Barthes published a book called *Mythologies*. It consisted of short essays, previously

published in French magazines, which dealt with a wide variety
of cultural phenomena, from wrestling matches to Greta Garbo,
from Citroen's latest car to steak and chips. These essays on
aspects of contemporary French culture sought to look beyond
the surface appearance of the object or practice which they discussed, and to decode its real significance as the bearer of particular meanings. What Barthes did was to read social life, with
the same close attention and critical force that had previously
been evident only in the study of 'high art', like literature, paint-
ing or classical music. *Mythologies* uses semiotics as the predom-
inant means of analysing aspects of everyday culture. The book
concluded with an essay called 'Myth Today', which drew
together the implications of the semiotic method Barthes was
using in his short essays, and showed why his reading of social
life was significant. *Mythologies* had a huge impact in France,
and later in the English-speaking world, and opened up everyday
popular culture to serious study. This section is devoted to the
discussion of one of the short essays in *Mythologies*. Then the
essay 'Myth Today' which provides a general framework for
the study of popular culture is more fully discussed. Many of the
analytical methods and critical concepts in 'Myth Today' will be
recurring in later chapters of this book.

The first essay in *Mythologies* is 'The World of Wrestling'.
Barthes discusses the meaning of the rather seedy wrestling
matches which at that time took place in small auditoria around
Paris. Something fairly similar can be seen today in the televised
WWF wrestling from the United States, where exotically named
and colourfully clad wrestlers perform very theatrically. The
modern television form of this type of wrestling is much more
glossy and widely marketed than the backstreet entertainment
Barthes discusses, however. Who wins and who loses in these
wrestling contests is insignificant compared to the excessive pos-
turing and the dramatic incidents which are displayed in the
bouts and in the stadium by the wrestlers. This form of wrestling
is not only popular enough to be televised recently, but has also
given rise to spin-off products: a TV cartoon featuring star
wrestlers, poseable toy action figures, T-shirts and other clothing,
and computer games. Clearly, something about this theatrical
wrestling spectacle has been significant and popular, in 1950s

Paris and in Britain and the United States today.

Barthes describes wrestling as a theatrical spectacle rather than a sport. The spectators, he finds, are interested primarily in the powerful emotions which the wrestlers simulate. These can be clearly read in their gesture, expression and movement, which are so many coded signs signifying inner passions. Wrestling becomes a kind of melodrama, a drama using exaggerated physical signs, and is characterised by an emphasis on emotion and questions of morality. Here Barthes describes some of the physical signs made by the wrestlers, and it is easy to read their connotations, since they belong to a very clear code:

> Sometimes the wrestler triumphs with a repulsive sneer while kneeling on the good sportsman; sometimes he gives the crowd a conceited smile which forebodes an early revenge; sometimes, pinned to the ground, he hits the floor ostentatiously to make evident to all the intolerable nature of his situation. (1973: 18)

For Barthes, wrestling is like ritual, pantomime, or Greek tragedy, where what is important is to see some struggle being played out by actors who do not represent realistic individual characters, but ideas or moral positions. The 'bad-guy' wrestler, the 'bastard' as Barthes calls him (1973: 17), appears to fight cruelly and unfairly, but is pursued by his opponent despite the 'bastard's' attempt to hide behind the ropes of the wrestling ring, and he is deservedly punished. The spectators enjoy both the outrageous cheating and cruelty of the 'bastard', and also the eventual punishment of the 'bastard' by the good-guy wrestler. The physical signs made by the wrestlers communicate all of this drama, and these signs belong to a code which is familiar to the audience. The audience's pleasure comes from reading and enjoying the wrestlers' coded signs.

Whether the good wrestler wins or not, the bout will have made Good and Evil easily readable through the medium of the coded signs the wrestlers use to communicate their roles and their emotions to the crowd. Grins, sneers, gestures and poses are all indexical signs which connote triumph, revenge, innocence, viciousness or some other meaning. A grin would be an indexical sign of triumph, or hitting the floor an indexical sign of submission in defeat, for instance. The wrestlers combine these signs together in syntagms and exaggerate them, so that there can be no doubt about how to read their connotations. The wrestling bout is much more like a pantomime than a fight, because highly coded signs are being presented for the enjoyment of the audience. Barthes' conclusion is that wrestling makes our confusing and ambiguous world intelligible, giving clearly readable meanings to the struggle between moral positions represented by the wrestlers. Once we look beyond the surface of wrestling, where it can appear to be a rather silly and pointless spectacle, we find that wrestling is a way of communicating about morality and justice, transgression and punishment, through signs which belong to a code. Wrestling is a medium which speaks about our culture in a highly codified (and entertaining) form.

Myth and social meanings

Having looked briefly at one of Barthes' short essays in *Mythologies*, the rest of this chapter explains and discusses the longer essay which concludes the volume, 'Myth Today'. In it, Barthes draws together some of the more general critical points which his analyses of cultural products have led him to, and explains a coherent method for going on to study more aspects of social life. At the beginning of 'Myth Today', Barthes declares that 'myth is a type of speech' (1973: 109). We saw above that wrestling can be regarded as a medium in which messages about morality and behaviour are communicated through a theatrical type of entertainment. The moves, gestures and expressions in wrestling are a form of coded communication through signs, used self-consciously by the wrestlers. Wrestling, as it were, speaks to us about our reality. On one level, the wrestlers' gestures can signify 'defeat' or 'helplessness'. They are signs for emotional or moral attitudes. But on another level, more abstractly, the whole wrestling match is itself a sign. It represents a moral terrain in which there is a crude and 'natural' form of justice. The 'bastard' is made to pay for his cheating and cruelty, and the match shows the spectators an exciting yet ordered world, compensating for the ordinariness and disorder of reality. The wrestling match makes good and evil, conflict and violence, intelligible by putting these ideas on stage in the artificial form of the match itself.

But is this way of understanding the world in moral terms natural, common sense, unchangeable? Should we understand behaviour in these moral terms? Barthes argues that in fact the wrestling match, with its moral structures and positions represented by the wrestlers, merely makes morality and justice seem as if they were natural. Wrestling, and morality, are both products of a specific culture (west European Christian culture). They are both tied to a certain historical period, and to a particular way of organising society in a particular place. The meanings in wrestling are not natural but cultural, not given but produced, not real but mythical. Myth, as Barthes uses the term, means things used as signs to communicate a social and political message about the world. The message always involves the distortion or forgetting of alternative messages, so that myth appears to be simply true, rather than one of a number of different possible messages.

The study of these myths, mythology, is part of the 'vast science of signs' which Saussure predicted, and called 'semiology' (or semiotics) (Barthes 1973: 111). Reading the messages in myth involves identifying the signs which it uses, and showing how they are built by means of codes into a structure which communicates particular messages and not others. This can be explained by discussing the main example Barthes uses in 'Myth Today'. Barthes imagines himself at the barber's, looking at the cover of an edition of the French glossy magazine *Paris-Match*. On the cover is a photograph of a black soldier in uniform, who is saluting the French flag. The signifiers, the shapes and colours in the photograph, can be easily read as meaningful iconic signs, which denote the message 'a black soldier is giving the French salute'. But the picture has a greater signification, which goes beyond what it denotes. The picture signifies that

> France is a great empire, that all her sons, without any colour discrimination, faithfully serve under her flag, and that there is no better answer to the detractors of an alleged colonialism than the zeal shown by this Negro in serving his so-called oppressors. (Barthes 1973: 116)

A set of iconic signs which already possess a meaning ('a black soldier is giving the French salute') becomes the basis for the imposition of an important social message, that French imperial rule is fair and egalitarian. This social message is myth, and a controversial one when Barthes wrote the essay in the 1950s. France's empire was disintegrating, and there was brutal military conflict in France's North African colony of Algeria where black Algerians fought and campaigned for independence. The crisis was the main political issue in France, and extensively debated in the media. The mythic signification of the picture on *Paris-Match*'s cover argues in favour of colonial control over Algeria, without appearing to do so.

The myths which are generated in a culture will change over time, and can only acquire their force because they relate to a certain context. In myth, the context and history of the signs are narrowed down and contained so that only a few features of their context and history have a signifying function. Where the photograph was taken, the name and life-experience of the soldier, who it was that took the photograph, are all historical and contextual issues which are irrelevant and neglected once the photographic sign is used as the signifier to promote the myth of French imperialism. Instead, the mythic signification invokes other concepts, like France's success as a colonial power, the contemporary conflict over Algeria, and issues of racial discrimination. What myth does is to hollow out the signs it uses, leaving only part of their meaning, and invest them with a new signification which directs us to read them in one way and no other. The photograph of the black soldier saluting makes the reader aware of the issue of French colonialism, and asks him or her to take it for granted that black soldiers should be loyal to the French flag, and that colonial rule is perfectly reasonable.

This is not the only way to read the mythic image of the soldier, though it is the reading which appears most 'natural'. Barthes suggests three ways of reading the photograph. First, the photograph could be seen as one of a potentially infinite number of possible images which support the myth of French imperialism. The black soldier is just one example of French imperialism in this case. Thinking of the image in this way, Barthes suggests, is how a journalist would think of it. Seeking to present a certain mythic signification on the cover of the magazine, the journalist would look for a suitable photograph which gives a concrete

form to this abstract concept, and creates the mythic signification.

Alternatively, a mythologist like Barthes himself, or someone
using the semiotic methods discussed here, would 'see through'
the myth. This critical reader would note the way that the black
soldier has had his meaning emptied out of the photograph,
except that he is an alibi, a justification, for the mythic signification. The rightness and naturalness of France's colonial power is
the dominant signification of the photograph, but one which the
semiologist is able to explain and unmask. The myth of French
imperialism has been imposed on the photograph, but the
mythologist is able to separate out the photograph and the myth,
the sign and the signification, to undo the effect which the myth
aims to produce. The mythologist 'deciphers the myth, he under-
stands a distortion' (Barthes 1973: 128).

Thirdly, an uncritical reader noticing the cover of *Paris-Match*
but not analysing it, would simply receive the mythic signification as an unremarkable and natural fact. The photographic sign
would seem to just show France's imperialism (translated in
Mythologies as 'imperiality') as a natural state of affairs, hardly
worth commenting on. The black soldier saluting would seem to
be 'the very presence of French imperiality' (Barthes 1973: 128).
The photograph in this case is neither an example chosen to
illustrate a point, nor a distortion trying to impose itself on us.
Instead, 'everything happens as if the picture naturally conjured
up the concept, as if the signifier gave a foundation to the signified: the myth exists from the precise moment when French
imperiality achieves the natural state' (Barthes 1973: 129–30).
For Barthes, the function of myth is to make particular ideas, like
France's colonial rule of other countries, seem natural. If these
ideas seem natural, they will not be resisted or fought against.
Myth makes particular social meanings acceptable as the
common-sense truth about the world. The function of the criticism and analysis of myth must then be to remove the impression of naturalness by showing how the myth is constructed, and
showing that it promotes one way of thinking while seeking to
eliminate all the alternative ways of thinking.

Myth and ideology

The analysis of myth to reveal its selectiveness and distortion is
obviously political in the broadest sense. In Barthes' work, and
in the work of many semiotic critics, the analysis of culture and
society is carried out from a left-wing perspective, and often
closely tied to Marxist ideas. In 'Myth Today', the later sections
of the essay take up the methods of semiotic analysis which have
been discussed so far, and relate them to a general political
analysis of society. The key concept in this analysis is 'ideology',
which will be discussed further in subsequent chapters of this
book as it relates to the study of the media. An ideology is a way
of perceiving reality and society which assumes that some ideas
are self-evidently true, while other ideas are self-evidently biased
or untrue. Ideologies are always shared by the members of a
group or groups in society, and one group's ideology will often
conflict with another's. Some of the arguments about ideology
which are advanced by Barthes and others will be subject to criticism later, as we investigate their usefulness in relation to concrete examples of contemporary media texts. In particular, I shall
argue that an ideology is not necessarily a false consciousness of
reality. But first, it is important to see how Barthes' analysis of
myth is connected to the concept of ideology.

Barthes proposes that myth serves the ideological interests of
a particular group in society, which he terms 'the bourgeoisie'
(1973: 137). This term refers to the class of people who own or
control the industrial, commercial, and political institutions of
the society. It is in the interests of this class to maintain the stability of society, in order that their ownership, power and control
can remain unchanged and unchallenged. Therefore, the current
ways of thinking about all kinds of questions and issues, which
allow the current state of economic and political affairs to continue unchallenged, need to be perpetuated. Although the existing state of society might sometimes be maintained by force, it is
most effective and convenient to maintain it by eliminating oppositional and alternative ways of thinking. The way that this is
done is by making the current system of beliefs about society, the
'dominant ideology', seem natural, common sense and necessary.

The dominant ideology of a society is subject to change, as the economic and political balance of power changes. Ideology then, is a historically contingent thing. If we look back, say, two hundred years, some features of the dominant ideology have obviously changed. Two hundred years ago, it would be self-evident that black people were inferior to whites, that women were inferior to men, that children could be employed to do manual labour. These ideas were made to seem natural, common sense. Today, each of these ideological views has been displaced. The ideology of today is different, but not necessarily any less unjust. However, it would by definition be difficult to perceive that current ideologies need to be changed, since the function of ideology is to make the existing system appear natural and acceptable to us all. Myth, for Barthes, is a type of speech about social realities which supports ideology by taking these realities outside of the arena of political debate.

> In the case of the soldier-Negro, for example, what is got rid of is certainly not French imperiality (on the contrary, since what must be actualized is its presence); it is the contingent, historical, in one word: fabricated, quality of colonialism. Myth does not deny things, on the contrary, its function is to talk about them; simply, it purifies them, it makes them innocent, it gives them a natural and eternal justification, it gives them a clarity which is not that of explanation but that of a statement of fact. If I state the fact of French imperiality without explaining it, I am very near to finding that it is natural and goes without saying: I am reassured. (Barthes 1973: 143)

The function of the photograph of the black soldier saluting the flag is to make French imperialism ('imperiality' in the quotation) seem like a neutral fact. It discourages us from asking questions or raising objections to colonialism. It serves the interests of a dominant ideology. The way that it is able to do this is by functioning as myth, presenting a historically specific situation as a natural and unremarkable one. Today, more than forty years after Barthes published *Mythologies*, colonial rule is regarded by most people as an outdated and embarrassing episode in European history. It is much easier to see how myths like French imperialism are constructed once they become distanced from the prevailing ideology. When analysing contemporary examples of myth in the media, the task of the mythologist in analysing the semiotic construction of myth becomes more difficult, since the very naturalness and self-evident quality of myth's ideological messages have to be overcome.

Semiotic methods are not always used to analyse cultural meanings from a left-wing point of view. For example, advertising agencies in continental Europe (e.g. Italy) and a few in Britain use semiotics to design more effective advertisements. Just as Barthes argued that a photographer might look for an image which conveys the myth of French imperialism, advertising copywriters might look for linguistic and visual signs which support the mythic meanings of a product. Both verbal and visual signs are used in ads to generate messages about products and their users, and semiotics can provide a framework for precise discussion of how these signs work. But it will also become clear that advertisements have a highly ideological role, since 'by nature' they are encouraging their readers to consume products, and consumption is one of the fundamental principles of contemporary culture, part of our dominant ideology. In advertisements, consumption is naturalised and 'goes without saying'. In order to accomplish this ideological effect, we will see that advertisements make use of myth, attempting to attach mythic significations to products by taking up already-meaningful signs in a similar way to the photograph on the cover of *Paris-Match*. The investigation of advertisements will involve further discussion of myth and ideology, and introduce some of the problems with the concepts of myth and ideology which have not so far been addressed.

Sources and further reading

The theories of the sign in Saussure (1974) and Peirce (1958) are considerably more complex than the outlines of them in this chapter. For other explanations and discussions of the sign, see Culler (1976), from a linguistic and literary perspective Hawkes (1983) and Eagleton (1983), and from a media studies perspective Ellis (1992), Burton (2000) and Tolson (1996). Branston and Stafford (1999) draw on the first edition of this book in their first chapter, and provide explanation, discussion and suggestions for further work on signs and myth.

Barthes (1973) contains many entertaining short essays in addition
to those discussed in this chapter and is not too difficult, although some
of his references to French culture and theorists may be obscure to a pre-
sent-day reader. Danesi (1999) is a more recent and entertaining use of
semiotics to decode social behaviour. Three books which analyse aspects
of culture in a similar way to Barthes are Blonsky (1985), Hebdige
(1988), and Hall (1997). Masterman (1984) contains short essays discussing myth and social meaning with reference to television. Barthes'
work is discussed by Culler (1983) and Lavers (1982).

Suggestions for further work

1   Make a selection of road signs from the Highway Code or from obser-
    vation of your local area. Which features of the signs are iconic,
    indexical or symbolic (some may be combinations of these)? Why do
    you think these signs were selected?
2   Analyse the front and back covers of this book and two others you
    are using on your course, or two others you use in different contexts
    (like cookbooks or leisure reading). What is denoted and connoted
    by the signs you find, and why?
3   Note the clothing, hairstyles and other adornments of two people
    you encounter. What do these signs connote, and what knowledge
    of cultural codes do you need in order to read the connotations?
4   Find an example of a short text written in one linguistic code (like
    a love poem, or the instructions for operating a video recorder) and
    try to 'translate' the text into another code (like the condensed style
    of SMS phone text-messaging, or a police report). Why are some
    signs and meanings more resistant to 'translation' than others?
5   There are cultural codes governing the 'natural' combinations of
    foods in each course in a meal (paradigmatic choices), or the order
    of courses in a meal (syntagmatic choices). How do the cultural
    codes of foods and eating you are familiar with differ from those of
    other cultures (for example, Indian, Chinese, French) whose foods
    you have sampled?
6   Analyse the layout, decor, music, staff uniforms, and displays etc. in
    your local supermarket. How do the connotations of these signs con-
    tribute to mythic meanings about the shop, shoppers, and shopping?
7   Analyse the physical attributes, accessories and packaging of dolls
    and action figures like Sindy, Barbie, Action Man and G.I. Joe. In
    what ways do their connotations encode ideological assumptions
    about each gender?

2

Advertisements

Introduction

This chapter introduces the semiotic study of advertisements. The combination of linguistic signs with visual, often photographic signs in ads allows us to explore the terms and ideas outlined in the previous chapter, and to begin to question them. The discussion of advertisements here is mainly focused on magazine and poster ads, and I have made this decision for several reasons, some of them pragmatic and some academic. Ads in magazines often take up a whole two-page spread in a magazine, and can be thought of, for the moment, as relatively self-contained. Two ads are reproduced as illustrations in this chapter so you can see the ad I am discussing, whereas TV or cinema ads, for instance, are composed of a syntagmatic sequence of images, sounds and words. It is much harder to get a grip on these syntagms of moving images when you can't see and hear them in their original form. The ads discussed here appeared in magazines, and glossy magazines are the subject of my next chapter. So the context of ads like those discussed here can be more fully explained in chapter 3. There have been several influential academic books dealing with ads from a semiotic point of view, so my focus on magazine ads allows me introduce some of the key findings which have previously emerged from semiotic work on ads, and identify some of the problems which semiotic analysis has encountered.

The beginning of this chapter gives an overview of advertising as an industry and of the socio-economic functions of ads. Then we move on to the types of signs and codes which can be found in ads themselves, and consider a theoretical model of how ads are read. The remaining part of the chapter deals with the problems which semiotic analysis faces when it attempts to justify its findings and apply them to the experience of real readers of ads, rather than using an abstract theoretical model of what readers do. I shall be using the two ads reproduced in this book to show how semiotic methods can be applied to ads, and to point out how semiotic methods often have to reduce the complexity of what reading an ad is really like.

The advertising business

Advertising is very common and is found in a range of media. If we begin to list the places where advertisements are found, it soon becomes obvious that they are both widespread and diverse. Ads are found in magazines, and in local and national newspapers, where we encounter brief 'small ads' which are mainly linguistic, and much larger 'display ads' placed by businesses, comprising images and words. There are small posters on walls, in shop windows, on railway platforms, and huge poster hoardings next to roads and railway lines. There are advertisements on radio, on television and on film. All these kinds of advertisement are usually recognisable as ads and not something else, but there are other more subtle kinds of advertisement. We will note later in this book, in the chapters dealing with television and cinema, how products 'tying in' with films and TV programmes, can also fulfil advertising functions. In the next chapter, we will encounter self-contained advertisements in the pages of magazines, as well as advertisements embedded in editorial material, and advertisements for magazines themselves within their pages. As we shall see, it can be difficult to determine what is an ad and what is not.

Advertising is highly professionalised and competitive, and the people who work in the advertising business are very often highly creative and well-educated. Many of them have studied semiotics as part of their formal education, and there is even a British advertising agency called Semiotic Solutions, which uses semiotic methods to design advertisements. While semiotic analysis has been used in the past for a critique of advertising, it can also be used in the industry to help make ads more effective.

Companies spend very large amounts of money on advertising. It is not unusual for a large manufacturer or financial corporation to spend several million pounds on advertising in Britain each year. But it is not only businesses that buy advertising; government agencies, for instance, also advertise. The media monitoring service A. C. Nielsen MMS reported in February 2001, for example, that the Central Office of Information (a government agency) spent over £16 million on advertising in the preceding year. Campaigns against cigarette smoking, drug use, or drink driving, and campaigns promoting healthy exercise, are all government-funded advertising. Other major advertisers in 2000 were Unilever (makers of household cleaning products) who spent over £12 million, Ford cars who spent nearly £9 million, Lloyds TSB Bank and the Orange mobile telephone company who spent nearly £6 million each. There are several different ways in which advertising campaigns are produced. Probably the most common model is for a company to employ an advertising agency, which will propose a campaign plan involving ads in one or more media, and perhaps other promotional activities like mailings direct to potential customers. Space for the ads will be bought from magazine publishers, newspapers, or TV companies for instance, for a specific placing and length of time. Publications which feature advertisements are therefore able to charge advertisers a considerable sum to place advertising material before their readers. Advertising is a significant commercial activity, and is evidently thought to be effective enough to warrant large financial commitments.

Analysing advertising

The semiotic analysis of advertising assumes that the meanings of ads are designed to move out from the page or screen on which they are carried, to shape and lend significance to our experience of reality. We are encouraged to see ourselves, the products or services which are advertised, and aspects of our social world, in terms of the mythic meanings which ads draw on and help to promote. As we saw in the last chapter, Barthes discussed the mythic meanings of the front cover of *Paris-Match*, and showed that signs and codes were used to represent French

colonial rule as natural and self-evident. This process of naturalising colonial rule had an ideological function, since the legitimacy of French colonialism was a political stance which the
mythic meaning encoded in the photograph made neutral and
scarcely noticeable. The photograph worked to support the ideological view that colonialism was normal, natural and uncon-
troversial. In the same way that Barthes uncovered the workings
of that image, the semiotic analysis of the signs and codes of
advertisements has also often been used to critique the mythic
structures of meaning which ads work to communicate. In her
classic study of the semiotics of advertisements, Judith
Williamson declares that advertising 'has a function, which is
to sell things to us. But it has another function, which I believe
in many ways replaces that traditionally fulfilled by art and
religion. It creates structures of meaning' (Williamson 1978:
11–12). As well as just asking us to buy something, Williamson
argues that ads ask us to participate in ideological ways of seeing
ourselves and the world.

In fact many contemporary ads do not directly ask us to buy
products at all. Ads often seem more concerned with amusing us,
setting a puzzle for us to work out, or demonstrating their own
sophistication. The aim of ads is to engage us in their structure
of meaning, to encourage us to participate by decoding their linguistic and visual signs and to enjoy this decoding activity. Ads
make use of signs, codes, and social myths which are already in
circulation, and ask us to recognise and often to enjoy them. At
the same time that we are reading and decoding the signs in ads,
we participate in the structures of meaning that ads use to represent us, the advertised product, and society. Many previous
studies of the semiotics of advertising use semiotic methods as
part of a critique of advertising's role in perpetuating particular
mythic meanings which reinforce a dominant ideology.

Analysing ads in semiotic terms involves a number of 'unnatural' tasks. In order to study them closely, we need to separate
ads from the real environment in which they exist, where they
often pass unnoticed or without analysis. We need to identify the
visual and linguistic signs in the ad, to see how the signs are
organised by paradigmatic and syntagmatic selection, and note
how the signs relate to each other through various coding sys-

tems. We need to decide which social myths the ad draws on, and whether these myths are reinforced or challenged. These are the main tasks which semiotic analysts of advertisements have concentrated on in the past, and which this chapter will explain. But since we cannot be certain that all readers read ads in the same way, we also need to examine two limiting factors which will complicate our ability to be sure of our findings. The first limiting factor is the potential ambiguity of the meanings of signs, and the second is that real readers of ads might decode signs differently, with a range of different results. These two limiting factors pose challenges to the semiotic methods outlined above, and we shall need to assess their importance later in this chapter. At this point, it is necessary to show how semiotic analysis has proceeded until quite recently.

The semiotic critique of ads

The first step in analysing an advertisement is to note the various signs in the advertisement itself. We can assume that anything which seems to carry a meaning for us in the ad is a sign. So linguistic signs (words) and iconic signs (visual representations) are likely to be found in ads, as well as some other nonrepresentational signs like graphics. At first sight, most of these signs simply seem to denote the things or people which the images represent, or to denote the referents of the linguistic signs. But the signs in ads very rarely just denote something. The signs in ads also have connotations, meanings which come from our culture, some of which we can easily recognise consciously, and others which are unconsciously recognised and only become clear once we look for them. Let's take a hypothetical example which reproduces the features of a large number of ads. A picture of a beautiful female model in a perfume ad is not simply a sign denoting a particular person who has been photographed. The picture of the model is also a sign which has connotations like youth, slimness, health etc. Because the sign has these positive connotations, it can work as the signifier for the mythic signified 'feminine beauty'. This concept belongs to our society's stock of positive myths concerning the attributes of sexually desirable women. The ad has presented us with a sign (the photographed model) which itself signifies a concept (feminine beauty). This concept of feminine beauty is what Barthes would describe as a mythic meaning. Yves Saint-Laurent's ad campaign for Opium perfume in 2000, for example, featured Sophie Dahl, described by *Marie Claire* magazine as 'realistically curvy'. The ads denoted Dahl reclining on her back with her knees raised and legs slightly apart, one hand on her left breast and her head thrown backward. She was completely naked except for heavy gold jewellery, and her pale skin, emerald green eye make-up, fuchsia lipstick and red hair contrasted with the deep blue fabric on which she lay. Clearly the sign 'Opium' has connotations of indulgent pleasure which derive from the codes for representing drugtaking and sexual abandonment, and the connotations of the ad's visual signs supported them. As Dee Amy-Chin (2001) has discussed, Sophie Dahl's pose and costume alluded to French nineteenth-century paintings representing harems, Turkish baths, and scenes in oriental palaces. The mythic meaning of the ad connected the perfume, feminine beauty, and exotic sensual pleasure.

As in the case of Barthes' black soldier saluting the flag, it does not matter who the model is, who the photographer was, where the picture was taken, etc. The only significant attribute of the photographed model is that she exhibits the physical qualities which enable her to function as a signifier for the mythic meaning 'feminine beauty'. The photographic sign has been emptied of its meaning except inasmuch as it leads the reader of the ad towards comprehending the myth. In analysing the signs in ads, we pass from the sign's denotative meaning to its connotative meanings. These connotative meanings are the ingredients of myth, the overall message about the meaning of the product which the ad is constructing by its use of the photographed model. The ad works by showing us a sign whose mythic meaning is easily readable (the photographed model is a sign for feminine beauty) and placing this sign next to another sign whose meaning is potentially ambiguous (the name of the perfume, for instance). The mythic meaning 'feminine beauty' which came from the photographic sign (the model) is carried over onto the name of the perfume, the linguistic sign which appears in the ad. So the name of the perfume becomes a linguistic sign that seems to connote feminine beauty as well. The product has been endowed with a mythic meaning.

This short example gives a sense of how the semiotic analysis of ads works at a basic level. We identify the signs in the ad, try to decide what social myths the connotations of the ad's signs invoke, and see how these mythic meanings are transferred to the product being advertised. The next step is to consider how the mythic meaning constructed in the ad relates to our understanding of the real world outside the ad. In other words, we need to ask what the ideological function of the ad might be. Our perfume ad invited us to recognise the connotations of the signs in the ad, and to transfer these connotations to the product being advertised. The perfume became a sign of feminine beauty, so that buying the product for ourselves (or as a present for someone else) seems to offer the wearer of the perfume a share in its meaning of feminine beauty for herself. As Williamson argued: 'The technique of advertising is to correlate feelings, moods or attributes to tangible objects, linking possible unattainable things with those that are attainable, and thus reassuring us that the former are within reach' (Williamson 1978: 31). Buying and using the product (an attainable thing) gives access to feminine beauty (a social meaning). To possess the product is to 'buy into' the myth, and to possess some of its social value for ourselves.

Ideology in ads

Our perfume ad, by placing the photographed woman next to the product, actively constructs a relationship between the woman and the product. It does this by placing an iconic sign (the photographed woman) and a linguistic sign (the name of the perfume) next to each other. It is this relationship between one sign and another which is important for the meaning of the ad, since the relationship involves the sharing of the mythic meaning 'feminine beauty' by both the product and the photographed model. The ad is constructed to make this sharing of the same mythic meaning appear automatic and unsurprising, whereas in fact it only exists by virtue of the ad's structure. So one point that a semiotic critic of ads would make is that the ad conceals the way that it works. Perfume ads do not literally announce that a perfume will make you seem beautiful (this claim would be illegal in many societies anyway). Instead this message is communicated by the structure of signs in the ad, by the way that we are asked to decode the ad's mythic meaning.

It is worth considering what would happen to the meaning of the ad if a different type of model had been photographed. We could list the different attributes of different photographic models, like youthful/mature, underweight/overweight, above average height/below average height, etc. The positive connotations of women used as signs in perfume ads derive from the positive connotations in our culture of the first sign in each of these pairs of opposites when they are applied to women in ads. The mythic meaning of 'feminine beauty' is much more likely to be perceived by the reader of the ad if the photographic sign calls on our social prejudices in favour of images of young, slim and tall women as signifiers of beauty. The iconic sign of the model can signify beauty because she is not elderly, overweight or below average height.

The ad presupposes that we can read the connotations of photographed women as if they were signs in a kind of restricted language, a code. Just as language works by establishing a system of differences, so that cat is not dog, red is not blue, youthful is not elderly, ads call on systems of differences which already exist in our culture, and which encode social values. One of the reasons I chose to discuss a hypothetical perfume ad featuring an iconic sign denoting a beautiful woman was that the example is controversial. Feminists have been critiquing ads and many other media texts for over three decades, showing that iconic signs denoting women in the media very often perpetuate oppressive ideological myths about real women. By calling on the positive social value of youth, slimness and tallness, for instance, our perfume ad could be described as supporting a dominant ideological myth of what feminine beauty is. It is easy to see that our ideological view of feminine beauty is not 'natural' but cultural if we look at representations of women in the past or in other cultures. In earlier historical periods, and in other parts of the world, the ideological myth of feminine beauty is not always signified by youth, slimness, tallness etc. Ideologies are specific to particular historical periods and to particular cultures.

The ideology of ads

The mythic meanings which ads generate are usually focused onto products. Ads endow products with a certain social significance so that they can function in our real social world as indexical signs connoting the buyer's good taste, trendiness, or some other ideologically valued quality. So ads give meanings to products, to buyers of products and to readers of ads, and to the social world in which we and the products exist. One central aspect of this process is the way in which ads address us as consumers of products. Critics of advertising have argued that real distinctions between people in our society are based on people's different relationships to the process of producing wealth. From this point of view, which derives from Marx's economic analysis of capitalist societies, it is economic distinctions between individuals and between classes of people that are the real basis on which society is organised. Some people are owners, and others are workers or people who service the work process. However, it has been argued that ads replace these real economic distinctions between people with a completely different way of regarding our relative status and value in society.

In ads, and in the ideology which ads reproduce, we are distinguished from others by means of the kinds of products which we consume. Social status, membership of particular social groups, and our sense of our special individuality, are all signified by the products which we choose to consume. Which beer you drink, which brand of jeans or perfume you wear, become indexical signs of your social identity. In any particular category of products, like perfumes, margarines, jeans or washing powders, there are only minimal differences between the various products available. The first function of an advertisement is 'to create a differentiation between one particular product and others in the same category' (Williamson 1978: 24). But ads not only differentiate one product from another, but also give different products different social meanings. Once products have different social meanings by virtue of the different mythic concepts they seem part of, products become signs with a certain social value. They signify something about their consumers, the people who buy and use them.

For critics influenced by this Marxist analysis, the real structure of society is based on relationships to the process of production. But far from making the real structure of society apparent, ads contribute to the myth that our identity is determined not by production but by consumption. Ads therefore mask the real structure of society, which is based on differences between those who own the means of production and those who sell their labour and earn wages in return. In a consumer society, these real economic differences between people and classes are overlaid with an alternative structure of mythic meanings oriented around buying and owning products (consumption). So according to this critical view ads have an ideological function, since they encourage us to view our consumption positively as an activity which grants us membership of lifestyle groups. But what ads are really doing is serving the interests of those who own and control the industries of consumer culture. Ideology consists of the meanings made necessary by the economic conditions of the society in which we live: a real way of looking at the world around us, which seems to be necessary and common sense. But this ideological way of perceiving the world is there to support and perpetuate our current social organisation: a consumer society. The individual subject's need to belong and to experience the world meaningfully is shaped, channelled and temporarily satisfied by ideology. In the sense that it provides meaning in our lives, ideology is necessary and useful. But the question is what kind of meanings ideology perpetuates, whether these meanings mask and naturalise an inequitable social system. Advertising has been critiqued as one of the social institutions which perform this function of naturalising dominant ideologies in our culture, for example that it naturalises ideologies based on consumption, or ideologies which oppress women.

Problems in the ideological analysis of ads

There are some theoretical problems with the ideological critique of ads outlined above. This critical discourse claims to 'see through' the ideological myths perpetuated in advertising. The critique of ideology claims to set itself apart from what it analyses, and to investigate the way that advertising (or any other social institution) perpetuates an ideology. This notion of setting oneself apart in order to criticise advertising is parallel to the way that scientists set themselves apart from something in order to understand it objectively. Indeed, the theorist who proposed the model of ideological critique discussed here, Louis Althusser, saw his analytical method as scientific and objective (Althusser 1971). But the scientific objectivity of the critique of ideology is easy to dispute, especially if you are not a Marxist as Althusser was. There seems to be no definite reason for a Marxist analysis of ideology to be any more scientific and objective than another theoretical approach to society.

Indeed, the discourse of science can be seen to be just another ideological view. The notion of a scientific viewpoint, standing outside of experience and endowed with a special ability to see into the truth of things, gives automatic priority to this point of view over all others. Science is a discourse, a way of using language which has its own codes and a particular social meaning. The discourse of science presupposes, for instance, that what we see on the surface is less true than what we see beneath the surface. Science passes from the observation of surface effects to proposing an underlying theory which accounts for these surface effects. Semiotic analysis borrows the assumptions of the scientific discourse when it moves from the signifier to the signified; from what we perceive in the material world (signifier) to the concept which it communicates (signified). Similarly, semiotics moves from the signs on the surface to the mythic meaning which the connotations of signs signify. And again, semiotics moves from the mythic meaning of a particular set of signs in a text to the ideological way of seeing the world that the myth naturalises. In each case, looking at what is on the surface leads the semiotician to what is beneath the surface. We move from observation to knowledge, from a particular instance to a general theory. Building on the same assumptions as scientific discourse, semiotics and the theory of ideology claim to reveal what is really true by going beyond, behind or underneath what appears to be true.

Scientific discourse has a high degree of status in contemporary culture, but we can critique its coded use of signs in the same way that we can critique the coded use of signs in our perfume ad. We saw that the mythic meaning 'feminine beauty' rested on the positive connotations of youthfulness, under-weightness, etc., in opposition to the connotations of elderliness or overweightness, etc. Scientific truth is a mythic meaning based on the positive connotations of objectivity and depth, in opposition to the connotations of subjectivity and surface, for instance. Scientific truth is a mythic meaning which comes from the use of signs with positively valued connotations, in the same way that the mythic meaning 'feminine beauty' works. Once we see that scientific truth is a cultural construct, a mythic mean-ing, its special status has to be acknowledged as cultural and not natural, not necessary but contingent on the way that our cul-ture perceives itself and its reality. Scientific truth must be equally as mythic as feminine beauty.

If scientific discourse is not necessarily superior to the dis-courses which it analyses, the scientific claims made by semiotic analysis and the theory of ideology must be treated with caution. The discourse of semiotic analysis, as I stated briefly at the begin-ning of this chapter, requires us to adopt some 'unnatural' pro-cedures. We have to separate an ad being studied from its context in order to study how its signs work. We have to pay more attention to the detail of how meaning is constructed in an ad than an ordinary reader probably would. We tend to come up with an underlying meaning of an ad, relating the ad to mythic meanings and ideological values, which is justified only by the rigour of our analysis, rather than by any other proof which would ensure that our reading is correct. These features of semi-otic analysis do not mean that it is useless, or that its results are wrong. But semioticians have to take account of the limitations which the semiotic method brings with it. Semiotics is a very powerful discourse of analysis, but it always has to struggle against other discourses and argue its case. We shall be consid-ering these issues further in later sections of this chapter, and in the other chapters of this book. It is now time to examine two ads in detail, and see what a semiotic analysis might reveal.

Volkswagen Golf Estate

First we need to identify the signs in this ad. There are iconic signs here, denoting three men, and the rear half of a car. There are linguistic signs, the copy written underneath the picture. There is also a graphic sign, the logo of VW cars. Taking the three men first, we can see that their poses and facial expressions are themselves signs which belong to familiar cultural codes. Their poses and expressions are signs which connote puzzlement. The standing figure is still, looking intently at the car, with the positions of his arms and hands signifying that he is deep in thought. The two crouching men are also looking intently inside the car, with expressions which connote curiosity and mystification. For these men, there is something puzzling about this car. To decode this ad more fully, we need to examine the linguistic signs which are placed beneath the picture. The function of the linguistic signs is to 'anchor' the various meanings of the image down, to selectively control the ways in which it can be decoded by a reader of the ad (Barthes 1977b: 39).

The copy text begins with the syntagm of linguistic signs 'We've doctored the Golf'. Drawing on the presence of the graphic sign on the right, the VW Cars logo, and the syntagm 'The new Golf Estate', we can assume that the car denoted in the picture, and the signified of 'Golf' in the first linguistic syntagm, is a new VW car. What does the signifier 'doctored' signify? To

1   Magazine advertisement for VW Golf Estate

doctor something is to conduct a medical procedure, often to remove an organ, or figuratively to doctor is to alter something by removing a part of it. So two related meanings of the syntagm 'We've doctored the Golf' are that Volkswagen have called some doctors in to conduct a procedure on their car, or that VW have altered their car by removing something from it. This meaning of the syntagm is constructed by referring to the value of the sign 'doctored' in the code of language. Moving back to the picture, we might assume that the three men are doctors, who have just altered the car. This decoding of the picture might seem to be supported by the next linguistic syntagm in the caption, 'The new estate is 41 per cent bigger on the inside than the hatchback version'. After being treated by the doctors, the car has been altered. But how could it become bigger if something has been removed from it? The meaning of the sign 'doctored' seems to contradict the meaning of the second syntagm in the ad.

There is a puzzle here, which can only be solved by referring to another media text. This ad can be described as 'intertextual', since it borrows from and refers to another text. The three men are iconic signs denoting actors who played fictional characters in the British television series *Doctor Who*. Each man appeared as the character Doctor Who, a traveller in time and space, in separate series of the programme in the 1970s and 1980s. So the sign 'doctor' signifies Doctor Who, and the car has been 'Doctor Who-ed' rather than just 'doctored' in the usual sense. To decode the meaning of 'Doctor Who-ed' it is necessary to know something about the television series. It involved travelling in space and time in a vehicle called the TARDIS, which appeared on the outside to be a blue police telephone box (something small) but on the inside was a very large spacecraft (something big). To 'Doctor Who' the VW Golf is to make it bigger on the inside than it appears on the outside.

Once we perceive the intertextual reference in the ad to *Doctor Who*, much more meaning becomes available to us. The car is blue, like the TARDIS. The car is for travelling in physical space, like the TARDIS. The Doctor Whos in the picture were incarnations of Doctor Who at different times, but they are together in the picture at the same time. The car seems to have acted like the TARDIS, which travelled in time, by bringing the Doctors together from their different times to the time the picture was taken. The Doctor Who character solves mysteries and problems. The three Doctors are now puzzling over the apparent mystery of the VW Golf Estate's bigger internal space. These further meanings of the ad are only communicated once we decode the intertextual reference to *Doctor Who* in the ad, and use this cultural knowledge to solve the puzzle set by the ad. Many of the signs in the ad function as clues to help us select the appropriate cultural knowledge, and to eliminate knowledge which is not appropriate. For instance, it does not matter whether we know the names of the actors who appear in the ad, the plots or other characters in *Doctor Who*, or even whether the men in the ad are real or waxwork dummies.

The ad empties out the meanings of *Doctor Who*, leaving only some of them behind. The mythic meaning of the ad, that the new VW Golf Estate is very roomy, is constructed from a few connotations of the iconic signs denoting the men looking at the car, and a few connotations of the linguistic signs 'doctored' and 'bigger on the inside'. The unexpected way that the ad communicates this message was one of the reasons that the ad was given an IPC Magazines Ads of Excellence award (*Campaign* supplement 16 December 1994), as the award judge, Tim Mellors, commented. The ad borrows signs and meanings from another media text, a process known as intertextuality. But it only borrows some meanings and not others, and the semiotic richness of the ad depends on the cultural currency of *Doctor Who* among readers of the ad. Without some knowledge of *Doctor Who*, the ad might seem rather mysterious. To 'doctor' the Golf might decode as to mutilate or castrate it, for instance. Perhaps the men looking at the car are working out how to steal it. Perhaps 'We've doctored the Golf' refers to the way that the photographer has cut off the front half of the car from the picture. The potential ambiguity of the visual signs and linguistic syntagms in the ad are reduced once the signs 'bigger on the inside' show us how to decode the ad. This linguistic syntagm anchors the meanings of the image and of other linguistic signs.

For someone unfamiliar with *Doctor Who*, the denoted linguistic message that the Golf estate is bigger than the hatchback version would still be meaningful, but the meanings of the picture would not be anchored down by the reference to *Doctor Who*. The back and forth movement of meaning between text and image, the 'relay' (Barthes 1977b: 41) of meaning between the two, would also be much less clear. It is evidently important to ask who the reader of this ad is assumed to be, since the reader's cultural experience of other media texts (specifically *Doctor Who*) is the basis of the ad's intertextual effectiveness.

The VW Golf Estate ad's contexts and readers

The ad was placed in these magazines: *Golf Monthly, Motor Boat & Yachting, Practical Boat Owner, Horse & Hound, Country Life, Amateur Photographer, The Field*, and *Camping & Caravanning*. The readers of these magazines probably carry equipment around when they are pursuing their leisure interests, or they are people who would like to indulge in the relatively expensive leisure interests featured in the magazines. An estate car would satisfy a real need for some readers, or, for aspiring readers, to own the car could function as a sign that they belong to the group who might need an estate car like this. So there are several functions of this ad, including announcing a new VW model, associating the VW Golf Estate with relatively expensive leisure pursuits, and encouraging readers to find out about the car (the ad includes a telephone contact number). The reader of the ad is 'positioned' by the ad as someone who needs or desires a VW Golf Estate.

But all of these functions of the ad in positioning its reader do not explain why the ad is structured as a puzzle that can be solved by someone familiar with *Doctor Who*. This is what Nigel Brotherton, marketing director of Volkswagen (UK) is quoted as saying:

> Estate cars are often seen as dull and boring. This is not helped by advertising which normally portrays them as the load carrying derivative of the range. We wanted the Golf Estate to be aspirational and not just a load lugger from Volkswagen. The target market was 'thirty-somethings' with young families whose lifestyle required an estate. These people were currently driving hatchbacks as the image of estate cars was not for them. By advertising the Golf Estate in a new and unusual way we hoped to convince them that the car was not like its dull and worthy rivals. (*Campaign* supplement, 16 December 1994)

So the *Dr Who* puzzle, because it is 'unusual', was chosen partly to establish a correlation between unusualness and the VW Golf Estate. The mythic meaning 'unusualness' is shared by the ad, by the car, and by the potential buyers of the car. The ad stands out from other less interesting competitors, and according to the message of the ad, the car and its potential purchasers stand out too. Furthermore, *Doctor Who* was a television series which was very popular in Britain in the 1970s and early 1980s when the Doctors in the ad appeared in the programme. People in their thirties in the early 1990s were very likely to know of the programme and to remember it with nostalgic affection. Decoding the ad's puzzle was probably a pleasurable experience for thirty-something readers, because they possess the appropriate cultural memory and this memory has pleasurable connotations for them.

It should now be clear that the intertextual reference to *Doctor Who* in the ad is not just amusing, not just unusual, and not just a puzzle. It is an unusual and amusing puzzle because this is a way of targeting a particular group of people. Aspiring thirty-somethings with families who are interested in certain leisure pursuits were 'ideal readers' of this ad. The ad is not simply asking these readers to buy a VW Golf Estate. It is endowing the car and these ideal readers with positive mythic meanings that can be attained only by decoding the ad appropriately. It is possible to decode the ad partially, incorrectly, or perversely. But the ad reduces the chances of these outcomes by virtue of the particular cultural knowledge it calls on, the context in which it appears, and the way that its visual and linguistic signs point the reader in the right direction, towards the correct position for understanding it.

This issue of positioning by the text is central to the way that ads (and other kinds of text) have been discussed by semiotic critics. In order to make sense of the signs in an ad, it is necessary for the reader to adopt a particular subject-position. The individual subject (the reader of the ad) positions himself or herself as a decoder of the ad's signs, and as the recipient of its meanings. The individual subject has to occupy the reading-position laid out by the structure of the ad, since this reading-position is the place from where the ad makes sense. The situation is like that of someone in an art gallery walking past a series of pictures. It is only possible to see a particular picture properly if you stand still, at an appropriate distance from the picture. If you walk past quickly, stand too close, too far away, or too much to one side, you can hardly see the picture. There is a particular position from which the picture 'makes sense', and to make sense of the picture you must occupy the position which it demands. Here it is a physical position in space which is important, but, returning to ads, it is not only physical position but also ideological position that counts. Ads position us as consumers, and as people who have a need or desire for certain products and the social meanings which these products have. There is a subjective identity which ads require us to take on, in order to make sense of ads' meanings.

But this notion of positioning by the text has several drawbacks as a way of describing how people read ads. It tends to treat all ads as if they were in the end the same, since all ads are regarded as positioning the individual subject in such a way as to naturalise a dominant ideology of consumerism. It tends to treat all real individuals as the same, since the positioning of subjects by the ad's structure of signs is a general model which applies to all readers. As we have seen, a quite well-defined group of readers were positioned by the VW Golf ad to receive all of its meaning. Other readers and groups of readers might easily decode the ad perversely, 'incorrectly', in which case the ad would still make a kind of 'sense', but a very different sense from the one the advertisers intended. The theory of textual positioning assumes that there is one 'correct' reading of any ad, which is its true meaning. It de-emphasises the ambiguity of signs (like 'doctored'), since all the signs in the ad seem to lead finally to the true meaning. It assumes that the 'scientific' discourses of semiotics and the theory of ideology are more objective than other analytical techniques, and can reveal a 'true' meaning of an ad which most real readers do not perceive because they are in the grip of ideology. We can see in more detail how some of these problems affect the analysis of ads by looking at an ad from one of the most successful campaigns of the 1990s, a Wonderbra ad.

Wonderbra

This ad can be read in a number of different ways, from different subject-positions, and problematises the distinction between an evident surface meaning and a concealed depth meaning which semiotic analysis can reveal. Like the VW Golf Estate ad, it draws on cultural knowledge of other media texts. It also appeals to an awareness of the critical discourses about advertising from feminist analysts and critics of ideology. It becomes very difficult to see what the 'true' or correct meaning of this ad might be. Discussing this ad brings us face to face with the limits of semiotic analysis, and of the theoretical model of media communication which has been developed earlier in this book.

Our first step must be to identify the signs in the ad, and then to decide how they relate to mythic meanings. The picture is an iconic sign denoting a woman, who is leaning against something, perhaps an open door. She is wearing a bra, and in the original picture the bra is bright green (this is the only colour in the picture, the rest of the picture is in tones of black and white). There is a syntagm of linguistic signs, 'Terrible thing, envy', and a further syntagm 'Now available in extravert green'. There is a further iconic sign denoting the brand label which would be attached to a Wonderbra when on sale. To read this ad, we would identify the connotations of the signs present in it, seeing how the anchorage between the picture and the text directs us towards the 'correct' reading of the ad. But there are several

TERRIBLE
THING, ENVY.

THE ONE AND ONLY
wonderbra

NOW AVAILABLE IN EXTRAVERT GREEN

2   Wonderbra poster advertisement

ways of reading the connotations of the signs in this ad, and several social myths which the ad invokes.

The relay between the bra denoted iconically in the ad and the linguistic sign 'Wonderbra' makes it easy to see that this an ad for a Wonderbra product. There is a further relay between the greenness of the bra and the linguistic sign 'envy', since green signifies envy in a cultural code (just as red signifies anger, for instance). But the iconic sign of the green bra does not anchor the meanings of 'envy' here in any obvious way. Let's assume that 'Terrible thing, envy' signifies the response of the reader of the ad to the picture. Perhaps a female reader would envy the woman because she owns this bra (the bra is signified as a desired object), but the reader's envy feels 'terrible'. Perhaps a female reader would envy the woman because of the sexual attractiveness which the bra gives the woman (the bra is a sign of desired sexual attractiveness), but the reader's envy feels 'terrible'. Perhaps a heterosexual male reader would envy the bra because it holds the breasts of the woman (the woman is signified as a desired object), but the reader's envy feels 'terrible'. Perhaps a male reader would envy the woman because she can display her sexual attractiveness by wearing this bra (female sexual display is signified as a desired mythic attribute of women but not men), but the reader's envy feels 'terrible'. Perhaps a heterosexual male reader would envy the person to whom the woman displays herself in the picture, her partner perhaps (the woman's partner is a desired subject-position), but to envy the partner is 'terrible'.

There is a range of possible meanings of the linguistic signs, and of possible relays between linguistic and iconic signs. But in each case, the relationship of the reading subject to the picture is one of desire, either a desire to have something or to be something, and in each case the reading subject feels terrible about this desire. Envy is signified in the ad as an attribute of the reader, but is at the same time acknowledged as an undesirable emotion. Another set of decodings of the ad would result if the syntagm 'Terrible thing, envy' represents the speech of the woman in the picture, but I shall not list them all here. This would affect the relay between the iconic and linguistic signs, and the way that the linguistic signs anchor the meanings of the

iconic signs. Once again there would be several ways of decoding the ad, and several subject-positions available for the reader.
As before, enviousness would be signified as an attribute of the
reader, but the condemnation of envy would come from the
woman rather than the reader. The ad would establish a desire
to have or to be something, but also withdraw permission for the
desire.

The ambiguity which I have noted briefly here is reinforced by
the connotations of the model's pose. Her arms are folded. This
gives greater prominence to the lifting up and pushing forward
of her breasts which the bra achieves, reinforcing the decodings
of the ad which focus on her sexual desirability. But her folded
arms also create a kind of barrier between her and the reader,
and this is a common connotation of folded arms in our culture
in general. Like the linguistic syntagm 'Terrible thing, envy', the
folded arms are an ambiguous sign, connoting that the woman
is to be envied, but that she is unattainable or critical of the one
who envies her. Similarly, the woman's sidelong glance might
connote flirtatiousness, or a sardonic attitude, or both at the
same time. The ad therefore exhibits a kind of give and take in
the possible decodings which it allows. It offers the reader a
range of possible subject-positions, but denies them to the reader
at the same time. This is a feature which is very common in ads,
and depends on irony. Ironic statements contain a denoted
meaning, and a connoted meaning which contradicts the
denoted meaning. The linguistic syntagm 'Terrible thing, envy'
denotes that envy is a negative emotion, but it connotes that its
speaker is envious or envied anyway, and doesn't really mind
being envious or envied. This ironic quality of the syntagm
means that envy is regretted but also enjoyed. The social meaning of envy is being made ambiguous by the ad in a very subtle
way. Envy, it seems, is bad, but it is also good in the sense that
it is pleasurable.

The irony of the linguistic syntagm is reinforced by a relay
between it and the picture, since the double decoding of the syntagm is parallel to the doubleness in the meaning of the woman's
gesture and expression. As noted above, her gesture and expression can be read in at least two ways. The mythic meaning of
the ad as a whole then seems to be that the woman, the bra, and

the reader, can mean several things at once. The woman, the bra and the reader are not single and fixed identities, but sites where several different coded social meanings overlap and oscillate back and forth. We do not need to decide on a single social meaning for the bra, the woman who wears it in the picture, or for ourselves as readers of the ad or buyers of the bra. The ad invites us to enjoy the unanchoredness of its signs, and the multiplicity of the bra's social meanings. This oscillation of meaning back and forth, which irony makes possible, has very major consequences for the semiotic analysis of the ad.

The outline of a critical semiotic analysis of the Wonderbra ad would be something like this. The ad addresses women, presenting them with a sign connoting sexual attractiveness and power (the woman wearing the bra). These social meanings, according to the ad, can be attained by women if they buy the bra. To buy the bra is to 'buy into' an ideological myth that women should present themselves as objects for men's sexual gratification. To critique the ad in this way is also to critique it as a mechanism for perpetuating an oppressive ideology. However, as we have seen, it is by no means certain that the ideological message of the ad revealed by such a critique is the 'true' meaning of the ad. There are a number of coherent alternative ways of reading the ad, and a number of possible subject-positions from which to understand it. The signs in the ad are too ambiguous, too 'polysemic' (multiple in their meanings), to decide on one 'true' message of the ad.

Furthermore, the ad seems to be constructed so that it can disarm an ideological critique of its meanings. The ad signifies (among other things) that women can choose whether or not to become 'extravert': sexually desirable, displaying their bras and themselves as signs of desirability. The irony in the ad signifies that women can both choose to become desirable and at the same time distance themselves from being perceived as objects of desire by others. Irony like this was used by Madonna, who popularised bras as fashion items and was also represented simultaneously as an object of desire and as the controller of her own image, for instance, and the ad's irony may therefore function as an intertextual borrowing, offering its readers clues about its relationship with representations of powerful and desirable women. To take on the identity of a desired object can be enjoyed by women, but they can also retain their power as subjects (and not just objects) by adopting an ironic attitude towards this status as a desired object. The Wonderbra ad takes on a feminist ideological critique which would see women as signs of desirability and objecthood, and is ironic about this critique. The wearer of Wonderbra has two kinds of pleasure; both the pleasure of being a desired object, and the pleasure of refusing to be perceived as a desired object while nevertheless being one. In fact, both of these pleasures can exist simultaneously. The Wonderbra product becomes a sign of a woman's power over the way she is perceived, for she is perceived as both desirable, and in control of the social meaning of her desirability, at the same time.

The Wonderbra ad's contexts and readers

The Wonderbra ad discussed here was one of a sequence, featuring the same model, similarly ironic slogans, and similarly ambiguous mythic meanings. The 'Terrible thing, envy' ad ran in a range of glossy women's magazines, and ads like it were also displayed on poster hoardings around Britain. The ad campaign began on St Valentine's Day, February 1994, a day on which romance is celebrated, so that the social meanings of St Valentine's Day clearly supported the codings of the ad. While the readers of women's magazines are mainly women, the poster versions of these ads would have been seen by a wide range of people of both sexes and of varying ages (which was one reason for offering the different reading-positions outlined above). For example, 40 per cent of perfume sales are to men for women at Christmas. Some perfume ads are targeted at women, to increase brand awareness and the desirability of a brand. But poster ads address men too, who can be prompted to recognise and select a brand for purchase as a gift. This is called 'overlook' in advertising terminology and refers to the targeting of one audience with an image apparently designed for another audience. The Wonderbra campaign was very successful. It reportedly cost £130,000 to put the first three Wonderbra posters on 900 hoardings around Britain for two weeks, and £200,000 to publish the same three ads in women's magazines until June (*Cam-*

paign, 9 January 1995: 21). This is a relatively small cost for a national advertising campaign. The response to the ads led to the production of a total of fifteen different ads by January 1995, and by then the campaign was running in ten countries.

The effects of the campaign are difficult to assess, and the responses of real readers of the ads are even more elusive. TBWA, the agency which created the ads, won Campaign of the Year for Wonderbra in 1994 (they also won silver at the 1994 Advertising Effectiveness Awards). UK sales of Wonderbras rose by 41 per cent and the manufacturer (Playtex) reported sales of 25,000 bras per week. It seems reasonable to deduce that the multiple meanings of Wonderbra signified in the ads were able to prompt at least some of these sales. But in addition, the campaign was mentioned in at least 400 stories in the local and national press, on radio and on television, supported by public relations initiatives. The woman denoted in the ads, Eva Herzigova, had previously been unknown but became the subject of extensive journalistic interest. Wonderbra ads were displayed in Times Square, New York, and during the football World Cup in Dublin, with puns and references specific to their location and occasion respectively. Kaliber beer ads were produced by another ad agency, Euro RSCG, which referred intertextually to the 'Hello Boys' Wonderbra ad by replacing Eva Herzigova with the Scottish comedian Billy Connolly pictured next to the slogan 'Hello Girls'. Giant Wonderbra ads were projected against the side of London's Battersea Power Station, with the line 'Happy Christmas from Wonderbra'.

In a situation like this, it becomes even more difficult to determine the 'correct' meaning of an ad. Even if a semiotic analysis claims to determine the 'correct' meaning which the signs and codes of a single ad construct, the ad is not a self-contained structure of signs. The meanings of the ad will be inflected and altered by the intertextual field of other ads, press stories, and media events which surround the ad. The Advertising Standards Authority, which ensures that ads are 'legal, decent, honest and truthful' received 959 complaints about the sexual suggestiveness of the poster ad for Opium perfume in 2000 (Amy-Chin 2001), and the ad was withdrawn. The ad did not generate controversy when printed in women's magazines, where its audience was assumed to be predominantly women. But the appearance of the ads in poster form, coupled with widespread coverage of them in newspapers, alerted many people to them. The Opium ad was reproduced on the front page of *The Sun* newspaper on 20 December, and was connected to previous erotic ads including the Wonderbra series, one of which was reproduced by *The Sun* on the same page. Readers of ads bring their decodings of related texts to their decoding of the ad. Indeed, when the Wonderbra campaign became a media event in itself, the effect of the ads may have been to advertise the campaign as much as to advertise the product. These factors, which have to do with the social context of ads and of their readers, make any reading of an ad as a self-contained system of signs with a determinable ideological effect very difficult to justify as 'true'.

This chapter has focused on the ways in which semiotic analysis helps us to decode the meanings of ads. Ads have been discussed here as relatively self-contained texts, although we have seen that the mythic meanings which ads draw on and promote are also dependent on cultural knowledge which exists for readers outside of the particular ad being read. The meanings of signs are always multiple or 'polysemic', and we have seen how some ads narrow down this polysemic quality of signs but do not eliminate it altogether, while other ads exploit polysemia. In the next chapter, which deals with a range of glossy magazines, we shall encounter polysemic signs and the importance of cultural codes again. We will also be considering the importance of models of how readers are positioned again too, drawing on some of the insights which psychoanalytic theories of subjective identity have contributed to semiotic analysis. As we have seen here in the case of theories of ideology and readership, it is always necessary to think about the limitations and assumptions behind our analytical techniques, as well as making use of the critical power they offer.

Sources and further reading

The first and still very perceptive use of semiotics to analyse advertisements is Williamson (1978), which is more theoretically dense than this chapter but illustrates its points with reference to a huge number of

magazine ads that are reproduced in its pages. Later studies of advertisements include Goffman (1979), Dyer (1982), Vestergaard and
Schrøeder (1985), Myers (1986), Goldman (1992), Cook (1992), Myers
(1994, 1999) and Cannon *et al.* (2000). There are also useful sections
on advertising in Alvarado and Thompson (1990), and Marris and
Thornham (1999). All of these books use semiotic methods to some
degree, and recent books also discuss the limitations of critical semiotic
studies of ads. Advertising producers' perspective on their business can
be found in *Campaign* and *Admap* magazines, White (1988) is an example of a book by an advertising practitioner on making ads, and Meech
(1999) discusses the advertising business. Umiker-Sebeok (1987) contains a series of essays on advertising, some of which present the case
for using semiotics to make more effective ads. Althusser's (1971)
theory of ideology is quite difficult. There are books like Fairclough
(1995) which contain explanations and discussions of ideology, and it
is often better to see how this concept is deployed in relation to concrete
media examples. This is done in the books listed above which use semiotics to critique advertisements, where ideology is discussed with specific
reference to ads.

Suggestions for further work

1 Note the situations in which ads can be found (on bus shelters, on
   trains, on hoardings, in magazines, etc.). How might the situation
   of an ad affect its meanings and the ways it is decoded?
2 Analyse the representations of men in a group of ads. How similar
   or different are the codes used to represent men to those used to represent women in ads you have seen? What are the reasons for these
   similarities and differences?
3 Choose three ads for a similar type of product (car, training shoe, pen-
   sion, or soft drink, for example). How similar and how different are
   the mythic meanings of the products in the three ads? Why is this?
4 Ads for some products (like cigarettes) are not allowed to recommend the product explicitly. What semiotic strategies are used to
   connote desirability, pleasure, or difference from competing products
   in these ads? Are the same strategies used in ads for other products
   which could be explicitly recommended?
5 Both ads discussed in this chapter contain linguistic signs as well as
   visual ones. How do ads with no words attempt to organise the multiple connotations of what is denoted visually in them?
6 Compare ads from earlier decades with contemporary ads for similar products (Williamson 1978 has many ads from the 1970s, and

Myers 1994 has some from before World War II if you cannot find your own). What similarities and differences do you find in the semi-otic strategies of each period? Why is this?

7   Analyse the connotations of the brand names and logos of five prod-ucts. Why were these names and logos chosen? Could any of them be used as the name of a product of a different type?

3

Magazines

Introduction

This chapter focuses on monthly style magazines aimed at women and men. As before, it will use the techniques of semiotic analysis discussed so far, together with some of the theoretical ideas which have been allied with semiotics in academic studies of the media. This chapter deals with the signs and codes at work in a range of magazines, to consider whether they encode a coherent mythic social identity for their readers. In other words, magazines might be argued to construct different social meanings for men and women by positioning them as readers of particular structures of signs in particular ways. To answer these questions, we will need to examine the editorial content of magazines (like their features, letters, horoscopes, interviews etc.), and advertising material (individual ads and advertising features). As we deal with these various signifying elements of magazines, we can also evaluate the semiotic methods used here and in earlier chapters.

When investigating a whole text like a magazine, we will need to think about how the process of reading the magazines affects the meanings of the signs which are used. We will need to ask how far polysemy, the multiple meanings of signs, is limited by the context and interrelationships of signs with each other. We will need to ask how the mythic meanings in magazines relate to ideologies, and whether these meanings are being naturalised in support of an ideology. I shall argue that magazines do not construct a single mythic meaning for masculine or feminine identity, or promote one ideological position for their readers. Instead, the discourses of magazines are mixed, sometimes contradictory, and involve the reader in choices about how to decode their signs. These choices are not infinite, and the concept of conscious choice needs to be evaluated in relation to subject-positions taken up by readers which are unconsciously structured.

We saw in the previous chapter that the theory of ideology is useful for the analysis of advertising, showing how ads promote mythic ideas about the individual subject as a consumer, and about social relations and consumer society. Although there are some conceptual problems with the theory of ideology, it goes a long way to explain the function of ads in society. In this chapter, one of the issues in our analysis of magazines is the role of the reader in constructing meanings. In the previous chapter, it was largely assumed that the reader, though active, is engaged in putting together the connotations of ads into relatively coherent structures of meaning. This chapter will show that the reader is positioned by the discourses of men's and women's magazines, but cannot take up a single coherent identity in relation to them because of the contradictions within and between these discourses. These issues of identity will be related to a discussion of theories of subjectivity. Discussing subjectivity, subject-positions, or the construction of individual subjects, is a way to approach the question of individual identity. Theories of subjectivity stress how social forces and structures constitute us as individuals in particular ways. Language, social and family relationships, and texts in the media are all structures which lay out subject-positions from which to experience things. But like ideology, subjectivity must be seen not as a unified sense of personal identity, but as relatively fluid and contradictory.

The magazine business

Women's magazines can be divided into several categories, according to the target group of readers which they address. There are, for instance, magazines aimed at pre-teens and adolescents (like *Seventeen*), magazines for women aged between eighteen and thirty-four, which focus mainly on fashion and beauty (like *Cosmopolitan*), magazines aimed at women aged between twenty-five and forty, which focus on the world of the home (like *Good Housekeeping*), magazines focusing on specific concerns involving health and fitness (like *Slimming*), magazines for particular minorities in society, and magazines focusing on other special interests in women's lives (like *Brides*, or *Parents*). Magazines aimed at men are more restricted in their focus. There are magazines with a particular focus on style (like *Arena*), on the body and well-being (like *Men's Health*) and on leisure and consumer culture (like *Loaded*), but there is considerable overlap between these groups. Men's style magazines are a much more recent media phenomenon than women's magazines (*Loaded*, for example, was launched in 1994) and I shall argue later on that the masculine identities which they shape and address are highly unstable.

The categorisation of readers by age-group or by relationship status (single or in a long-term relationship, for example) is used by magazine publishers and advertisers as a shorthand way of indicating the main issues discussed in the magazines' editorial material, the kind of reader the magazines are thought to have, and the kind of products advertised in the magazines. But it is misleading to think about magazines as divided up in such a simple way, for several reasons. As publishers and advertisers know, magazines are read not only by their purchaser, but often by between five and fifteen other readers as well. In general, the more expensive the magazine's cover price, the more additional readers see the magazine. Not all of the magazine's readers will belong to the group which the magazine targets: some readers of women's magazines are men, and vice versa. So while a semiotic analysis might reveal that a particular magazine has an 'ideal reader' corresponding to the man or woman whose interests are targeted and shaped by a magazine, there will be a large number of non-'ideal' readers of the magazine's signs and meanings. We cannot assume that a real reader corresponds to the reader we reconstruct from the ways in which a magazine's codes operate.

Publishers and advertisers divide readers into those who buy a single copy from a shop, and readers who subscribe to the magazine over a period of time. Sales of single copies to 'sample readers' are economically important to publishers and advertisers because they demonstrate an active choice to purchase the magazine, whereas subscribers might receive the magazine but not actually read it. On the other hand, subscriptions provide regular sales, and publishers can acquire information about known subscribers. This information can be used to create profiles of typical readers, to encourage advertisers to place ads in one magazine rather than another in order to target a certain market sector. Again, a profile of a magazine's typical subscriber might correspond to an 'ideal reader' or it might not, and there will be a very wide range of different sample readers for any single issue of a magazine. It is also quite common for people to buy or read more than one magazine. The magazines a person reads may be addressed to the same category of reader, but may not. The mythic masculine or feminine identities constructed in a range of magazines may be related but different, just as the identities and subject-positions adopted by real men and women are related but different. In order to acquire a significant share of the market for these different categories of magazine, the large corporations which own magazines often publish several titles which target a similar readership group, and magazines which target related but different readerships. In the 1990s, IPC Magazines published *Marie Claire* (jointly with European Magazines) as well as *Options*. Condé Nast published *Vogue* and *Vanity Fair*, as well as *GQ*. Emap publishes *Heat*, *FHM*, *Sky*, *Arena*, *Q*, *New Woman* and *Red*. As the publishing companies have tried to target a saturated market (where there are few new readers) by trying different combinations of content, kinds of address to the reader, and visual style, the number of titles has risen, and less successful magazines (like *Frank* or *Minx*) have ceased publication.

Both men's and women's magazines contain a large number of advertisements, and charges to advertisers provide about half the cost of producing a magazine. The other half comes from the purchase price of the magazine. The largest categories of products advertised in women's magazines are cosmetics, clothes and food, but women's magazines also include ads for cars, financial services, watches, and many other things. The largest categories of products advertised in men's magazines are cosmetics, clothes and cars, but there are also ads for electronic equipment, videos, and computer games. In her study of American women's magazines, McCracken (1993) includes editorial material recommending the purchase of products as advertising too, and she found that these concealed ads, as well as ads themselves, accounted for up to 95 per cent of the total number of items in the magazines. For McCracken, advertising is the key feature of women's magazines, and similar proportions of ads to editorial are found in men's magazines too. Magazines contain ads, editorial material contains ads, the front covers of magazines are ads for the magazine itself, editorial material 'advertises' mythic masculine or feminine identities to readers, and to complete the circuit, magazine publishers advertise the spending-power of their typical readers to advertisers in order to attract more ads. This emphasis, as we shall see, has major implications for a semiotic analysis which investigates how magazines relate to ideologies of consumerism and to ideological representations of masculine and feminine identity.

Myths of gender identity

We cannot assume that the representations of masculine or feminine identity found in men's and women's magazines accurately reflect the lives and identities of real men or women. Representations are composed of signs which are meaningful because they belong to socially accepted codes which readers can recognise and decode. Instead of simply criticising magazines for giving a false representation of men's and women's lives, a semiotic analysis would begin by discussing the way that the signs and codes of magazines construct mythic social meanings of masculinity and femininity. One of the ways in which this is done is for the signified concept 'femininity' to be differentiated from 'masculinity'. Women's magazines encode the difference between masculine and feminine identities inasmuch as they are different both from men's magazines like *Loaded* or *GQ*, and from the greater range of 'interest' magazines, like *Golf Monthly* or *MacUser*. This differentiation is signified by the placing of women's magazines in a specific section of newsagent shops and magazine stands. The point is not that all readers of women's magazines are women: about 15 to 30 per cent of readers of women's magazines are men. But women's magazines are signified as different from other kinds of magazine because of the coded way in which they are presented to potential readers. These coding systems permit the magazines to function as signifiers of a defined mythic signified of femininity. Similarly, men's style magazines make great efforts to differentiate masculine identities from feminine identities, and are displayed in shops in a different location to women's magazines.

Women's magazines delimit the shape of what Winship (1987) calls a 'women's world'. Winship argues that this world is mythical, a construct built out of signs; 'the "woman's world" which women's magazines represent is created precisely because it does not exist outside their pages' (Winship 1987: 7). From this point of view, the semiotic codes of women's magazines work to construct a mythic world of the feminine, which compensates for the lack of a satisfying social identity for real women. The function of women's magazines is to provide readers with a sense of community, comfort, and pride in this mythic feminine identity. So the magazines take up the really existing gender relations of culture, and work on them to produce a mythic femininity which supports real women and provides an identity for them. But for Winship and other critics, this mythic femininity has a negative side. It naturalises an ideological view of what being a woman means, and overlapping with this, it naturalises the consumer culture which magazines stimulate through advertising and editorial material. Women, it is argued, are positioned as consumers of products by the signs and codes of women's magazines, a role reinforced by the fact that magazines are themselves commodity products.

This critical account of the role of women's magazines considers that being feminine is a mythic identity constructed by the coded connotations of signs in society. Femininity is not a natural property of women, but a cultural construct. There is a position hollowed out by the codes of women's magazines, and real women fit themselves into this position as individual subjects. In positioning themselves as subjects in this way, women become subject to the ideologies encoded in women's magazines. Conscious choices, intentions and beliefs are seen as the effects of women's ideologically produced subject-position, rather than being freely chosen. But we know that it is possible for individual subjects to criticise ideology and the social order of which it is a part. After all, that is what semiotic critics and theorists of ideology do, and what feminism has done in relation to gender identity. Ideologies are not uniformly successful, and not always effective. Ideology is a site of struggle, where opposition and critique always threaten the edifice of naturalisation and conformity.

Men's magazines use signs and codes to delimit a 'men's world' in a similar way to the 'women's world' of women's magazines. Among the contents of this 'world' are sex, sport, gadgets, and fashion, a mix of ingredients which are linked by their relationship to leisure rather than work. Whereas historically men's role has been defined primarily through their employment, the 'men's world' of men's style magazines is centred on activities and interests pursued outside of work. The majority of these leisure activities and masculine roles are oriented around the purchase of consumer products or engagement with media representations. Clearly, ads and editorial articles about fashion, cars, food, alcoholic drinks and computer games are concerned with products which can be purchased. But even the photographs of scantily dressed women which make up a significant proportion of the visual signs in men's style magazines very often have a connection with consumer media culture. The women may be television actresses, film stars, or fashion models who appear in ads.

Men's magazines encode their readers as people who have considerable amounts of leisure time. The 'ideal reader' of a men's magazine would be a man who spends money on the latest electronic gadgets, clothes, music and video games, for instance. But this 'ideal reader' would also be aware of, and attracted to, the actresses and models who appear in contemporary visual culture, even if they appear in programmes, films or ads whose 'ideal reader' is feminine. The 'men's world' is a world of consumption, including not only buying but also 'consuming' by gazing at many kinds of media imagery. Similar ideologies of consumption which promise to fulfil a desire, to compensate for a lack of satisfaction, are evident in both men's and women's magazines, though in different ways. In a culture where traditionally masculine work (like manual and factory work) is decreasing, and where office work and work with technology are done by both women and men, the 'men's world' is oriented less around work and more around consumption. The 'men's world' of magazines comes increasingly to resemble the 'women's world' of non-work activities and consumer pleasures which women's magazines focus on.

In British culture today, it is not straightforward for men to be preoccupied with consumption and style, because this could be regarded as 'feminine' rather than 'masculine'. Similarly, it is not straightforward for men to be preoccupied with looking at women's bodies as sexual objects, since this would be sexist and insulting to many women. The way in which men's style magazines maintain the 'men's world' of consumption is through the use of the kind of ironic linguistic codes which we encountered in the Wonderbra ad in the previous chapter, and by a particular mode of address to the reader which emphasises heterosexual masculinity in contrast to both femininity and homosexuality. While I shall argue that the ideological significance of the mythic 'men's world' in men's magazines is to reinforce ideologies of consumption and eroticism, the magazines' codes demonstrate an acknowledgement that men may 'see through' these ideologies. Being ironic about an ideological position is a means of preserving that ideology while also admitting the contradictions and problems which it involves.

The inability of ideologies to be permanent structures, and the ability of actual individual subjects to see through some of the discourses which support them, means that we can show not only how media texts support ideology, but also how they might expose cracks and fissures in it. The ability of readers to decode texts 'against the grain', to diagnose and evade their ideological subject-positionings as readers, means that there is always a conflict of interpretations in relation to every text. The ways in which specific individual subjects read and decode signs and meanings will exhibit important differences. These oppositional possibilities must derive from somewhere, and are made available by the specific nature of an individual's place in society, perhaps a contradictory and ambiguous place. Nevertheless, as readers of codes we are always shifting between decodings which are complicit with a dominant ideology, to oppositional or alternative decodings of texts. In this chapter, we shall have to take account of the range of possible decodings of magazines, and note the fissures within and between the discourses of magazines.

The reading subject

The meanings which are decoded by readers depend in part on how a magazine is read. When first getting a magazine, you might leaf through it quite rapidly, stopping briefly to glance at an ad or an editorial page. In this reading pattern, which is syntagmatic (linear) and where concentration is evenly focused through the reading, visual signs and large-type linguistic signs are likely to be noticed most. Because of their size, colour and simplicity, ads may be most likely to attract your attention. Then, you might choose to read particular editorial articles closely. In this second reading pattern, which may not follow the sequential order of the magazine's pages, linguistic syntagms become the focus of attention. Next, having had the magazine for a few days, and read some of it in detail, you might leaf through it again, stopping at interesting ads or articles, reading them again or noticing them for the first time. This third reading pattern is relatively linear, evenly focused on linguistic and visual signs, and depends to some extent on a memory of the first two readings. Each of these reading patterns will affect the decoding process, both in what is read, and how it is read. The reader is controlling the speed and intensity of reading, as well as what is chosen for reading. It is difficult for semiotic analysis to take proper account of these different reading patterns, except by noting connections between the signifiers of the various ads and articles, and the various evident and more complex levels of signification in the part of the magazine under analysis. The way we read (quickly, slowly, superficially, attentively etc.) has significant effects on how signs are decoded. Furthermore, all texts attempt to contain the multiple connotations of their signs by linking them in coded ways. Finally, every text (an ad, a magazine feature, etc.) is prone to 'contamination' of its meaning by adjacent and related texts. Reading magazines in order to conduct a semiotic analysis is not a typical context for reading them.

Reading a women's magazine may be a diversion or an escape from your surroundings, at the doctor's or on a train, for instance, relaxing at home, or at work during a break. Reading may be a relief from domestic work, or a way of expressing independence from a partner or children who are doing something else. Reading magazines always takes place in a concrete social context, and this context (as some of the examples in this paragraph indicate) derives in part from the place of women in society, as mothers, partners, workers etc. Women's magazines not only represent these social contexts by referring to them in the ads and articles they contain, they also shape the meanings of these social contexts for the women who read them. Many of the contexts in which magazines are read help to encode reading as both pleasurable (a private pleasure) and defensive (a way of holding something at bay). McCracken sees women's magazines as constructing a shared consensual myth about femininity which is complicit with ideological roles that real women play out. But she draws attention to the concrete social context of reading, which may often be in conflict with the positive connotations which women's magazines give to femininity.

> Readers are not force-fed a constellation of negative images that naturalize male dominance; rather, women's magazines exert a cultural leadership to shape consensus in which highly pleasurable codes work to naturalize social relations of power. This ostensibly common agreement about what constitutes the feminine is only achieved through a discursive struggle in which words, photos, and sometimes olfactory signs wage a semiotic battle against the everyday world which, by its mere presence, often fights back as an existential corrective to the magazine's ideal images. (McCracken 1993: 3)

As McCracken indicates, pleasures belonging to the 'women's world' are encoded in the contents of magazines, and also in the physical nature of magazines. They have larger pages than most books and may comprise up to 250 pages, connoting abundance and luxury. These connotations are reinforced by the frequent presence of additional free supplements which are attached to the body of the magazine itself. Magazines are glossy and colourful, connoting pleasure and relaxation rather than seriousness, just as Sunday magazine supplements and additional sections do in the newspaper medium. The smell and feel of the glossy paper connotes luxury, and the smells of perfume samples in the magazine connote femininity and its pleasures of self-adornment. The page layouts and typefaces of magazine articles, in contrast to newspapers, for instance, are often as varied, sophisticated, and interesting to decode as the ads which surround them.

The physical nature of women's magazines has connotations which help to encode their purchase and their reading as enjoyable private pleasures offered specifically to a woman reader. But the features which McCracken identified are also shared with men's magazines: they too have glossy colourful pages and complex layouts, samples of men's perfumes and free additional sections. The same physical signs which McCracken found in women's magazines are present in men's style magazines, and this suggests that the same pleasures may be offered to male readers. These pleasures are differentiated from work, and include relaxation, diversion from a less pleasurable activity (like cleaning the house), and enjoying dreams of having or being the people and products denoted in the magazine. To buy a magazine is itself an anticipation of pleasure and can be both regular and controlled, unlike the lack of control over pleasure in many other aspects of people's lives. A magazine is a sign which connects pleasure with the mythic meanings of masculinity or femininity. So there are ways in which buying and reading a magazine can function as a private resistance to the domestic and public roles marked out for men and women. At the same time, buying and reading a magazine reinforces mythic meanings of masculinity or femininity by offering subject-positions which are complicit with the ideological positioning of men and women as particular kinds of consumer, nurturer, lover, or worker, for instance. For McCracken, magazines invite women to share in the pleasures of femininity, but also naturalise the ideological injunction to express one's individuality through the purchase of products. 'If women, at the magazines' urging, experience a sometimes real and sometimes utopian sense of community while reading these texts, confident of participating in normal, expected feminine culture, they are at the same time learning consumerist competitiveness and reified individualism' (McCracken 1993: 299). I have argued in this chapter that men's magazines offer a signified concept of masculinity which men are invited to participate in, and that it is oriented around buying and possessing. Men's magazines differentiate masculinity from femininity, but also share the semiotic mechanisms which women's magazines use. One issue which arises from this argument is that men's magazines might 'feminise' their reader as the same time that they 'masculinise' him.

Address and identity

On the front cover of magazines we often find linguistic signs which encode mythic meanings of masculinity or femininity in their address to the reader. The May 2001 issue of *Cosmopolitan*, for example, announces a feature inside with the linguistic syntagm 'How to have RED HOT SEX ... 44 rude and raunchy foreplay tricks for bad girls only. The 24-hour sex clock – discover your body's passion pattern'. This address to 'you' is also used in ads, and in both media it invites the reader to recognise herself as the individual being spoken to, and also to recognise herself as a member of a group, 'women like you', since 'you' is both singular and plural in English. The visual space and perspective of the magazine cover (or ad) performs the same function since the reader is positioned in front of it as an individual decoder of its visual and linguistic signs, but this position can be occupied by anyone. While magazine covers and ads can address anybody, they claim to address individuals with unique desires and needs, promising that the contents of the magazine or the product in an ad will fulfil the needs of the individual and her group. The cover of the April 2001 issue of *Maxim* addresses men not by using the sign 'you' but by listing series of metonymic items which are components of the signified 'men's world'. At the top of the cover the list is 'SEX SPORT LADIES CLOTHES GADGETS BEER SKITTLES'. These diverse signifiers appear to signify quite distinct signifieds, but what unites them is the absent signifier 'man' whose masculine identity, interests and aspirations are signified by them. There is a mythic masculinity composed from these signs (and potentially composed out of many more signs too) which the magazine and reader are expected to fit into and make complete.

Referring to ads, Williamson argues that 'What the advertisement clearly does is thus to signify, to represent to us, the object of desire' (Williamson 1978: 60). The ad is therefore not just selling us a product with a meaning for us. The ad is also selling us

a future image of ourselves as happier, more desirable, or whatever. The object being advertised stands in for the self which we
desire to become. 'Since that object is the self, this means that,
while ensnaring/creating the subject through his or her
exchange of signs, the advertisement is actually feeding off that
subject's own desire for coherence and meaning in him or her
self' (Williamson 1978: 60). Magazines address 'you', both an
individual man or woman and as a member of a gender group.
The linguistic syntagms on the cover position the reader as a
subject who will be interested, excited, amused, or assisted by the
articles in the magazine which are being advertised on the cover.
The magazine cover, like an ad, is offering something and at the
same time coding the reader as a particular kind of subject, a
gendered subject. In one way or another, all the linguistic signs
on the cover signify that the magazine will make 'you' happier
or better in your gender identity. So as in the case of ads, magazines address a reader who desires to have or to be a more complete self than he or she has or is now.

   This notion that individual subjects are lacking something and
desire to be more perfect selves, can be clarified by a theoretical
model of human subjectivity which derives from psychoanalysis
and shares some of its principles with semiotics. The French psychoanalyst Jacques Lacan developed these ideas in work done in
the 1950s and after (Lacan 1977), and they have since become
allied to semiotic theories because they help to explain how signs,
like the signs in ads, magazines or other media, latch onto fundamental forces in our inner selves. Lacan argued that the
human child is born into a lack in being, a wanting-to-be.
Throughout his or her life, the individual subject attempts to
master this sense of lack, to come to terms with it and overcome
it, but can never succeed in doing so. The subject projects back
the impression that originally, in his or her union with the
mother in early childhood, there was nothing lacking. This is the
imaginary unity and wholeness which the subject tries to recap-
ture throughout his or her life. The thing which would apparently restore the lost pre-lacking state, Lacan calls 'the Other'.
Since there is actually no thing which could really defeat the
sense of lack, the Other is always a representation, an image of
totality rather than something actually graspable.

In order to explain how people come to suffer from this sense of lack, Lacan (1977) gives an account of early child development. The child begins to think of himself or herself as an individual between the ages of six and eighteen months, at a point known as the 'mirror stage'. This stage describes a moment when the child recognises himself or herself in a mirror, and sees himself or herself as just as whole and coordinated as the image which he or she sees, even though the child is in reality physically uncoordinated, and his or her experience is a mass of uncontrolled feelings and instincts. In the mirror, the child sees himself or herself as an independent entity existing in time and space, rather than as the dependent and fragmented being of his or her actual experience. The image the child sees is more whole than the child really feels, and the child's identification of himself or herself with the mirror image in this way is a misrecognition of what the child really is. The child is 'narcissistic': admiring and desiring to be the better self which he or she sees in the mirror, deluding himself or herself that he or she really is this better self. Because the child sees that he or she can become an image that can be seen, he or she can now realise that he or she appears as an image for someone else too, for an Other person, just as the mirror image was an image or Other for the child.

This rather complicated aspect of psychoanalytic theory provides a model for understanding why we identify with images of other people, like the images of beautiful models on the covers of women's magazines. These images are iconic signs which represent the better self which every woman desires to become. The desire to become the better self represented by the visual sign is a desire to overcome the lack which all human subjects experience. Since the model signified in the photograph is made to appear as she does by the various cosmetic products, hair stylists, and clothes which are detailed on the inside page of the magazine, the connotation is that the reader can become like the model by using these products. The eyes of the models signified on magazine covers always look out at the viewer, just as a reflection in a mirror looks back at us. The linguistic syntagms on the cover address the reader as 'you', offering to make 'you' happier, better. In the same way, the cover's iconic sign addresses the viewer, offering an image which signifies a better, happier self, like the image of the better self in Lacan's mirror stage theory. Both linguistic and visual signs position the woman reader as a lacking subject, and simultaneously connote that her desire to overcome lack can be satisfied.

Men's style magazines rarely denote images of men on their covers who could represent the better selves which men desire to be. Instead they denote celebrity women or models who pose in their underwear, adopting the static and languid poses often seen in the topless 'glamour' photographs of 'soft-core porn' magazines. The models are posed and lit to emphasise their faces, breasts and buttocks, and most of their bodies can be seen (whereas women's magazines usually denote only faces). The viewer of the cover image is being positioned as the man to whom the model displays herself. The denoted woman opens herself up to a look which seizes her as an object of heterosexual masculine desire. It is the glamour model Jordan who is denoted on the April 2001 issue of *Maxim*, for example, wearing only black underwear and gazing out at the viewer. A linguistic syntagm on the cover anchors the meaning of the photograph, stating 'Hello Big Boy it's... Jordan. Shy, quiet and reclining'. The linguistic and iconic signs hollow out a subject-position for the viewer where Jordan is a passive and available ('shy, quiet and reclining') object for the viewer, who is sexually dominant ('Big Boy'), though the humorous tone of the syntagm tames this rapacious relationship somewhat. The cover image has presented Jordan as an Other for the viewer to desire. Furthermore, to desire Jordan and to have her (by possessing her sexually) promises to satisfy the viewer's desire, to make him more complete and more fully masculine than he is now. The image of Jordan and the cover's linguistic signs are there to be seen and read from a particular masculine subject-position, which actual men are called to take up.

It is no accident that psychoanalytic theory has the same kind of underlying structure as the theory of ideology which we have been using. In each case, the theory argues that individual subjects are positioned by a structure which they cannot control, and which precedes them. In each case, individual subjects are positioned as lacking something, and desiring to have or to be something. In fact, Althusser's theory of ideology (1971) used Lacan's psychoanalytic concept of the mirror stage to explain how ideology acts on us. Ideology calls each person to take on the image of himself or herself as a subject, to be a woman and not a man, to be 'I' and not 'you', to be a consumer and not a producer, etc. Like the mirror stage, ideology gives the individual subject a social identity. But like the image in the mirror, the subject's ideological identity is a misrecognition of what he or she really is.

The image of himself or herself which the child sees in the mirror in Lacan's theory is of course a sign. It is an iconic sign which represents the child. Lacan uses the term 'imaginary' to refer to the various signs, like the mirror image, which a subject identifies with in the quest to overcome lack and see himself or herself as a better and more complete self. So we can say that the iconic and linguistic signs in magazines are addressed to the imaginaries of masculine and feminine subjects, because the magazines offer better, happier selves which might be attainable by having or being the Other things and people which magazines represent. The imaginaries coded in magazines are also ideological, since the connotations of the magazine's signs construct mythic pleasurable identities for real men or women to identify with. Despite the problems for real people in society, the mythic gender identities signified in magazines provide imaginary satisfaction for men and women. Magazines' mythic masculinities and femininities are 'worlds' which the reader of the magazine is invited to share in. Since these 'worlds' are imaginary representations built out of signs, they can hardly be condemned for being unlike the reality which real men and women experience. On the other hand, since these imaginaries are composed of mythic gender identities that feed off men's and women's real sense of lack and unhappiness, magazines can be criticised for offering people forms of pleasure that do little to make their real lives any better or happier. McCracken puts this point succinctly: 'within this discursive structure, to be beautiful, one must fear being non-beautiful; to be in fashion, one must fear being out of fashion; to be self-confident, one must first feel insecure' (McCracken 1993: 136).

Masculine and feminine 'worlds'

The cover models gaze at the buyers of magazines, connoting the complicity of the model and the reader in constructing the mythic masculinities and femininities in men's and women's magazines. Since it is for men that attractive images of women are usually presented, there is, we could say, an absent male gaze structuring the look of the cover model and the corresponding look back by the buyer, whether this is a woman buyer or a man, and whether the magazine is for men or for women. The cover images are constructed with reference to a wider social code in which being feminine means taking pleasure in looking at oneself, and taking pleasure in being looked at by men. The 'women's world' and 'men's world' in magazines are not self-sufficient things, but imaginary worlds constituted by their different relationships with masculinity. For instance, the May 2001 issue of *Cosmopolitan* includes these features: 'Is He Mr Right Or Just Mr Tonight?' and 'The New Celibacy. When women give up lust in the name of love'. One feature codes men as possible partners versus objects of desire, while the other focuses on romance with men in contrast to sex with them. There are numerous other regular features and occasional articles in which the magazine's discourses addressed to women define feminine experience as a set of possible relations to masculinity. As the titles of the features above indicate, the myth of feminine identity does not consist of a single way of relating to masculinity. Men and masculinity are coded as desired, feared, pitied, and a host of other positionings. Each of these coded ways of representing masculinity requires the reader of the article to adopt a particular subject-position in order to decode the 'correct' meaning of the article. But the subject-positions constructed for the reader are different in different articles. To take a simple example, some articles encode the reader as single but seeking a partner, while others code the reader as either married or in a long-term relationship.

But despite these differences in subject-position, the mythic meaning of femininity is given its meaningfulness, its value as a signified, by a distinction between the feminine and the masculine. Heterosexual sexuality is one of the key aspects of social life which involves the distinction between femininity and masculinity as well as the interrelation of the two gender roles. Therefore much of the mythic meaning of femininity is signified in terms of desire and sexuality between men and women. In *Cosmopolitan*, writes Winship: 'Sex is a means for self-discovery, sex is the centre of a relationship; sex is a step to other things; sex is always something that can be bettered or varied; sex is potentially always a problem; sex is something you-never-can-forget' (Winship 1987: 112). Sex is not an activity with a fixed 'natural' meaning. Its meaning is constructed through the ways in which it is defined and coded as meaningful by discourses. Feminine and masculine sexuality are therefore mythic social meanings which magazines work to shape. The shaping of feminine identity is preoccupied with men and masculinity because femininity and masculinity are defined in relation to each other, and the same is true for the shaping of masculine identity in men's magazines.

In the April 2001 issue of *Maxim*, many of the editorial features help to shape the masculinity of the 'men's world' in relation to women. One feature, 'What She Wants' is about 'Lies, farts and vomit. Strangely, not what your good lady wants (unless you're lucky) – but what she loathes'. The feature promises to help men understand what women like and dislike about men, in the context of a sexual relationship. In the feature 'Welcome to the pleasure domes', '*Maxim* pays tribute to the wonders of the bosom' as a key component in men's sexual attraction to women. Some features focus on women as objects of sexual desire, while others assume that men wish to improve existing emotional relationships. There are also features based around interviews with men who are represented as icons of masculinity (like the footballer and actor Vinnie Jones) and features which represent masculinity in relation to unlikely physical challenges (like how to survive on a desert island). The numerous fashion and style pages in men's magazines connote that masculinity may be as narcissistic as femininity, since it is associated with adornment, self-display and bodily improvement. But magazines' emphasis on heterosexual desire, sexual performance, and physical testing signify resistance to, and refusal of, this potentially 'feminine' subject-position. Similarly, the ironic and mocking tone of much of the linguistic material in men's magazines distances them from the contradiction between being excessively masculine (aggressive, sexist, rapacious) and threateningly feminine (narcissistic, insecure, passive). The masculinity signified in men's magazines is a fragile construction uniting contradictory meanings.

The notion that femininity and masculinity are defined in relation to each other is much the same as Saussure's contention that signs acquire their capacity to mean for us because of their position in *langue*, the system of differences which underlies language. Just as 'cat' is not 'dog', femininity is not masculinity. Gender identity can be seen as a structure of meaning in which each gender acquires its meaningfulness by being different from the other gender. The ideological component of this process is that magazines encode the identities they offer in certain ways and not others. Some gender identities are coded as 'natural' while others are not. The naturalisation of gender identities is accomplished by several means. In relation to the codes which structure linguistic signs, the inclusion of the reader as a friend and an equal is a significant example of naturalisation. The discourse of the articles in magazines connotes conversation. It is a representation of the ways that people speak when they know each other and share the same world, the 'woman's world' or 'men's world'. An article in *Cosmopolitan*, '44 sizzling pre-sex secrets' begins by referring to the conversational code immediately: 'To have mind-blowing sex, you need memorable foreplay. But having one or two tried and tested techniques isn't the key to eternal arousal' (May 2001: 139). Conversation is connoted here by, for instance, the use of contractions ('isn't'), cliché ('mind-blowing sex'), and non-literary sentence structure (beginning a sentence with 'But'). Similar conversational devices are used in the *Maxim* article 'So, you're a breast man', which begins 'So why are breasts so damn sexy? Because they remind us of bottoms, according to San Francisco evolutionary biologist Brian Miele' (April 2001: 91). Unlike most newspapers, magazines feature a personal editorial address by the editor to the reader, often accompanied by the editor's photograph. As on the cover, the reader is addressed as 'you', and the editor refers to the magazine staff, its readers, and men or women in general as 'we'.

Magazines signify the mythic community of the 'women's world' or 'men's world' in the linguistic signs and codes of their articles, which enable the discourse to overcome contradictions. They create a mythic community in which men or women share the same opinions and invite individual readers to recognise themselves and their opinions as part of a gendered 'world'. Furthermore, it is the magazine which creates the bridge between individual men or women and a community of the same gender, and denotes the parameters of the 'world'. The magazine becomes a metonymic sign standing in for the 'men's world' or 'women's world'. By buying the magazine, readers are 'buying into' the gendered 'world' and the community it represents, although this community is a mythic construct generated by the reader's interaction with the signs, codes and myths of the magazine's discourse. Community is also signified by surveys, letters, and other interactive devices like makeovers, competitions or reader offers. Each of these features of the magazines' discourse involves an exchange between the magazine and the reader, where the reader actively responds to the magazine. The function of these interactive devices is to reinforce the mythic interchange between the real world of the reader and the imaginary 'world' of the magazine.

All style and fashion magazines associate the attainment of a desired imaginary self with products. McCracken (1993) gives a very full account of the various strategies of advertising, while only a brief list can be given here. Articles may contain recommendations of products, so that the article is in effect an ad itself. For the magazine, recommending a product may also help to secure advertising from the makers of the product, a process called 'brand reciprocity'. For the reader, a continuum is established between the codes of ads and of articles, so ads are not perceived as an interruption to the reading experience. Ads which use the linguistic and visual codes of the magazine, 'advertorials', are the clearest example of the intertextual merging of the codes of ads with the codes of articles. The credibility connoted by editorial recommendations of products helps give credibility to ads for these products, a meaning reinforced by the placing of ads in appropriate articles or sections of the magazine. Breaking an article on different pages of the magazine forces the reader of the article to pass through a series of ads to get to the conclusion of the article, setting up a relay between ads and the article. All of these relationships between ads and articles confuse the distinction between the two kinds of discourse. The effect of this confusion is for the whole magazine to encode the 'women's world' or 'men's world' as a world of desired mythic meanings which are attached to products.

The limits of the imaginary

In the account of Lacan's theory of the mirror stage above, the ungendered sign 'child' and the phrases 'himself or herself', 'he or she' etc. were used to explain how individual subjects come to experience a sense of lack in being or wanting-to-be. The gender of the child was not significant, because the theory applies to all human beings of either gender. The theory showed that the experience of lack gave rise to a desire to have and to be a better self. The theory accounts for the desired images presented in magazines, and the better self which the magazines offer as part of their mythic 'women's world' or 'men's world'. It was also noted that the child seeing his or her image in a mirror realises that the child can be an image seen by someone else, just as the child sees himself or herself as an image. The child is positioned in time and space as an individual subject, an Other to someone, just like the individual subjects in the world around it who are also Other. The child begins to have a social existence and an identity.

It is the difference between the child's real self and the better self represented by the mirror image of the child which establishes a lack in the child's sense of himself or herself. As soon as the child recognises that he or she can be represented by a sign, something that stands in for him or her, he or she has made the first step towards the system of language. Language is of course a system in which something (a signifier) stands in for something which it represents (a signified). Just as the child's mirror image signifies the child, so the signifier 'cat' signifies the concept of a furry four-legged creature. When we use language, the signifier 'I' stands in for our individual subjective identity. Each individual subject can represent his or her identity in language by using the signifier 'I' to signify him or her. Everything we can under-

stand and communicate about our reality has to pass through
the medium of the linguistic signs we use to think, speak and
write about it, and this applies also to our identity. The individual subject's identity has to be understood, represented and communicated by signs.

But the system of language, and the world which it enables us
to know and speak about, are two different things. The system of
language is Other to the world of the real, but we can only gain
access to the real in thought and experience by apprehending it
in language. We are forced to live, think, and know in the realm
of the Other, the realm of signs. Lacan called this realm of the
Other, the realm of signs, the 'symbolic', because a symbol represents something (as a sign does) but is not the same as what it
symbolises. The symbolic is the opposite of the imaginary. The
imaginary is a realm where there would be no lack, where there
would be no difference between a signifier and its signified. We
have already seen that the imaginary for the child in the mirror
stage is a realm where the child and the mirror image, the signifier and the signified, are imagined to be the same thing. But
this imaginary realm where there is no lack, no difference
between signifier and signified, is illusory. The child and its
mirror image are not really the same. In the same way, the imaginary of magazines' 'women's world' or 'men's world' is a world
of better selves which a reader aspires to be part of, a world in
which his or her real sense of lack would be abolished. Despite
the pleasure of identifying with the imaginary 'men's world' or
'women's world', the magazine cannot deliver a new and perfect
identity to its reader. After all, the magazine is just a collection
of signs. Magazines are addressed to the reader's imaginary,
offering a better self, but magazines have to exist in the symbolic
order, the world we all exist in. Magazines communicate their
mythic meanings by means of signs, thus their representations of
the imaginary are dependent on the symbolic, the signs which
do the communicating.

The discourse of magazines, comprising the discourses of articles and ads, constructs an imaginary for the reader. This imaginary consists of a gendered 'world' in which femininity or
masculinity is both satisfying and attainable as an identity. The
discourses of magazines construct subject-positions for their read-

ers by means of codes which address the reader as a lacking subject of the symbolic order, whose gender identity is constructed as Other to masculinity (for women) or femininity (for men). By constructing a mythic community for men or women, magazines delineate the social meaning of gender which the reader is invited to participate in. Although the imaginary identity offered by the magazine discourse is pleasurable and secure, it can only be communicated by signs. As a structure of signs, imaginary gender identity is brought into the realm of the Other, where by definition it cannot satisfy the lack which all individual subjects experience. So there is a perpetual movement back and forth for the reader between identifying with the better self which the magazine's imaginary offers, and having to exist in the symbolic world of signs and social meanings. In the social world which individual subjects inhabit, there is always a difference between what we are and what we desire to be. So there are always more images of better selves which can be constructed in magazines, and more products which promise to lead us towards this unattainable better self.

Sources and further reading

McCracken (1993) is a long and detailed analysis of women's magazines partly based on semiotic methods, though her examples are of American magazines, and with the exception of her final chapter the magazines discussed were published in the early 1980s. More recent magazines are discussed in essays in the collection edited by Ballaster *et al.* (1991). Winship (1987) is a less explicitly theoretical study, emphasising the pleasure which readers (and Winship herself) derive from reading magazines, and contrasts with very critical work from a feminist point of view like Ferguson (1983). Hermes (1995) focuses on the pleasure of reading magazines and is based on interviews with Dutch women (ethnographic research) rather than semiotics. Men's style culture and men's magazines are addressed by Mort (1996) and Nixon (1996), and teen magazines for girls are analysed by Stokes (1999).

The psychoanalytic theory in this chapter derives mainly from Lacan (1977), but readers wishing to follow this up are advised to start with other secondary writing before tackling the original. Introductions and discussions of psychoanalytic theory include Moi (1985), Butler (1990), the introductory essays in Mitchell and Rose (1982), and part one of

Macdonald (1995) which also uses these concepts in analyses of a wide range of media texts. Williamson (1978) also has discussions of the concepts explained in this chapter.

Suggestions for further work

1 Analyse the covers of three magazines aimed at either men or women. What signs on the covers justify or contradict your assumptions about their readers? Is there a single 'ideal reader' constructed by the signs in each case?

2 Analyse some of the signs and codes in three magazines which seem to address teenage girl readers. In what ways does a mythic 'teen world' resemble or differ from the 'women's world' constructed in women's magazines?

3 If you are already a reader of magazines, how is your usual reading pattern similar or different to that of a semiotic analyst? Can a semiotic analysis adequately explain the ways you usually read, for instance by emphasising the way of reading which seems to be invited by the magazine's format, arrangement, layout etc?

4 Select some examples of editorial discourse discussing men in women's magazines, or discussing women in men's magazines. What functions do mythic representations of the other gender perform?

5 This chapter focuses on monthly magazines. How should the analysis you have read be altered to account for the semiotics of weekly women's magazines?

6 Which aspects of the editorial discourses of women's magazines are common to other kinds of media text (like romance fiction, self-help books, or chat shows on TV, for instance)? What are the shared myths and ideological assumptions of these discourses in the different media?

7 Look for ads in magazines where the placing of the ad in relation to editorial material seems significant to you. Analyse the relationship of ad and editorial in semiotic terms.

4

Newspapers

Introduction

This chapter discusses the ways in which semiotic analysis approaches newspapers as a medium. We shall be considering the linguistic signs used in newspapers, the iconic and other visual signs in newspapers, and the relationship between linguistic and visual signs. The front pages of two British newspapers published on the same day (Wednesday 7 February 2001) are reproduced in this chapter, and many of the specific examples used here are drawn from those newspaper editions.

Before considering how signs are used in newspapers, we need to define what news is. News does not consist of lists of facts or events. News is not just facts, but representations produced in language and other signs like photographs. A semiotic analysis of news discourse will therefore include discussion of the connotations of the linguistic and visual signs used in news stories. Connotation shapes the meanings of a news story, and connotations can only be perceived when they belong to coded ways of using signs which the reader can recognise. So codes have a social dimension, they are ways of using signs which are more or less familiar to groups of people in society. As we shall see, some codes are specific to newspapers and others are more widely used. One of the most common codes in the media and social life generally is the narrative code. News in newspapers is presented in stories, and stories are narratives about people and events. How something is narrated using the narrative code will be just as significant as what is narrated by a news story.

Codes more specific to the newspaper medium are found in newspaper photographs, which commonly connote actuality and

evidence. One of the issues this chapter deals with is the relationship between linguistic signs, photographic signs, and
graphic signs in the pages of newspapers. Each of these kinds of
sign and their coded connotations play a role in establishing the
mythic meanings of what is reported in the news. As we have
seen with the media discussed so far in this book, mythic meanings have a relationship to ideology. We shall need to consider
how the mythic meanings of the news are related to ideologies,
and the ideological status of news as a specific set of ways of communicating. Newspapers and other news media shape what can
be thought of as news, by reporting some events and excluding
others. So news discourse is an ideological representation of the
world because it selects what will be reported, and sets the terms
of what is significant. A semiotic analysis of newspapers will need
to consider what kinds of message are communicated by the
codes of news discourse, the contexts in which these messages
are produced by news professionals and decoded by newspaper
readers, and the ideological significance of news discourse.

The newspaper business

News is a commercial product, in that newspapers are businesses
controlled by corporations whose aim is to generate profit for
their shareholders. Of the twenty-one British national daily
newspapers and Sunday newspapers, eleven are owned by two
corporations, News International and Mirror Group. News Corporation owns *The Times*, *The Sunday Times*, *The Sun*, *News of the
World*, and also has TV interests including Sky, Granada Sky, Fox
Kids and Sky Box Office, with a 40 per cent share of the satellite
TV broadcaster BSkyB. Similarly, Daily Mail and General Trust
owns the *Daily Mail*, *Mail on Sunday*, *Evening Standard* and
twenty other daily newspapers in Britain, and in television the
corporation owns Teletext, British Pathé, the Performance
Channel, New Era Television, and 20 per cent of the ITN TV
news company. News International and Mirror Group between
them control about two-thirds of the national newspaper market.
Newspapers make money through sales, and need to maintain
large circulation figures to stay profitable. Figures provided by
the Audit Bureau of Circulations showed national newspaper cir-

culations in January 2001 as: *The Sun* 3,624,563; *The Mirror* 2,113,705; *Daily Mail* 2,441,398; *The Daily Telegraph* 975,890; *Daily Express* 943,898; *The Times* 686,618; *Daily Star* 637,826; *Financial Times* 458,292; *The Guardian* 400,708; *The Independent* 197,075. These figures record the number of copies of each newspaper actually purchased, but in September 2000, for example, the recorded sales of both 'quality' and 'popular' newspapers were boosted by 'sampling exercises' where 350,000 free copies were provided on trains and aeroplanes, and bulk sales were made at a discounted price to restaurants and hotels. Some newspapers reduce their cover price even further on particular days to incrcase opportunist sales. As a result of these changes sales appear relatively stable, but the underlying trend in the British newspaper market is down. Market pressures have led to the copying by competing titles of sales-boosting techniques like new formats, extra sections, or prize quizzes.

These economic factors have affected the contents of newspapers. Broadsheet 'quality' papers have become more like the mass-market 'popular' newspapers, with fewer front-page stories, more photographs, bigger headlines, and many 'blurbs' advertising the features on inside pages. In recent years, the sport sections of British 'quality' newspapers have increased in size significantly, and 'lifestyle' sections have been added to attract a wider range of advertising. The traditionally sober style of 'quality' newspapers has given way to the forms of self-advertisement which have been common in 'popular' newspapers for many years, caused by the increased competitiveness and falling profitability of the newspaper industry. As in the case of women's magazines, small newspaper circulations can be viable if the readership is an attractive market for advertisers. Large circulation figures mean that ads reach large numbers of consumers, but a small and significant readership group (like businesspeople who control their companies' purchasing decisions) may be enough to attract advertising income. Just as newspapers are commercial products which gather income from sales, the purchasing-power of their readers is also a kind of product, which is offered to advertisers. As an industry producing newspapers and readerships, newspapers are part of consumer culture. This context is reflected in the ideologies which are naturalised in newspaper discourse, as a semiotic analysis can reveal.

News value

Newspapers are produced by professional workers who select some events for reporting as news, and exclude others. The pattern of inclusion–exclusion differs from one paper to another and from one news cycle (usually one day's news) to another. 'Qualities' have more foreign news for instance, 'popular' tabloids have more crime-based or personality-based news. So clearly,

3   *The Sun*, front page 7 February 2001

news is not a fixed category which arises naturally. News is neither found nor gathered, as if it were already there. It is the product of professional ways of thinking, writing, and composing
which are all codes of behaviour learned by news workers. These
general points about what news is and how it is produced need
to be substantiated by a closer examination of what can become
news, and the codes which structure news discourse. Then we
can see how these structures of news encoded the meanings of

4   *The Times*, front page 7 February 2001

news in some news stories, and consider how the readers of newspapers might make sense of the news.

There are an infinite number of possible facts about the world which could be reported, but news discourse reports only a selection of facts. What is reported is the selection of facts assumed to be significant. But it is obvious when looking at a group of newspapers that what counts as most significant for one newspaper is often quite different from what counts as significant for another newspaper. As you can see from figures 3 and 4, the front-page stories in *The Sun* and *The Times* are all different. So one of the first questions we need to ask about news discourse is how news is constructed by the use of criteria for selection. This selection process depends on criteria which give greater 'news value' to some facts and events than others. Galtung and Ruge (1973) described the criteria used informally and unconsciously by journalists and editors to decide which events are newsworthy, and which are more newsworthy than others. In other words, these criteria form a code shared consensually by news workers which enables them to determine the degree of news value which any event has. Events which can be narrated by news discourse in terms of these criteria are likely to become printed news stories, and the more criteria which an event satisfies, the greater news value it possesses. Here are outlines of the main criteria for encoding news which Galtung and Ruge discovered:

1 Frequency: short-duration events (like a conference on ozone depletion in the atmosphere) are close to the daily frequency of newspaper publication and are more likely to be reported than long processes (like the progressive depletion itself).
2 Threshold: the volume of an event (like a multi-car pile-up) or degree of increased intensity (like an escalation in deaths from AIDS) must be high to be reported.
3 Unambiguity: the event must be clearly interpretable by news codes (like the Queen suddenly goes into hospital – a 'royal story'), even if its meaning is itself ambiguous (no-one knows what is wrong with her).
4 Meaningfulness: to the assumed reader (an event occurring in or close to Britain, or which is relevant to current pre-occupations in the British news).

5 Consonance: the expectedness of an event (like more soccer violence at an international match), or assumed reader demand for news about it (like a royal marriage).

6 Unexpectedness: the surprising unpredictability of an event (the Foreign Secretary suddenly resigns, for instance), or the scarcity of such events (major floods in London).

7 Continuity: the persistence in the news of a story deemed newsworthy in the past (like the persistence of stories about the royal family).

8 Composition: a full newspaper will exclude other stories due to lack of space, whereas an empty newspaper will pull in stories to fill it.

9 Reference to elite nations: news relating to nations of world importance (like the United States, Germany, Russia, etc.).

10 Reference to elite persons: news relating to important figures (like the President of the United States, the Queen, Michael Jackson, etc.).

11 Reference to persons: the simplification of processes by reference to a person who is used as a sign of something abstract (Miners' leader Arthur Scargill, for instance, appeared in the 1980s as a sign of the negative value of union militancy).

12 Reference to something negative: disasters are more newsworthy than successes, for instance.

It is obvious from reading the list of criteria for news value that events in the world do not 'naturally' exist as news. What is selected as news depends on the usually daily rhythm of a newspaper office and the shared professional codes of journalists. News is dependent on the organisation of news institutions, and the construction of a mythic reading subject whose interest newspapers aim to engage. On the front page of *The Times*, the story 'Russell "killer" may be freed' exhibits Unambiguity (its dominant code is that of court reporting, and although a decision about the freeing of a murder suspect has not yet been reached, this is a dramatic development in the case), Meaningfulness (the murder of Lin Russell and her daughter was a consistent interest for all British newspapers), Consonance (the story updates the reader about the case), Continuity (part of the ongoing news discourse about violence against children), and Unexpectedness (a presumed killer may be found not guilty). The apparently quite different story in *The Sun*, 'BANNED', can be accounted for by many of the same criteria. The story exhibits Unambiguity (the exclusion of *The Sun*'s drug-detecting dog from a royal event is partly a 'royal story'), Meaningfulness (the story is connected both to concerns over drug-use and to the royal family), Consonance (assumed demand for news of the royal family), Unexpectedness (it is surprising that a drug-detecting dog is unwelcome at the event), Continuity (*The Sun*'s drug dog and the royal family have featured in previous stories in the newspaper), and Reference to elite persons (members of the royal family).

The criteria of news value are useful in showing that despite the different referents of news stories, news stories exhibit a number of consistent and repeated features. So the news value criteria can be regarded as a coding system which is knowingly or unknowingly used by journalists in order to structure and shape the meanings of events as news. One of the consequences of this must be that journalistic 'objectivity' is a mythic meaning for news discourse which is created by the assumptions about news that underpin the professional activities of newspaper workers. Since journalists narrate news using the codes of news value in general and of their newspaper in particular, the news discourse which they produce cannot be the 'natural' way of understanding news or an 'objective' account of facts. For over twenty-five years, critical analysis of news by, among others, the Glasgow Media Group (1976, 1980, 1986), has shown that news is shaped by the commercial, ideological and semiotic structures through which it is produced. This is not at all to accuse journalists of 'bias' or distortion, since that accusation assumes that there is such a thing as an 'unbiased' news story. As we have seen in previous chapters of this book, signs never simply denote a reality 'objectively'. They always encode connoted meanings, drawing on mythic social meanings which support a particular ideological point of view.

So news value criteria are a code which can be usefully tested against the stories which have appeared in particular newspapers, to see which news stories have more news value than others in journalistic professional codes. But there are also a number of drawbacks to the use of the news value criteria. As the two examples of news stories above indicate, they do not discriminate between the kinds of news story in different kinds of newspapers. They tell us little about the linguistic and visual signs, the codes of newspaper discourses, in which news stories are represented. They tell us even less about how newspaper readers make sense of the news, although the criteria are based on assumptions held by journalists about what readers are interested in.

In representing newsworthy events in news stories, newspapers make use of familiar narrative codes, ways of narrating stories with different contents in similar terms. For instance, the stories 'Cruise v Cruise' in *The Sun*, and 'IMF advises Britain to hold off on euro' in *The Times* are both narratives presented in terms of conflict. The divorcing film stars Tom Cruise and Nicole Kidman are said to 'battle over their £300 million fortune', while campaigners for a referendum on Britain's entry into the European monetary system are said to have been 'dealt a blow' by International Monetary Fund advice. The connotations of the narrative code being used are significant in shaping and containing the meanings of news in particular ways. Although, by definition, the content of each news story must be different to all others, the contents of stories are given meaning by invoking narrative codes which define, order, and shape the contents. An event attains news value not simply because of what it is, but also because it can be narrated in the terms of an existing narrative code. News events, when narrated as news stories, reinforce existing narrative codes, and familiar narrative codes attract stories which exemplify them. So selecting events for the news cannot be thought of as neutral, nor can it be prior to the representation of the event in a narrative code. The activity of selection already involves an awareness of the narrative codes in news discourse.

As well as noting what news discourse represents, and how it represents by means of connotation, we need to consider the coding systems used by different newspapers. Just by glancing at a few newspapers in a newsagent's shop, it is easy to see that newspapers do not all look the same, because they use page layout, photographs, or headlines differently. A closer look will reveal that their linguistic registers and 'tones of voice' are different. Although there are some mythic meanings which are common to news discourse in general (news is immediate, relevant, and significant, for instance), there are varied ways that news is encoded by linguistic and visual signs. These differences not only affect the meanings of news stories, but also affect the ways in which the newspapers can be read. Later in this chapter, we shall need to consider the reading patterns which real readers adopt, and the contexts in which reading newspapers takes place.

News discourse

Because newspapers are organised institutions with habitual ways of doing their job, and because they have to generate news stories quickly, efficiently and almost continuously, they rely on information relayed to them by existing and accessible news sources or by news agencies which gather news. The news sources, as Whitaker lists them (1981: 31–2) include Parliament, local councils, the police and emergency services, law courts, royal press offices, 'diary' events which happen each year (like sporting events or party conferences), and other news media. Newspapers also receive news from organisations which issue press releases and give press conferences, including government departments and local authorities, companies, trades unions, charities and lobby groups, and the armed forces. Some individuals (like people in newsworthy court cases) also make public statements, and news might also be acquired from them.

These bodies are organised, established by status, and maintained by funding. They are 'accessed voices', to whom the media have access, and who expect access to the media. The discourses of these groups therefore become the raw material for the language of news stories, since news language is parasitic on their discursive codes and ideological assumptions. News is intertextually related to, and permeated by, the discourse of these news sources' press releases and public statements. Organisations usually train their press officers (who produce news information for newspapers) to write press releases in the style and language of news discourse, so that the distinction between newspaper discourse and public relations discourse can be difficult to draw. But the linguistic codes used in newspapers are not all the same. Particular linguistic signs, narrative forms, and mythic meanings deriving from a news source must be assimilated into the habitual discourse of an individual newspaper.

One of the most interesting aspects of newspaper discourses is the way that they address their readers. Particular linguistic signs and ways of combining them according to socially accepted codes connote that newspaper discourse is a sign of the reader's discourse, a representation of the reader's own discursive idiom. Newspaper discourse cannot be the same as the reader's real discourse, since the newspaper does not know who the reader is, and newspaper language is written, not spoken. But newspaper discourse takes the form of a coded discourse which stands in the place of the reader, asking the reader to identify with the subject-position implied by the code. 'Popular' tabloids use an orally-based, restricted set of vocabulary and sentence structures, while 'quality' newspapers use a more elaborated and complex set of codes which have more in common with written communication than spoken communication. This does not mean that 'popular' newspaper readers cannot write, or that they do not understand long words. The orally-based discourses of 'popular' newspapers connote familiarity, camaraderie, and entertainingness, as opposed to the connotations of authority, formality, and seriousness which are present in the discourses of 'quality' newspapers.

Orality is connoted by the use of deliberate misspelling, contrastive stress (like italics or bold letters in contrast to the standard typeface), paralanguage (features of spoken discourse, like writing words in ways that connote slurred or hesitant speech, for instance), information structure (the use of short or incomplete sentences), slang words ('bash' to mean party in *The Sun*'s 'BANNED' story), idioms, clichés, first names and nicknames ('Lady V' in *The Sun*), contractions (like 'don't' etc.), deixis (words like here, now, you, we, this, which make reference to the situation of a speaker), modality (implying a speaker's subjective judgement with words like correct, should, might, regrettable, certainly etc.), and the use of words which constitute speech acts (questions, commands, accusations, demands, where the word is also performing an action in itself). Alliteration is very common

('Cruise v Cruise'), as are puns. It is not just particular linguistic signs which connote speech, but also typography and layout. Typographic devices break up the linear appearance of print, and such devices include variation of typeface, and dots or dashes connoting unfinished sentences or shifts of thought in the same sentence. Fowler (1991), from whom this analysis derives, has a much fuller discussion of these linguistic features.

On the other hand, 'quality' newspapers use longer sentences (the six-line first paragraph of *The Times*'s 'IMF advises Britain' story is a single sentence), no misspelling or contrastive stress within stories, no signifiers of paralanguage, no incomplete sentences, and fewer of the other devices mentioned above. This may not mean that 'quality' newspapers are better because they appear more 'authoritative' than 'popular' tabloids. Authority is a mythic meaning connoted by the discourse of the 'quality' press, and is no less a mythic meaning than the 'entertainingness' connoted by the discourse of 'popular' newspapers. To make a value-judgement about the two kinds of discourse would be to assume that there is a discourse which is 'transparent' and uncoded. This assumption is itself a mythic meaning of news 'objectivity' which is constructed in discourse.

The mythic equivalence between a reader's speech codes and the newspaper's written discursive codes enables the newspaper to seem to engage in dialogue with the reader. This establishes an imaginary community of readers, reader loyalty to the paper's identity as manifested in its discourse, and a familiar environment in which ideological values circulate between newspaper and reader. Dialogic modes of discourse have the effect of presupposing an ongoing, comprehensible reality which is the referent of a conversation between newspaper and reader. Both parties, it seems, know what they are referring to, and do not need to analyse or define the subject of their 'conversation'. For the assumed reader of *The Sun* there is no need to explain who 'Lady V' is, and for the reader of *The Times* the debate over the 'euro' currency is taken for granted. The ideological function of this way of using linguistic signs and their connotations of speech is to make the referent of the news story (the news event) seem naturally given. When consensual agreement between newspaper and reader is established by the news discourse, there is no apparent need for an analysis of how the meaning of the news event has been constructed, coded by the signs used to represent it.

The desire for items of high news value will militate against the presentation of consensus, of a smoothly running and coherent reality, because news stories are so often about events which seem to threaten stability. In the context of this contradiction in news discourse, the maintenance of the ideology of stability is displaced onto the linguistic structuring of the discourse. Stability is evident in the consistent use of the same news discourse for all the stories and in every issue of the newspaper. 'Quality' newspapers demonstrate discursive stability by the relatively formal language and considered tone of their stories, connoting the measured assessment and objective reporting of the mythic 'responsible' journalist, and the supposed good sense of their readers. Tabloid newspapers demonstrate stability in the maintenance of the orally-based language used, connoting a consistent 'tone of voice' which stands in for their reader's assumed discourse. There is also consistency in the repeated use of the same narrative forms in newspaper stories, despite the perpetually different events which are being reported.

News stories use a lot of personalisation (reference to individuals) in stories where the individual is a representative of some larger news issue relating to an ideological meaning. If we recall Barthes' example of a black soldier saluting the flag on the cover of *Paris-Match*, a particular person was pictured because he became the instance of the myth of French imperialism. In news stories, personalisation techniques include the use of linguistic signs like names, ages, job-descriptions, and gender roles. However, as in the case of the black soldier, this personalisation is not only connoting the uniqueness of the person, but relating him or her to a category of person (like pop-star, mother, spokesman, premier etc.) with a mythic meaning, as in *The Sun*'s personalisation of Tom Cruise and Nicole Kidman, mentioning names, ages, and the description 'Hollywood couple', for instance. The personalisation here signifies membership of a particular social group with mythic meanings, rather than uniqueness, since the 'showbiz' wealth and status of the couple make them newsworthy.

Both the 'Lady V topless at last!' story in *The Sun* and the 'Just William bows out of princely protocol' story in *The Times* concern the boundaries between ordinariness and extraordinariness. Part of their newsworthiness derives from the contemporary concern with how high-status individuals might be the same or different from the 'ordinary person'. Lady Victoria Hervey is the sister of the Marquess of Bristol but she is photographed on the front page of *The Sun* in a pose connoting sexual availability, and the linguistic signs in the feature on page three of the paper play on the contrast between her distance from the ordinary person due to her aristocratic status, and this availability as a sexual object of the reader's gaze: *'The Sun ... feels jolly privileged to offer this exclusive peek'*, and *'there is no finer candidate for the peer-age'*. Both 'peek' and *'peer'* connote illicit erotic looking, while 'exclusive' and *'peer'* also belong to a discursive code of social status (as in 'peer of the realm'). The 'Just William' story in *The Times* concerns Prince William's desire to be addressed simply as 'William' while at university, rather than by his full royal title. The story quotes the accessed voice of a St James's Palace spokeswoman to confirm this, 'William decided he did not want to adopt the HRH title at 18', a discourse which is very similar in vocabulary, tone and structure to *The Times*'s own discursive register. While the discourses of *The Sun* and *The Times* are very different, each of the two stories concerns the accessibility of privileged figures, and the contemporary issue of supposedly increasing classlessness in British culture.

Headlines and graphics

The function of the linguistic syntagms of headlines is to draw the attention of the reader to the topic of each news story, and through the connotations of the linguistic signs to propose some of the social codes appropriate for understanding it. The five main headlines on the front page of *The Times* are all almost-complete sentences whose connotations refer us to our existing knowledge about particular news stories. 'Russell "killer" may be freed' connotes controversy in a court case, and the attribution of the quote 'killer' is substantiated by the opening line of the story, 'Michael Stone, jailed for life for the murders of Lin and

Megan Russell, could walk free tomorrow after the Court of Appeal ruled yesterday that the evidence of a key witness at his trial was unsafe'. The headline relies on the reader's existing knowledge of the court case, and the first paragraph of the news story confirms that this is the correct context for the headline. The relatively polysemic headlines and relatively unequivocal text work together to both open out and close down decodings of the story. For example, some of the narratives activated here concern miscarriages of justice, failures to catch perpetrators of violent crimes, and the vulnerability of women and children. 'Asylum "run as criminal racket"' activates several narrative codes. It invokes narratives about the legitimacy of asylum-seekers' claims for protection in Britain, and the signs 'criminal racket' offer to confirm the widespread prejudice against immigrants as people taking advantage of supposed British goodwill and generosity. The fact that the phrase 'criminal racket' is a quotation, however, protects *The Times* from potential accusations of pandering to these prejudices, and preserves the paper's authoritative broadsheet discourse.

The headlines on *The Sun*'s front page also denote the news topics concerned, and connote the mythic social meanings to be brought to each story. But whereas the stories on *The Times*'s front page concern the conventional news topics of politics, economics and foreign affairs, *The Sun*'s stories are concerned with celebrities, though the royal family appear on both newspapers' front pages. The 'Lady V' headline has been discussed above, and like that story, 'Cruise v Cruise' concerns high-status personalities. The headline codes the stars' divorce as conflict, and invites the reader to note potential similarities between the misfortunes of the stars and those which might be experienced by readers, at the same time as the story highlights their '£300 million fortune' and 'four houses and a plane'. *The Sun*'s sniffer dog Charlie in the 'BANNED' story unites several of the paper's characteristic concerns. The dog is described as a 'loveable labrador', and the endearing qualities of pets are further signified by the humorous framing of the word 'EXCLUSIVE' in a bone-shaped graphic. The paper's interest in stories about the royal family is connected with this by the dog's 'regal red coat trimmed with ermine to prepare for his brush with royalty', and by the presence at the party

of Prince William. *The Sun*'s editorial stance against drugs is signified by the dog's role as a detector of them, so that Charlie
stands in for the paper metonymically, partaking of *The Sun*'s
own self-identity, its 'brand image'. The dog is made 'royal' by
its special coat, but it is 'rejected' by the royal family (themselves
lovers of dogs) whose interests it was trained to serve by pro-
tecting the 'bash' from drugs. The 'EXCLUSIVE' bone connects
the discourse of the story to the dog, which, like the story itself,
is already the property of the newspaper. So in some ways the
story can be read as a humorous protest by *The Sun* against its
exclusion from the 'PARTY OF THE YEAR'. This is particularly
important because the party is hosted by the Press Complaints
Commission, the regulatory body which protects the privacy of
celebrities (like the royal family) from intrusive reporting such as
that which might be practiced by 'news-hounds' from *The Sun*.
The story about Charlie is a way of positioning *The Sun* in relation to the royal family, pets, the Press Complaints Commission,
and drugs, by using humour and satire.

Photographs in the news

This section is a discussion of the signs and codes of news photographs, based on an essay by Roland Barthes called 'The photographic message' (1977) which deals with newspaper
photographs in semiotic terms. Some of the issues considered
here have already been touched on in earlier chapters of this
book, for instance the fundamental argument that photographs
always denote something, but that what is of more interest in
decoding their meanings are the connotations which photographs generate. The connoted message of these iconic signs
depends on what is denoted, but goes much further in providing
a mythic significance which contains and shapes the decoding of
a photograph's connotations.

Press photographs will have been carefully selected from a
number of possible choices, and may have been 'cropped' (cut
down to emphasise particular parts of the image), or technically
processed to alter contrast, colour or some other aspect of the
photograph. So the photograph 'is an object that has been
worked on, chosen, composed, constructed, treated according to

professional, aesthetic or ideological norms which are so many factors of connotation' (Barthes 1977: 19). Each photograph will not be a 'pure', 'natural' image, but one which has been selected and processed in order to generate particular connotations. This recalls the status of photographic signs in advertising, where obviously the picture is used because its connotations support particular mythic meanings. The photograph denoting Charlie the dog in *The Sun*, for example, has been separated from its background so that the dog appears to be looking soulfully at the reader, supporting the connotation that he is sad to be excluded from the party.

Photographs must gain some of their meaningfulness from the newspaper context in which they appear. This context is the channel through which their messages are transmitted, which shapes their significance for us. The newspaper is a message too, or more accurately a collection of various messages which surround the photograph. The newspaper in which the photograph appears will give rise to certain expectations about the kinds of picture we expect to see (pictures of royalty, criminals, pop-stars, or politicians, foreign wars, diplomats etc.). One kind of photograph may seem 'out of place' in a particular newspaper, but be routinely used in another paper. For instance, it would be unusual for a photograph of the topless Lady Victoria Hervey to appear on the front page of *The Times*, but not unusual in *The Sun*. In the same way, different pages and sections of newspapers deal with different kinds of news. So a photograph may connote different meanings when used on a 'hard news' page than when it is used on a page dealing with personality stories.

Photographs usually appear with a news story, and the text of the story will 'anchor' the meanings of the photograph, supporting some readings of the photograph while discounting others. From the point of view of our analysis of the photograph, the text will provide connotations from its linguistic signs that set limits to the meanings of the picture, and direct us to construct its mythic significance in a certain way; 'the text loads the image, burdening it with a culture, a moral, an imagination' (Barthes 1977: 26). The caption underneath it similarly provides a set of linguistic meanings which shape our reading of the picture. The role of the linguistic message is to load down the image with particular cultural meanings. But since photographs bring with them the assumption that they simply record something which 'naturally' happened, the meanings which the text loads onto the photograph are themselves 'naturalized', rendered innocent and apparently self-evident. The photograph functions as the 'proof' that the text's message is true.

Moving to a more detailed analysis of the meanings of photographs, Barthes proposes six procedures through which connotations are generated. The first three procedures relate to the particular choices about what is in the photograph, and the ways in which the photograph was produced condition the ways in which the photo is decoded. These three procedures therefore affect what the photograph denotes, and thus how we read the connotations of what it shows. The final three connotation procedures relate to the context of the picture, and depend on the relationship between the signs in the photograph and other signs outside it.

The first connotation procedure which Barthes identifies is what he calls 'trick effects'. Here the photograph has been altered specifically to produce a particular mythic meaning. Perhaps parts of two photographs have been combined, so that two people who never actually met appear to be present in the same place, or the facial expression of the subject of the picture has been altered to give the person a guilty, evil or dangerous look. The use of trick effects in such a blatant manner is rare, but is sometimes discovered in the sensationalising coverage of crimes, for instance. This kind of trick effect is now much easier because of the widespead use of computer technology to 'brush out' unwanted blemishes in pictures, or to enhance the colour or definition of the picture. Trick effects then, 'intervene without warning in the plane of denotation' (Barthes 1977: 21), using our assumption that photographs simply denote what was really there to load the image with connotations, to code it in a particular way.

The second coding system in Barthes' list of connotation procedures is pose (1977: 22). In photographs of people, their physical pose very often provides connotations which affect our reading of the picture, and thus the mythic meanings attached to the person. These gestures and facial expressions mean something to us because they belong to a code or language of gesture and expression which is recognised in our culture. Denoting someone's hands clasped together connotes 'praying' for us, and might generate the mythic meaning 'piety' for the person in the picture. The photograph of Lady Victoria Hervey on the front page of *The Sun* denotes her with her shorts unzipped to expose her knickers, and with no other clothes, looking out at the viewer. This pose is commonly seen in men's magazines (like those discussed in the previous chapter) and in the 'glamour' photographs regularly published on page three of *The Sun*. Like the Wonderbra ad discussed in chapter 2, it invites to viewer to regard her a sexual object, but Lady Victoria's confrontational gaze also challenges the viewer. Clearly, these connoted meanings support and relay the connotations of the story as discussed above, in terms of the distance from the reader which is connoted, at the same time as an intimate and erotic invitation is made. The choice of which pose to photograph someone in is a choice of what to denote in the picture, but also a choice about which cultural codes are brought to bear when constructing the connoted meaning of the photograph.

The third connotation procedure Barthes proposes is 'objects' (1977: 22), the denotation of particular objects in the photograph. The presence of certain denoted objects which already possess cultural connotations can enable the transfer of these connotations from the objects to the news story. The photograph on the front page of *The Times* denotes the handcuffs worn by Michael Stone, and these are given further prominence by his pose with outstretched arms. The handcuffs connote 'imprisonment', and perhaps also 'guilt', which might lead the viewer to connect these meanings with the linguistic sign 'killer' in the accompanying headline. While the story concerns the possibility that Stone is innocent, the handcuffs may contribute to the reader's assumption that he is guilty of the crime of which he was accused.

The three connotation procedures so far discussed relate to what is denoted in the photograph, and the connotations of what is denoted. The next three connotation procedures refer to the manner of the photograph and its context. The first of these Barthes calls '*photogénie*' (translated as 'photogenia'), which denotes the quality of photographing well, or looking good in photographs. The connoted message of *photogénie*, Barthes suggests is 'the image itself, "embellished" ... by techniques of lighting, exposure and printing' (1977: 23). Because of the hurried nature of much press photography, *photogénie* is not often seen in newspaper pictures. It is sometimes seen in non-news sections of newspapers, where photogenic models are photographed simply because they look attractive in photographs. The photographs of Lady Victoria Hervey in *The Sun* do not adopt the conventions of news photography, but rather of erotic magazine photography, for example in the contrast of her skin with the dark leather sofa on which she is lying, and the highlighting of the curves of her face, shoulder and buttocks. The photograph of Michael Stone in *The Times*, by contrast, has no connotations of photogenia, and adopts the conventions of news photography.

The next connotation procedure Barthes outlines is 'aestheticism', where photographs borrow the coding systems of another art form, giving the picture an aesthetic, or self-consciously artistic quality (1977: 24). News photographs rarely use aesthetic codes in this self-conscious way, since they would conflict with mythic meanings of objectivity and immediacy. Aestheticism is a connotation procedure used in other media like advertising, and the 'lifestyle' sections of newspapers use 'aesthetic' photographs when the articles concern fashion or holidays, for instance, where the aesthetic codes of advertising images can be intertextually referred to. But the photograph of Lady Victoria refers to the conventions of nude portraiture by its adoption of pose and lighting conventions inherited from this medium.

Finally, Barthes discusses 'syntax', a connotation procedure relating to the placing of one photograph next to another, like the placing of words next to each other according to the syntax of a language (1977: 24). Sequences of photographs are sometimes found in newspapers when they record a dramatic event, like an earthquake or a sports event. Each photograph may well contain a multiplicity of coded connotations individually, but clearly the meaning of the sequence of pictures depends on the differences of one from the next as the event unfolds in time. The repetition and variation of the signs in the pictures 'add up' to produce particular connotations for the sequence as a whole, which become the signifiers of the mythic meaning of the event, like 'tragedy' or 'triumph' for instance.

Barthes returns at the end of his essay on press photographs to the thrust of Saussure's analysis of language; that language shapes thought and experience by providing the signs and codes which give form and meaning to our social reality. Language, Saussure argued, cuts up the world and its meaning into specific shapes. Language 'cuts out' the signifieds and signifiers which are available to us for thinking and experiencing. Therefore, even though photographs appear to denote the things they show, and simply record what is in front of the camera without the intervention of language and culture, there can be no such thing as a purely denotative photograph. Once we perceive what the photograph denotes – man, tree, the Houses of Parliament etc. – we perceive it through the linguistic code which gives us the signs 'man', 'tree', 'the Houses of Parliament' and so on. Since thought and perception are enabled by the language system, the meanings of every photographic image depend on the system of language despite the fact that they are made up of iconic and not linguistic signs. Photographs, because they mechanically reproduce what was in front of the camera, claim to denote reality. But as we have seen, this denotative aspect of photographs is a mythic foundation on which connotations are built. The cultural significance of photography as a medium rests on this 'double message' of photographs. They appear to denote their subject without coding it, but when subjected to a semiotic analysis, they reveal the cultural codes of connotation at work to produce mythic meanings.

Newspaper readers

At the beginning of this chapter, I quoted some figures showing the circulations of a number of British daily newspapers. This numerical data is helpful in getting an idea of the various titles currently available, and their relative popularity. But the figures tell us nothing about what kinds of people read which newspapers, and nothing about how newspapers are read in concrete social contexts. It is startling to discover, for instance, that the most popular British newspaper, *The Sun*, is read by a quarter of all adult males and one-fifth of all adult females (not all of these people will have actually bought the newspaper themselves). This statistic seems to show that *The Sun* has a huge influence on the news people perceive, and how they perceive it. Critics of the news media have often bemoaned these apparent influences, and have also attacked the legal framework which allows a few corporations to own several mass-market newspapers and therefore perhaps to exert significant political influence. But once we go beyond this raw statistical information, and think about the ways in which newspapers fit into people's life experiences, the picture becomes more complex.

Some individuals and households buy more than one newspaper, or buy different newspapers on different days in the week, so that at least some of the time more than one narrative encoding of a news item can be compared, contrasted and intertextually mixed. News is now consumed by many people from television news programmes, radio, teletext, or online news services, as well as or instead of newspapers, adding other media to the intertextual mix. Newspapers are often read at work, and on journeys to work or elsewhere. In these work and domestic situations, news items are discussed, extracts are read out and commented on, so that the meanings of news are negotiated between a reader and the newspaper, and between several readers and the newspaper, and between several readers and several encodings of the same item in different newspapers. Aside from the ways in which these contexts affect the meanings of news items, talking about the news and about newspapers is itself a medium of social communication. Conversations relating to news items become a medium in which the news is not foregrounded as 'content', and the form of the conversation as a medium of social exchange is what is significant. In this social situation and in others, neither newspapers nor news may be 'taken seriously', so that reading and discussing news involves recoding news discourse in a quite different way to its original presentation in the newspaper.

Even in the most close reading of news discourse, the reader is an active participant in constructing the meanings of the text, not only by decoding signs and meanings, but also by anticipating the codes needed to make sense of the discourse, and checking the mythic meanings constructed by the text's connotations against the reader's own ideological assumptions. The reader is not only a consumer of already-encoded meanings, but also a producer of the meanings of the text. Readers of 'popular' tabloids may become expert in the discursive codes used in the paper, where language is often used in foregrounded ways including puns, metaphors, alliteration etc. On one level, these features work against the reader's consumption of the 'content' of the discourse, since the linguistic signs through which news is conveyed are being self-consciously displayed as artifice. The reader can actively enjoy decoding the text and its almost 'literary' discourse. However, this pleasure reinforces the paper's 'brand identity', and allows the reader pleasure in the newspaper as an entertainment medium as well as an information medium. The pleasure of reading might either reinforce or work against the newspaper's ideological coding of news events.

As we have seen, news discourse frames events as significant by a variety of semiotic processes, but the practices of reading newspapers in concrete social contexts will always be a significant factor which semiotic analysis cannot deal with adequately. By conducting a detailed analysis of newspaper stories, much can be discovered about how newspaper discourse is structured and how it constructs news and the meanings of news. But there are some limitations to the certainty with which we can discover the meanings of news stories by using semiotic methods, since semiotics cannot reproduce the ways newspapers are read in real social contexts. One quite successful response to this problem is a sociological approach known as the encoding/decoding model (Hall 1980). It concerns the ways in which messages are encoded by a sender (like a newspaper journalist) and decoded by a receiver (like a newspaper reader). First, both senders and receivers probably share a number of common codes, like language, gesture, and occasion (certain signs carry meanings dependent on their situation in time and place) as long as they live in the same culture. But because the fit between the sender's and the receiver's knowledge and familiarity with codes can never in principle be exact, it is not possible to argue that an encoder's 'preferred meaning' will always be understood by the decoder.

This way of understanding communication acknowledges that

all signs are polysemic, open to a range of different interpretations. Preferred meanings are more likely to be encoded and decoded with the same result when both parties in the communication share common codes and ideological positions. Decoders who take up different codes and ideological positions will probably construct 'oppositional' or 'aberrant' decodings, which may be far from identical to the sender's encoded meanings. Indeed, much of the academic writing about newspapers has discussed news stories and photographs to try to reconstruct what the preferred meanings of news stories might be, whether the journalists who wrote the stories knew that they were encoding these meanings or not. The meanings uncovered by academic studies of news have often been very much oppositional decodings, which have critiqued news discourse for its ideological naturalisation of particular social meanings. But preferred meanings have a very uncertain usefulness as knowledge, since it is unclear whether they are meanings necessarily produced by the signs within a text, or the meanings most commonly perceived by real readers, or whether preferred meanings are only evident to academic analysts looking below the surface meanings of signs to the mythic social meanings they support.

Over the years that semiotic analysis has developed, it has shifted its emphasis as far as this problem of decoding and preferred readings is concerned. The earlier phase of semiotic analysis, known as 'structuralism', assumed that there are 'correct' meanings of signs which can be discovered by looking at the relationships between signs and codes in particular texts. Structuralist semiotics would claim to reveal the preferred meaning of a text. But later, in a variant known as 'social semiotics', semiotic analysis acknowledged that it is only one of many ways of investigating the meanings of signs. As only one discourse among many competing discourses, the results of a semiotic analysis may not reveal the 'correct' meaning of signs, but merely the meaning which the discourse of semiotic analysis allows it to reveal. Here the preferred reading is simply the one which the discourse of semiotics is likely to discover. Once it was accepted that real readers, with their own discourses, are likely to decode meanings in a wide variety of ways, research on the responses of real readers seemed to be necessary.

One way to draw together these different approaches to meaning is to acknowledge that each way of analysing meaning is likely to produce a different preferred reading of what the meaning of a text is. The only way to decide which account of the meaning of a text is better than another is to see how effective it is. The discussion of newspapers in this chapter shows how semiotic analysis can determine the meanings produced within a text made up of linguistic and visual signs, by looking at the structural relationships of signs to each other, and of signs to wider social codes. The limitation of this approach is that it can only partially take account of how real readers construct meanings for themselves in concrete social contexts. But on the other hand, the advantage of this approach is that it shows how news discourse attempts to close down the range of possible decodings of its signs, by relaying together the connotations of, for instance, photographs and captions, or headlines and news stories. This book argues here and in the other chapters that semiotic analysis is highly effective in revealing how meanings are communicated by signs, read in relation to social codes, and related to wider ideological positions in society. But although this kind of semiotic analysis is effective in these terms, it must always be acknowledged as one kind of discourse among a range of other competing ways of dealing with the media.

Sources and further reading

Earlier studies of news focused on its ideological assumptions and economic and institutional organisation. Cohen and Young (1973), the Glasgow Media Group (1976, 1980, 1986) and Hall *et al.* (1978) are examples of this approach. The discussion of news discourse from a semiotic point of view in this chapter is indebted to the still persuasive Hartley (1982) and the rather different form of semiotic analysis used by Fowler (1991). Part 1 of McNair (1994) discusses the evolution and various methodologies of academic research on news in print and on television, though the book does not contain semiotic analyses and focuses instead on the political, institutional and professional organisation of news in Britain.

Some of the books listed in the *Sources and further reading* section of the next chapter are also relevant to the study of newspapers, and some of the books listed above also contain sections on TV news.

Suggestions for further work

1   Compare the treatment of the same news event in two different
    newspapers published on the same day. How similar or different are
    the relationships between headlines, text, picture, layout, etc.? What
    effects do the connotations of different coded ways of presenting the
    story have on its meanings?

2   Compare an edition of a local newspaper with an edition of a
    national newspaper. How do news values appear to differ between
    the two papers? Why is this?

3   Choose a news photograph which is interesting to analyse in terms
    of the codes and conventions outlined in this chapter. How do these
    relate to the accompanying story, caption and headline?

4   Cut out three photographs from a newspaper. Try to devise three
    captions for each photograph which anchor their connotations in
    quite different ways from each other and from the original caption.
    How resistant were the photographs to your re-encoding of them,
    and why?

5   Analyse the advertisements in a 'quality' broadsheet and a 'popular'
    tabloid newspaper. How much similarity is there in the products or
    services advertised in each paper, and how much difference is there
    between the semiotic codes of the ads in the two papers? Why is
    this?

6   Compare a current newspaper with a newspaper from decades ago
    (Hartley 1982 reproduces pages of past newspapers if you cannot
    obtain your own). What changes are evident in the codes of lan-
    guage, layout, photographs, etc.? How much change do you find in
    the naturalised ideologies of then and now?

7   Analyse the signs in a newspaper of 'you' the reader, your demands,
    pleasures, linguistic codes and ways of reading. How coherent or
    contradictory are these representations of 'you'? Is there an 'ideal
    reader' of the newspaper?

5

Television news

Introduction

This chapter is primarily about evening news programmes on British television. It follows on from the chapter on newspapers by discussing the semiotic analysis of the linguistic and visual signs which communicate news, and the mythic social meanings and ideological significance of news discourse. The detailed analysis of TV news draws on some of the items in two news programmes on different TV channels, the *BBC News* and the *ITV News at Ten* broadcast on the same day, Wednesday 7 February 2001. This was the same day on which the two newspapers whose front pages are reproduced in the last chapter were published. So one of the issues considered in this chapter is how the news items on TV news relate to the news items in the newspapers which some viewers will have read on the same day. This is also the first chapter in this book in which moving images are discussed in detail. It will be necessary to start discussing how semiotic analysis approaches the mix of spoken and written linguistic signs, still and moving images, music, and graphics which are all present in TV news and in the television medium in general.

Some conceptual issues relating to the television medium are introduced here, and are followed up more fully in the next chapter, which is about a range of reality-based television programmes. In particular, this chapter begins to address the facts that television is a broadcast medium received by a mass audience, and that television is not exclusively national, but also transnational or global in its reach. Because of the wide variation in audience groups which this situation produces, the issues of polysemy and audience decoding are given further discussion in this chapter. A related issue is the fact that TV news is not often watched in isolation from the other kinds of programmes on TV. While this chapter primarily explains a semiotic approach to TV news in particular, it sometimes becomes essential to see how the meanings of TV news interrelate with the meanings of other TV programmes. This way of writing the chapter is designed to allow for a clear discussion of TV news as a specific genre or category of television programme. But my aim is also to begin to introduce the idea that much can be learned by thinking of television not as a set of self-contained programmes, but as an intertextual field in which programmes interrelate and affect each other.

So first the role of news as part of the heterogeneous television output will be discussed, to see what role news plays in the total TV schedule. Then we move on to the coding systems which organise the signs and meanings of TV news. News is a specific genre of TV discourse which is highly coded as we shall see, and it is easy to recognise a news programme when we switch on the TV because of this restricted repertoire of codes. A reminder of the discussion of codes of news value in the previous chapter will show that news value works rather differently in TV news from newspapers, and this issue will lead into some preliminary remarks about the semiotics of television as a medium. As the word 'medium' itself connotes, TV news is a mediator between the viewer and a reality constructed by signs. A semiotic analysis of TV news will show how particular mythic meanings of reality are shaped by signs and codes, and how watching TV news also shapes the subjective identity of viewers in different ways. As we consider the role of the viewer as a decoder of signs, we shall again encounter questions about the power of semiotics to discover the 'correct' meanings of signs in real social contexts.

News in the television schedule

News has a significant role in the broadcast output of television channels. Satellite and cable offer all-day news channels, and all terrestrial television stations in Britain broadcast news several times each day. The longest news bulletins are in the early evening, the time when people return from work, and at the end of the 'prime-time' mid-evening period when family entertainment programmes give way to programmes aimed at a more adult audience. From the point of view of television stations, news not only serves to fulfil the requirement that they inform their audience about contemporary events, but is also used to manage the TV audience's patterns of viewing. A popular early-evening news programme may encourage viewers to remain watching that channel for subsequent entertainment programmes in the prime time which follows the news. Late-evening news bulletins occur at times when adult-oriented programmes are shown, after the 9.00 p.m. 'watershed', when children are presumed not to be watching, and watching the long late-evening news bulletin may encourage viewers to remain on that channel for subsequent programmes. *BBC News* at ten o'clock began in October 2000, replacing the former *Nine O'Clock News*, and usually draws about five million viewers. On 7 February 2001, BBC1's evening news at 10.00 p.m. occurred after a popular factual programme, *Thief Catchers: A Car Wars Special* (about police units which target car crime) and the *National Lottery Update* revealing the winning numbers for that day's draw. About 80 per cent of news viewers have watched the preceding programme. On 7 February 2001 the start of the news was preceded by trailers for two programmes: the drama serial *The Best of Both Worlds* beginning on Sunday, and the *Omnibus* arts programme following the news. These trailers aim to retain viewers for other BBC1 programmes, since some viewers will have just tuned in to watch *BBC News* and can be invited to remain on the channel afterwards, while other viewers may be tempted to switch channels away from the news and are reminded of other BBC1 programmes they might return to.

ITV's late-evening news bulletin was at 10.30 p.m. on 7 February 2001, but the news was broadcast even later in the evening for nearly two years under the name *ITN Nightly News*, after ITV executives had campaigned for more than five years to shift their news timeslot. The reason for placing the news later in the evening was to make room for popular programmes, films and football matches in the mid-evening period. But in July 2000, the Independent Television Commission which regulates commercial television operations ordered ITV to return *News at Ten* to its 10.00 p.m. slot in early 2001. The current *ITV News at Ten* is 20 minutes long and is uninterrupted by commercial breaks. The programme can be moved to a later slot on Fridays and on one other day during the week, but is always named *News at Ten* because of the high recognition of this name among TV audiences. The newly repositioned news allows ITV to add 2.5 minutes of advertising to its peak time programming, and 20 seconds of extra trails for forthcoming programmes. This is significant because news is watched by comparatively high numbers of viewers in the ABC1 social categories (professional, managerial and skilled workers) who are the preferred audience for ads for such high-cost products as cars. So although ITV gained about £70 million a year from moving its news to 11.00 p.m., the inclusion of these additional ads around *News at Ten* will offset the loss incurred from shifting the news back to 10.00 p.m.

TV news is usually regarded as authoritative, with most people in Britain gaining their knowledge of news through TV rather than newspapers. The dominance of TV as a news medium comes in part from the perceived impartiality of news broadcasting. There are rules of 'balance' and 'objectivity' in the regulations governing television broadcasting, and we shall consider what balance and objectivity connote later in this chapter. Newspapers are not subject to these rules. The increasing dominance of TV as a news medium has been reinforced by a shift in newspaper coverage to other kinds of material, like lifestyle features or sensational stories, or to greater coverage of areas not extensively covered by TV news, like sport. The dominance of TV news derives also from its immediacy, since newspapers must be produced several hours before being distributed, while TV news can incorporate new reports even during the programme broadcast. On Wednesday 7 February 2001, almost all national newspapers carried stories on the newly elected Prime Minister of Israel, Ariel Sharon, who featured in the main stories of ITV's and BBC's news programmes. The continuing story of his equivocal support for peace with Palestinians was featured in both TV news programmes, but no newspaper had the opportunity to present a story about the arrest of a man who fired shots at the White

House in Washington DC on 7 February 2001 because the event occurred after newspaper publication deadlines.

So while there are evident parallels between the news values of newspaper journalists and television journalists, there are constraints imposed by the different timing of news production in the two media which determine the degree of immediacy which can be connoted in each. The different stories on the front pages of 'quality' and 'popular' newspapers also show that the news values of television news programmes are more similar to those of 'quality' newspapers than to 'popular' ones. This sharing of news values by 'quality' newspapers and TV news is also paralleled by the authoritativeness, objectivity and balance which are connoted in TV news discourses and in 'quality' newspapers' discourses. These mythic meanings are discussed later in this chapter. Like newspapers, television channels compete to attract audiences and advertisers, but the differences in funding arrangements for British television channels make a direct comparison between them, and between television news and newspapers, much less straightforward.

In Britain, the BBC's two terrestrial channels are funded by a licence fee which must be paid by all owners of television sets. The regional TV companies broadcasting on the ITV channel, and the other terrestrial channels Channel Four and Channel Five gain their income from advertisements. There are TV commercials before ITV's *News at Ten*. TV broadcasting companies funded by commercial advertising need to attract audiences for advertisers, and TV broadcasters funded by licence fee need to justify the compulsory payment of the licence fee by attracting large audiences. So broadcasters continually compete against each other to achieve large audiences for their programmes ('ratings'), and to encourage viewing of their own programmes rather than the competing programmes from other channels which are shown at the same time ('audience share'). On 7 February 2001 the *ITV News at Ten* was preceded by a trailer for the comedy drama serial *At Home with the Braithwaites* and *The Big Match* football coverage which followed the news, plus details of that evening's ITV programmes. These trailers can be regarded as an advertisement for the ITV channel (and the Carlton television company which broadcasts on this channel), attempting

to attract audience share. Within *News at Ten* itself, results of
football matches to be seen on *The Big Match* were broadcast
without sound and viewers were reminded that *The Big Match*
would follow (so that the results could remain a surprise for *Big
Match* viewers), thus further advertising this ITV programme as
well as informing viewers of sports news. News on TV is not only
significant in itself, but also has an important role in the daily
schedule and in the attraction and control of audiences.

Defining television news

As we have seen in the discussion of newspaper discourse, news
is a mediator of events, defining, shaping and representing the
real by the use of linguistic and visual codes. The discourse of TV
news is composed of language and visual images, organised by
codes and conventions which the news viewer has to perceive
and recognise in order for the viewer to construct sense. This
competence in decoding news derives in part from the viewer's
competence in the discourses which the news borrows from
society at large. For instance, the presenters of TV news programmes adopt a formal dress code. Men wear suits, and women
wear business clothes (blouses, jackets, unobtrusive jewellery).
On 7 February 2001 both Peter Sissons, presenting the *BBC
News* (see figure 6), and Trevor Macdonald, presenting *ITV News
at Ten*, wore ties and jackets. News presenters are thus coded as
professional, serious, and authorititative. These connoted meanings are supported by the impersonal linguistic codes used in
news presenters' speech (they hardly ever say 'I'), and the lack
of gestural signs which might connote emotion or involvement
in the news stories they present. The mythic meaning that news
presenters are neutral and authoritative is constructed from
these connotations, which viewers recognise from other aspects
of social life and not only from the codes of television.

Viewers of TV news will also make use of their knowledge of
codes specific to the medium in which the news is broadcast. Like
all other TV programmes, TV news is separated from other programmes and commercials by title sequences. Title sequences
are syntagms of signs which signify boundaries between one
part of the continual flow of TV material and the rest of it. News

programmes contain interviews which are visually coded in similar ways to current affairs programmes and some sports programmes. Camera shots alternate back and forth between speakers, signifying the to and fro of conversation, or unseen speakers put questions to people denoted in studio or outside locations. The news presenter's head-on address to the camera is also found in current affairs, sports, and quiz programmes, signifying the presenter's role in mediating between the viewer and the other components of the programme. News programmes feature actuality film with voice-over, which is also found in documentary programmes and signifies 'observed reality'. These examples show that TV news is not a unique television form, but rather a genre of television whose codes draw on the viewer's knowledge of the codes of other genres of programme. The meanings of TV news derive from some codes which are borrowed from social life in general, and from codes used in the TV medium.

As in the case of newspaper discourse, TV news does not consist of lists of facts, but of narrative reports of events. Like newspapers, TV news makes use of criteria of news value, where the set of priorities and assumptions shared by news broadcasters determines which news reports are given greatest significance within the news bulletin. In general, reports with high news value are those which appear near the beginning of the bulletin, just as the front pages of newspapers present stories with high perceived news value to readers. All four of the headline news stories announced at the beginning of *ITV News at Ten* and *BBC News* were the same stories on each programme (a White House gunman was arrested, a man imprisoned for murder was released after evidence was revealed as flawed, Prime Minister Tony Blair spoke about Britain's entry into the Euro currency zone, and Prince William attended a party). But these headline stories were present in a different order on each programme, and appeared in greater length at different points in each bulletin. Each news programme will contain a hierarchy of news items, with the first item in each segment having greater news value than the items which follow it. As in newspapers, the ranking of reports according to their perceived news value gives us an insight into the ideology of TV news, and the ideology of society in general.

The representation of reality offered by TV news is not reality itself, but reality mediated by the signs, codes, myths and ideologies of news. News both shapes and reflects the dominant common sense notion of what is significant (because what is significant is what is in the news), and also therefore contributes to the ongoing process of constructing a dominant ideology through which we perceive our reality. One obvious example of this ideological function of TV news is to naturalise the myth that what is significant is what happens from day to day in the public arenas of politics, business, and international affairs. Four of the nine news stories in the 7 February 2001 *News at Ten*, and seven of the thirteen stories in the *BBC News* concerned politics, business, or international affairs. Several of the other stories concerned court cases. This encoding of events as of high news value in TV news is closer to the discourse of 'quality' newspapers than to 'popular' tabloid newspapers, particularly in the scarcity of news about celebrities in TV news.

Mythic meanings in television news

Immediacy is a key mythic meaning of TV news. While newspapers have to be printed and distributed several hours before they can be read, electronic news gathering (ENG) techniques like the use of satellite links allow images and sound to be almost instantaneously incorporated into TV news programmes. Immediacy is connoted by the use of signs like the on-screen caption 'live' denoting the simultaneous occurrence and broadcast of an event, or by a spoken linguistic syntagm from the news presenter introducing a live satellite link: 'And John Simpson is in Jerusalem now. John, as we've heard ...' (*BBC News*, 7 February 2001). The organisational chaos potentially caused by the incorporation of immediately occurring events makes broadcasters use it sparingly. News programmes have to be meticulously planned and operate under powerful constraints of timing, so that there must always be a conflict between the desire to connote immediacy and the desire to connote orderliness and authority. Compromises between these two impulses include the use of 'packages', where distant reporters beam pre-made sequences of pictures with voice-over reports to the news organisation just in time for broadcasting in a pre-arranged timeslot, and live interviews in which a certain time is allowed for live discussion of a news story.

The mythic meaning 'authority' in TV news is connoted by a variety of means. One of these is the structuring of news stories, which is discussed in the next section of this chapter. Another coded use of signs connoting authority is the title sequence of the news programme itself. TV news programmes tend to use music featuring loud major chords, often played on brass instruments, with connotations of importance, dignity and drama. Visually, title sequences often use computer graphics in fast-moving syntagms which connote technological sophistication and contemporaneity. Each news programme's title sequence establishes the mythic status of news as significant and authoritative, while simultaneously giving each channel's news programmes a recognisable 'brand image' which differentiates it from its competitors. *BBC News* begins as a clock graphic's second-hand reaches 10.00 p.m. precisely. First Peter Sissons is shown at his desk, with the large figure 10 and the *BBC News* logo on the screen to his right. He outlines four main news stories, each anchored by brief actuality footage. This is followed by another news presenter introducing the headlines in the viewer's local BBC region, in my own region this was Gillian Joseph presenting *Newsroom South East* headlines in a very similar studio set to Peter Sissons'. At the end of this syntagm, an animated graphic sequence begins showing dark red concentric rings over a yellow background. These rings merge and expand while maps of Britain and Europe fade in and out of view, with the rings sometimes centring on London, Cardiff and Edinburgh. The names of world capital cities appear and disappear, until a clock face showing ten o'clock occupies the centre of the rings. Finally a large figure 10 appears in the centre of the image and revolves, with the logo of *BBC News* underneath it. Brass and percussion music accompany the entire sequence, having been heard accompanying the presenters' introductions and the brief headline sequences, and during the title animation the sound of an electronic time signal is also heard.

This title sequence signifies the authority of BBC news through the connotations of, for example, the maps and names of world capitals (national and international coverage of news), and the

radiating rings (the radiating broadcast TV signal covering the
nation). The title sequence of *News at Ten* also has brass and percussion music, with a voice-over announcing 'From ITN, The
ITV News at Ten, with Trevor Macdonald'. ITN, Independent Television News, is the company which produces news for the ITV
channel, funded jointly by the regional companies like Carlton
television which broadcast on the ITV channel. Trevor Macdonald announces four news stories, each accompanied by brief
visual sequences, and divided by the sound of the Big Ben bell
chiming the hour. Like the title sequence of *BBC News*, the *News
at Ten* sequence connotes authority and immediacy. Iconic signs
denote the face of Big Ben's clock showing ten o'clock. Big Ben
is a metonymic sign which stands for the Houses of Parliament
complex, thus connoting national political affairs. Aural signs
denoting the clock chiming 10.00 p.m. connote immediacy,
while a graphic sign of a globe moves across the screen, connoting worldwide coverage of news.

The title sequences of news programmes share many of the
functions of ads, in differentiating similar products and providing

5   Martyn Lewis reading BBC news

6 Peter Sissons reading BBC news

them with a consistent identity. As this brief look at the title sequences of the two main evening news programmes has shown, each sequence constructs similar mythic meanings, through the connotations of different sets of signs. Both BBC and ITV news have changed their title sequences in recent years, but the same mythic meanings of news have persisted. In the now discontinued BBC *Nine O'Clock News*, the title sequence showed a revolving globe, connoting worldwide coverage, and as the camera pulled back and panned to the right the globe was revealed as the centrepiece of a huge shield set in a coat of arms, connoting authority and tradition (see figure 5). In the previous title sequence for *News at Ten* the ITN logo was superimposed over an airborne shot of the top of the Big Ben clock tower in London, and the camera tilted down to its clock showing 10.00 p.m., and panned over the Houses of Parliament. The signifiers in the sequence are similar to those used in 2001's *News at Ten*, with similar connotations, though the signifiers were used differently in the past. Different signs have been used in news programme sequences to connote a restricted range of mythic meanings for TV news.

Balance and objectivity are shared mythic meanings which are also connoted in several different ways. The neutral vocal delivery of news presenters has already been mentioned, a sign con-

noting the mythic objectivity of the presenter and the news institution he or she represents. News programmes seek to connote
balance by quoting or describing the responses of conflicting
parties and interested groups to the news events narrated in
news stories. For instance, in *News at Ten* on 7 February 2001
the item on Tony Blair's announcement that Britain might join
the Euro currency area within two years showed Blair speaking
from the Labour party benches in Parliament, and Conservative
leader William Hague and Liberal Democrat leader Charles
Kennedy giving their different opinions to ITN's reporter. The
mythic meanings 'balance' and 'objectivity' are constructed by
the codes which organise the structure of news programmes and
also of individual news stories, as outlined in the following section. The ideological significance of these mythic meanings is
that balance and objectivity can only be defined in relation to a
'common sense' view held consensually in society. A common
sense view is of course a naturalised ideological position, rather
than an opinion which is necessarily true.

The structure of television news

Events in the world are always potentially interpretable in different ways because events only become meaningful when they are
represented by signs, and signs are organised by codes which
establish the framework of meanings that are brought to bear in
decoding signs. TV news discourse always attempts to deal with
the ambiguity of reality by containing events within the codes of
conventional subject-categories, and conventional codes of narrative. News programmes very often divide news reports into
categories like 'foreign news' or 'business news', reflecting the
institutional divisions of their reporters into specialist staffs. Both
BBC and ITN programmes on 7 February 2001 denoted their
news stories partly by captions like 'White House shooting' or
'Court Hearing', which appear next to the news presenter on the
TV screen, connoting the specificity and uniqueness of each news
story. But the majority of the stories are narrated by correspondents in terms of their specialist area of knowledge, like 'foreign
affairs' or 'economic' news. One important effect of this categorisation is to restrict the discursive codes through which news is

represented. Even though news events often have very wide-ranging effects in different places and on different groups of people, the placing of news reports in coded discursive categories produces the mythic meaning that news events are unique but are significant in the terms of only one discursive code. For instance, a 'foreign news' story about an African famine may omit issues like the structural causes of the disaster (deforestation, debt crisis, trade barriers etc.) because these causes 'belong' in other news categories like 'environment news', or 'business news'. The containment of news reports in categories of news discourse gives mythic meanings to news stories, and has ideological effects, since it naturalises the mythic meanings proposed and precludes decoding the news story from alternative points of view.

By definition, all news events are new and different to what has gone before, but TV news discourse represents events by means of narrative functions which are established by convention. As Hartley shows (1982: 118–19) TV news stories make use of four main narrative functions. These are 'framing', 'focusing', 'realising', and 'closing'. By means of framing, the topic is established by a 'mediator', usually the news presenter, in the discursive code which will contain the story (for instance political news is usually coded as adversarial). The neutral language of the mediator encodes the mediator and the news organisation as neutral, with the effect of naturalising or rendering invisible the ideological significance of the mediator's framing or closing of the news story. The news stories in both the *BBC News* and *News at Ten* are framed by the news presenters in the 'headlines' at the start of the programmes and again by the news presenters when the news stories are more fully narrated in the main body of the news.

Peter Sissons frames the White House shooting story in *BBC News* by the syntagm 'Security scare at the White House as guards shoot and disable a gunman', and by this syntagm in the main body of the bulletin:

> There's been a major security scare at the White House; a man who appeared near the perimeter fence brandishing a gun was shot and wounded by secret service agents. President Bush was in the White House at the time but was never in any danger.

So the discursive frame of this story encodes its meaning as both a challenge to White House security arrangements and a dramatic story about the violent response to this threat. On *News at Ten*, Trevor Macdonald frames the story by the syntagm 'Gunfire at the White House – a man is shot and wounded' in the 'headline' sequence, and by this syntagm in the main body of *News at Ten*:

> There was a major security scare at the White House in Washington today, when a man carrying a handgun fired shots near the building's perimeter fence. Police officers cornered him, and for ten minutes tried to talk the man into giving up. He refused, and was shot in the leg. President Bush was in the White House at the time, though he was never in danger.

The framing of the story here is very similar to that in *BBC News*, proposing that the story is about an individual's wrongdoing, but focuses less on threats to White House security and more on the dramatic narrative of the man's capture.

The topic is 'focused' by reporters and correspondents, who are 'institutional voices' (Hartley 1982: 110–11) speaking with the authority of the news institution. The reporter's institutional voice explains the significance of the news event in detail, and draws out issues in the news story which were coded as significant by the discursive frame. Tom Carver, BBC Washington Correspondent, presents a report which includes the syntagms 'Sub-machine guns and confusion in the grounds of the White House', and 'It seems that this was more like a botched suicide attempt than any direct attack on President Bush'. The reporter's institutional voice confirms the framing of the story as dramatic, centred on an individual, and an instance of the inability of security services to deal with unpredictable behaviour. Similarly, James Mates, ITN's Washington reporter, describes the shooting as 'the sort of incident which no-one could predict, but which the secret service is on constant guard against'. He concludes 'as today proved, no security can ever be a hundred percent.'

'Realising' is the process of lending authenticity to the story and confirming it as real by the use of actuality footage, interviews and 'accessed voices' (Hartley 1982: 111), the contributions of individuals invited to put their views on the story. These realising techniques tend to confirm the frame and focus which have already been established. The two versions of the White House shooting story use a wide range of realising techniques, including shots of the exterior of the White House, footage from a White House press briefing, and interviews with eye-witnesses. These linguistic and visual syntagms anchor and relay each other's meanings, wrapping the news story up in a consistent narrative.

Finally, 'closing' refers to the movement throughout the news story towards one discursive construction of the story, a preferred meaning. This closure can be achieved by discounting alternative points of view on the news story, or by repeating and insisting on the point of view already connoted by the frame or focus, if there is a marked absence of competing discursive positions in the story itself. Closing will occur not only at the end of the story, but will be ongoing throughout it. As you can probably see from the necessarily brief extracts given here, the focusing and realising functions in the White House shooting story confirm the mythic meanings proposed by the frame in each news programme. Despite the various points of view on the story accessed linguistically and visually, the coverage of the shooting represents the actions of an individual (the gunman) as an instance of unpredictable violence which security organisations cannot fully protect against. Ideologically, this mythic meaning of the news story relies on a series of naturalised assumptions. It takes for granted the presence of weapons in American society and the need to respond violently against a violent threat, the propensity of individuals to act unpredictably, especially if they are mentally unbalanced (the gunman was described as prone to depression and bearing a grudge against government institutions), and the necessity for security institutions despite the recurrent failure of these institutions.

TV news stories are almost always dependent on the use of different kinds of visual syntagm, and the use of a variety of denoted speakers. To make the news more varied and interesting, the maximum number of stories in a TV news bulletin will be constructed as a visual syntagm, a sequence of pictures, as well as a linguistic syntagm. The dominance of iconic visual signs has a significant effect on the news value of TV news stories. News stories which are lacking in pictures will be less likely to be included in a news bulletin than stories which can be illustrated by actuality footage which connotes drama. While actuality pictures could be regarded as the dominant type of sign in TV news, it is extremely rare for pictures to be shown without accompanying voice-over by an institutional voice (like a reporter). As we have seen in relation to news photographs in newspapers, iconic photographic signs like these are potentially ambiguous in their meaning because of their denotative dimension. In the *News at Ten* White House shooting story, images denote, for example, armed police running, and the wounded gunman being wheeled into hospital on a stretcher. The visual syntagm connotes violent response to violence, and chaotic activity, but its meaning for the news story narrative has to be anchored by James Mates's voice-over. The story's emphasis on dramatic violence is supported by the inclusion in the report of library footage of a small plane crashed on the White House lawn in a failed attempt some years ago to attack President Clinton, and footage of a previous gunman shooting an automatic weapon into the White House grounds. So the connotations which support the framing and closing narratives of a news story are provided by iconic signs and linguistic signs supporting each other. Interviews in news programmes are visual as well as linguistic. In his or her mythic role as the representative of the viewer, interviews are conducted by the mediator with accessed voices who are either 'live' in the studio or 'live' via satellite link. Here the mediator puts questions which represent the questions which could be asked by an informed viewer. The mediator him- or herself must not appear to hold any opinion, but will reflect the assumed concerns of the audience.

As the last chapter described in relation to newspaper photographs, the meanings of particular shots in TV news sequences will be generated by the connotations of composition within the shot, framing, colour and lighting. Movement of the subject in the shot, pose, objects shown, and movement by the camera are also coded signs with connotations. TV news pictures are often heavily coded, constructed according to recognisable conventions. There are conventional, coded ways of representing press conferences, the arrival of the accused at a sensational court case, starving children in developing countries, etc. Each conventional code will trigger the mythic meanings, of authority, victimhood, dismay, etc. which are regularly signified in each case. In the studio, similarly familiar and repeated visual codes are used in TV news. The news presenter is shot in medium close-up, full face, and is neutrally lit. Through these coded signs, the news presenter is endowed with the mythic role of mediator of events, addressing us as viewers but also making the link between the news organisation, its reporters in the field, and the personalities in the news. The mediator is a link between the domestic world of the viewer and the public worlds of news events. The context and surroundings in interviews with accessed voices often have significant connotations, connotations which are likely to support the framing and closing of the news story in the studio by the mediator. In a story where there are interviews with three different accessed voices, the connotations deriving from the situation of the interview could significantly affect the viewer's assessment of their authority. For instance, prominent people like politicians or businessmen may be in plush offices, spokespeople for protesters may be in a rainy street surrounded by noise and commotion, and an independent expert may be sitting next to the newsreader in the TV studio. Accessed voices in TV news can be either empowered or disempowered by the connotations produced by the signs of situation which are present in the shots.

Myth and ideology in television news

In conducting a semiotic analysis of TV news, it is important to bear in mind not only the mythic and ideological meanings produced in individual news programmes, but also the intertextual context of TV news. TV news programmes are part of the daily television schedule, and part of their meaning must derive from the way in which they work as TV, as well as the way they work as news. Television literally means 'seeing at a distance', and the TV medium has always been used to bring distant events and uncommon sights into the private arena of the home. TV news participates in this mythic identity of the television medium. Most people have very little direct experience of the political decisionmaking, wars, disasters, and business affairs which TV news reports narrate. TV proclaims its ability to bring what is different, strange and interesting into the viewer's familiar and domestic world. The TV medium has a mythic identity as a technology which bridges this gap between public and private, and TV news is one component of it. This mythic identity of TV has ideological significance, since, for instance, it naturalises the idea that the TV viewer can be informed and aware of affairs outside the private sphere, but can have no direct effect on the wider public world. TV (and TV news in particular) involves the viewer, but disempowers the viewer, positions him or her as passive, at the same time.

News programmes have to be entertaining and interesting to watch, like any other programme. The newsreader's address to the viewer and direct look at the camera are ways of demanding our attention, while the rapid alternation of studio settings with filmed reports and interviews encourages the viewer to actively assemble these segments for himself or herself. News programmes also use increasingly sophisticated graphics, montage and image manipulation for visual interest and to connote sophistication.

Some of the structuring of news programmes is interestingly similar to that of fictional programmes, thus invoking known codes used in other kinds of TV. News programmes feature a quite consistent set of characters from one day to the next, the news presenters and reporters who give continuity to TV news in the way that the protagonists of TV fiction programmes do. While news is perpetually different, the cast and format of news programmes are consistent. This pattern of repetition and difference is part of TV news programmes' mythic identity, their 'brand image'. The news programme's 'newsness' is personalised, in the way that advertised products are personalised by the use of recurring models, TV stars etc. in advertisements, or like the personalisation of the law in police fiction series, where Inspector Morse, for example, becomes the mythic representative of justice.

TV police fiction sets up the narrative opposition of law versus crime, where the audience is aligned with the law and the protagonist, and crime and criminals are 'other' to 'us', different, and negatively presented. TV news sets up the narrative opposition between 'us', including the viewer, the general public, the news presenter and news organisation, versus 'them', including other nations, bureaucratic institutions, criminals, and fate, which are all 'other' entities which appear to cause the mainly negative news events to happen. As we have seen, the 7 February 2001 news programmes report events which are either caused or exacerbated by 'others' like the White House gunman, and further 'others' are found in the news stories not discussed in this chapter. Clearly, this mythic narrative structure has ideological significance, since it naturalises 'us' and presents 'the other' as the source of disruption and disorder. The requirement to connote objectivity and balance in news narratives reduces the potential for the viewer to intervene with his or her own discourse about the events reported in the news, and instead passively aligns the viewer with the news institution presenting the news.

News generally constructs the mythic identity of life in our society as something which is fragmented into different spheres (like business, sport, politics, or family life). Society is also represented as naturally hierarchical, since some events, people, places, or issues, are coded as more important than others. News discourse regards society as consensual, or operating by the informal agreement and cooperation of its members. The nation is unified but it is seen as diverse, plural, and fragmented. It is assumed in news discourse that the democratic system provides for equality before the law, shared interests among the population, equality of opportunity, and a common heritage and culture, which are the bases of a consensual model of society. But this mythic consensual model cannot therefore explain dissent within the culture, except by coding it as irrational or criminal. Dissident actions (by animal rights protesters, anti-capitalist demonstrators, terrorists, criminals etc.) are often framed in relation to actual or potential violence, which is a concrete way of encoding these groups' perceived threat to the consensual and democratic process. News constructs a mythic norm, against which disorder and disruption are measured.

The ideological role of news, then, is to construct a mythic 'climate of opinion' about life in our society, and this mythic reality is produced by the structure and form of news discourse, as well as its language and images. News's mythic definition of normality, since it is a cultural construct and is not natural, will therefore shift and change according to the current balance of power. In the 1970s for instance, the nationalisation of major British industries was a tenable political position which reporters and interviewers could discuss pragmatically with politicians. This is far from true today, after the introduction and normalisation of competitiveness and the free market into previously publicly owned industries. News discourse, even in the apparently 'balanced' and 'objective' context of TV news, will use the currently dominant ideological myths about society as its 'neutral' way of perceiving news events. What is presented as factual and neutral is a mythic construction determined by the dominant ideology.

Making sense of television news

The ideological myths of TV news cannot always succeed in imposing themselves on the viewer of TV news, however. For the viewer of TV news, the meanings of news stories will always be negotiated with reference to the connotations and myths proposed by the news discourse, since whatever other meanings are brought to bear on the TV news story by the viewer, the viewer will decode at least some of the meanings which TV news discourse constructs. But negotiation can take a very wide range of forms. One form of negotiation of meaning relates to the way in which viewing takes place. Tunstall (1983) distinguished between primary, secondary, and tertiary involvement with media sources. Primary involvement is where watching the TV news is done attentively and with concentration. The analysis of TV news in this chapter has been done by a special kind of primary involvement, watching attentively and critically. Secondary involvement denotes ways of watching where something else is going on, like doing your ironing or flicking through a magazine. All kinds of TV programme are very commonly watched in this way. Tertiary involvement denotes a very inattentive way of watching, where for instance you are deeply engaged in a conversation while the news is switched on, or even half-listening to the TV news switched on in your living-room while you are making a cup of tea in the kitchen. The degree of attention given to the TV news programme will obviously affect the sense made of the news.

TV news programmes are constructed in order to attract and reward primary involvement with them. The loud and dramatic music in their title sequences is a sign which calls for your attention because it connotes the importance of the programme, and the dramatic connotations of news. The news presenter's address to the viewer as 'you', which is even implied by the opening remark 'good evening' which most news presenters begin with, also calls to the viewer as an individual. Indeed, this address calls the viewer to adopt a subject-position in which he or she plays the role of the addressee of the news discourse, and is invited to accept its naturalised ideological framework. As the news programme proceeds, primary involvement is rewarded by the fuller decoding of news discourse which will result. News stories assume at least some primary involvement with past news programmes and with earlier moments in the news programme. Primary involvement in the TV news discourse might enable the decoding of a much greater range of meanings from the various sequences and accessed voices presented in the news. But primary, secondary and tertiary involvements in the White House shooting news story share the same ideological subtext. The story is encoded as a concrete instance of the inability of institutions to protect society from eruptions of violence, the regrettable but inevitable tendency toward violence in some individuals, and the ability of news institutions to bring the viewer an 'objective' account of a distant reality.

Most of the time, the framing, focusing, realising and closing in news narratives probably succeed at least partially in delimiting news stories, and offering mythic connotations for news events. But it is difficult to know how much of this ideological coding of the news is consciously retained by viewers, and how much is unconsciously retained in a muddled and partial form. Because of the density of news discourse, which contains a very large number of short syntagms comprising written and spoken linguistic signs, still and moving iconic images, and graphic signs, it is very unlikely that the TV news could be remembered and described in detail after it has been broadcast, even by the most attentive viewer. On 7 February 2001 *BBC News* comprised thirteen news stories, and *News at Ten* comprised nine stories. Each news story contained linguistic and visual signs, and many stories used maps, still images, graphics, the voices of interviewees, reporters and the news presenter, and several short sequences of actuality film. Each news story is a highly complex and rapidly changing text.

Many viewers of TV news probably decode a mythic 'newsness', made up of fragments of narrative, and individual linguistic and visual signs. The 'newsness' of TV news, in combination with newspaper encodings of news and other kinds of discourse like conversations, becomes the basis of a cultural knowledge of events. Some of this cultural knowledge of 'newsness' must be widely shared, but some of it must be specific to the media involvements of individuals. It is this mix of shared and specific news knowledge which enables TV news quizzes, for instance, like *Have I Got News for You* (a satirical programme based on current news stories), or current affairs phone-in programmes, to be comprehensible and entertaining. Despite the various negotiations with TV news discourse made by viewers in making sense of it, the meanings proposed by TV news discourse evidently become part of a naturalised 'newsness' which pervades social life.

Global news

This chapter has concentrated so far on evening TV news programmes in a British cultural context. Many of the semiotic structures outlined here are similar to those in the news programmes broadcast in other nations, despite differences in the particular news stories which are broadcast. The structure of news programmes is shared in other cultures because the professional codes of news broadcasters which determine news value are now largely shared by the news journalists of many national and international TV institutions. We can investigate this phenomenon further by a brief discussion of the globalisation of news. Globalisation has been seen from two dominant but opposed points of view; either positively or negatively. The availability of new technologies like satellite broadcasting allows very large and diverse groups to have access to media products. News and other current events can be broadcast globally and this appears to provide unprecedented 'open' and 'democratic' access to information. This is the positive view. But clearly, there must be a global code of news value operating here which assumes that some news stories exhibit sufficient news value for them to be worthy of global dissemination. Globalisation can be evaluated negatively as the monopoly control over information and broadcasting by a few multinational media owners, where global news imposes Western cultural values across the world and local cultures are drowned out by globally dominant ideologies. This is the negative view. However, even if ownership and control of news networks is concentrated in the hands of a few corporations, it does not follow that different audiences simply consume the same ideological meanings encoded in news programmes. Both the positive and negative evaluations of global news need to be analysed more closely by looking at the forms of global and international news broadcasting, since these forms and the institutions which control them are different and varied.

International news agencies like Reuters have been distributing news around the world mainly in linguistic forms since the mid-nineteenth century, but the use of satellite technology has altered the nature of this distribution process. International agencies provide news material for television, and operate twenty-four hours a day, sending both raw footage and complete news packages to national and regional TV stations. Because the international news agencies deal mainly in pictures rather than words, it is common for their news material to be perceived by the news editors of broadcasting companies as denotative and 'objective' because it consists largely of iconic denotative visual sequences. The visual rather than verbal satellite news material now being used is more open to polysemic interpretation and thus to different uses by the broadcasters who include it in their news story syntagms. Since the visual material provided by the agency does not arrive with an obvious mythic meaning, it is easy to impose a range of different mythic meanings on it, particularly through the connotations of the linguistic signs in an accompanying voice-over. The connotations of the linguistic signs in a voice-over can be used to construct mythic meaning, even though visual footage may not itself determine the meanings of news stories.

News services which broadcast complete news programmes by satellite include Cable News Network (the largest, broadcast to over 130 countries) and Britain's Sky News and BBC News 24. CNN provides news from an American ideological viewpoint, covering domestic American news and foreign news. Because its programmes are complete, CNN news is not subject to recoding by national broadcasters. Because CNN broadcasts the same news globally, its criteria of news value influence the professional codes of news value used by broadcasters in particular nations. If a news story is broadcast by CNN news, it carries the mythic meaning of global significance simply because CNN broadcast the story. In addition, the fact that CNN news coverage is broadcast virtually 'live' back into the countries in which these events are occurring can also have the effect of 'making' news events happen, by alerting viewers to a news event (like a political demonstration) and encouraging them to participate in it. CNN news coverage also shapes the responses of politicians and institutions inside the country to what is being reported, as well as shaping the mythic meanings of news for other distant nations. For this reason, politicians and interested groups either impose restrictions on CNN reporters, or invite them to film particular events for CNN news stories which will provide support for one or another political strategy. The management of news by political organisations has always happened at national level, but global news gives news management greater significance. News agencies and global news broadcasters provide national news broadcasters with access to a wide range of footage from distant places which they could not afford to send their own reporters or crews to. For the audience, there is more news, and more broadcast packages of news from different sources. But as news from a greater number of places and social contexts is made available, the importance of the news broadcasters in making sense of the news through their professional coding systems becomes more significant. The audience is assumed to need familiar and simple codes to make sense of so much news, so that the distinctiveness and significance of events is reduced. The ways that the medium of news works (its narrative codes, news values, and mythic meanings) may appear to take precedence over the 'content' which the news medium communicates.

Sources and further reading

Hartley (1982) discusses both TV news and newspapers using a semiotic approach, but many analyses of TV news are in chapters of books covering a range of genres of TV programme. Examples of these which make use of semiotics are Fiske (1987), Fiske and Hartley (1978), Lewis (1985) and Tolson (1996) who includes a case study on the semiotics of TV news. Corner (1995) discusses British TV news coverage with some implicit use of semiotics. Very influential but also controversial work on news was done by the sociologists of the Glasgow University Media Group (1976, 1980, 1986), who mapped out the content of British TV news, aiming to show political bias, but who also used some semiotic methods to discuss the textual forms of news discourse. The contribution made by their work is assessed by Harrison (1985) and Philo (1987), and samples of it are published in Eldridge (1995) and Philo (1995).

From other analytical points of view, Dahlgren (1985) presents research on viewers' decodings of news as academics and 'ordinary viewers', Schlesinger (1978), McNair (1994) and Harrison (2000) discuss the professional practices, ideologies and economics of TV news, and van Dijk (1988) discusses the discursive structures of news communication. The globalisation of the media is discussed by Gurevitch (1991) and MacGregor (1997) in relation to news and by Lorimer and Scannell (1994), though with little reference to semiotics. There is a bibliography on news, focusing on American sources and broadcasting, in Jacobson (1995).

Suggestions for further work

1   Watch an evening TV news bulletin. An hour or so after you have done this, how much of the news and the way it was encoded can you remember? Are there any shared characteristics of the signs and meanings which you remember?
2   Obtain a newspaper on two successive days, and watch the evening news on the evening of the first day, analysing the news stories which appear in more than one of these three texts. Are the stories treated differently in the two media? Why is this?

3   Analyse the news bulletins on as many TV channels as you can. How are the mythic meanings of news programmes signified in their title sequences? How much similarity is there in the signs and codes of the title sequences?

4   Select a TV news story which is presented by several linguistic and visual sequences (newsreader, filmed report, interview etc.). How do framing, focusing, realising, and closing operate? What ideological viewpoints emerge from your analysis?

5   Which of the semiotic codes of TV news outlined in this chapter are common to other genres of TV programme? How and why are their connoted meanings the same or different in these different contexts?

6   Compare a local TV news bulletin and a national TV news bulletin. What similarities and differences in their semiotic codes and their assumptions about the viewer do you find? Why is this?

7   If you have access to TV news programmes from satellite or cable as well as terrestrial channels, compare and contrast the stories covered and the discourses used to make sense of the news. What conclusions do you draw from your analysis?

6

Television realisms

Introduction

The chapter on TV news considered only one kind of programme, and treated news as a relatively discrete form of text. The television medium broadcasts a very wide range of different kinds of programme and here further critical issues in the semiotic analysis of television are exemplified through short discussions of programmes which exhibit different forms of realism. This chapter is mainly concerned with programmes in which unscripted events involving non-actors in actual locations are represented. Programmes like this are called 'factual' in the television industry, and they clearly have an important relationship to realism. Factual programming includes documentary, drama-documentary, and docusoap programmes, which respectively claim to represent an authentic reality, to dramatise events which actually happened, or to follow a cast of real people in real locations in an ongoing character-driven narrative. In each case, it seems as though television is used simply as a medium for recording and broadcasting people and events which were already there in the real world. But although people would have learned to drive whether or not the docusoap *Driving School* was being made, several programmes discussed in this chapter involve situations deliberately created for television. The 'reality TV' serial *Big Brother* is a clear example of this, and it is discussed later in the chapter. The chapter also discusses programmes which contain scripted sequences performed by actors, but which claim to reproduce or reconstruct events that really happened. *Crimewatch UK* is a factual programme which includes these kinds of fictionalised real events.

Programmes which are factual contain fictional or fictionalised elements, and fictional programmes often construct 'realistic' fictional stories (as discussed in the next chapter). So it must be the case that realism is not a property solely of fact-based programmes. The codes of narrative, editing, music or shot composition which connote realism are discussed in this chapter, and are found in both factual and fictional programmes. If realism is an effect which cannot be pinned down to what has been filmed, or even how it is filmed, realism must be a set of ways of using television codes which audiences recognise as realistic, and which the makers of television use in order to address and involve the audience in particular ways. Realism depends on the shared acceptance of codes by the television industry and audience, which allows realism to be connoted and understood. This notion of a consensual code, shared between the different groups who communicate with it, is the same as Saussure's semiotic definition of how language works. Realism, in the same way as language, depends on a socially accepted code in which signs are used and shared to communicate meanings. We can say therefore that there are 'languages of realism' in television, which both producers and audiences learn to use and read. How these languages of realism work, and how they can be analysed, are the main subjects of this chapter.

We begin with a section containing factual and statistical information about contemporary non-fiction television. Then the section called *Codes of TV realism* explains how the semiotic concepts of code and convention illuminate the claims of television programmes to represent realities. The *Television and society* section extends this by considering how factually-based programmes relate to real issues in society, while the *Dramatising the real* section discusses how fictional codes appear in realist factual programmes. The semiotic study of television, in common with semiotic approaches to the other media discussed in this book, involves particular attention to the television 'text'. But Television Studies has also focused on the television audience, and how actual viewers engage with television programmes. The focus of analysis shifts in the final section of this chapter, on *Viewer involvement*, to ways of thinking about how actual viewers relate to realist television programmes.

Contexts of non-fiction television

In Britain, the average person spends more than twenty-one hours per week watching television, so watching TV is evidently a very significant activity for most people. 99 per cent of British households possess a television, and more than half of all households have more than one TV set. About two-thirds of households also have a video cassette recorder. The television broadcasting of live real events is a significant motivation for people to buy television equipment and to watch television. When television broadcast the coronation of Queen Elizabeth II in 1953, sales of television sets increased significantly. More recently, when the wedding of Prince Charles and Lady Diana Spencer was covered in July 1981, five and a half hours of live coverage was shown on BBC and ITV, attracting 39 million viewers watching live in the UK. The coverage was also broadcast live to 74 countries. In the year preceding the event, sales of video recorders doubled to 1.5 million. The popularity of live broadcasting shows that the television medium is particularly associated with documenting the occurrence of events which are deemed significant by and for society. The concept of news value was described in the previous chapter as a code which determines which events are important enough to become news. The events which are broadcast live (like royal events, international sports, or the government's annual budget speech) share many of the attributes of events which have high news value. They concern elite persons, are consonant with the assumed interests of the audience, and are often expected public occasions, for example. Just as news has a mythic identity as a discourse which serves the public by informing them about events, live broadcasting also has connotations of service, information, and public significance. Live broadcasting is part of the public service culture of British television, where television has a responsibility to the audience and the nation.

The academic discipline of Television Studies has attempted to determine what is specific about television as a medium, and part of this effort involves the importance of live broadcasting of real events. Television shares some features with radio: it is broadcast widely across a geographical area, many of its programmes are

'live', and many of its programmes address viewers as members
of society and provide information and comment about current
events. On the other hand, television shares some features with
cinema, for instance both cinema and television involve moving
pictures, and both media engage viewers in fictional narratives.
Television is a hybrid medium, which combines the features of
other media. In a sense, what is unique about television is its
inclusiveness, drawing on many other meaning-making forms in
our culture. A further kind of inclusiveness derives specifically
from television's broadcasting of factual programmes, like documentaries. Documentary television has a history of presenting
information about people and events which are outside of most
viewers' experience. Documentary reveals realities which may be
little known, and shows evidence which may lead to changes in
viewers' attitudes. In this way, documentary includes people and
events which seem 'other' to a norm, and includes its viewers in
a community invited to reflect on the evidence which television
can denote. Realist television, therefore, has connotations of
responsibility, inclusion and community, as well as simply
authenticity or truth to life. Television has a political, ideological
role because of its claim to denote realities in non-fiction
programmes.

The significance of non-fictional programming to British television can be glimpsed by examining the budget of BBC in the
1999/2000 year (as detailed in the BBC's booklet *We Promise...:
The BBC's Promises to You 2000–2001*, published in 2000). The
BBC is a 'public service broadcaster', informing the audience and
serving society. Factual programmes are an important part of the
BBC's mythic identity as responsible to society, because factual
programmes often denote that society and show it to itself in
ways which encourage reflection on contemporary social life. In
the 1999–2000 financial year, the BBC spent £2,318 million on
all its services, with £823 million spent on BBC1, and £421 million on BBC2. Regional television, which often includes news and
other factual programmes, cost £207 million, while the new
digital channels BBC News 24 and BBC Knowledge (which
broadcasts factual programmes) cost £50 million and £21 million respectively. The BBC spent significant amounts on making
non-fictional programmes for television and radio. Factual and

learning programmes cost £350 million, news cost £310 million, sport cost £178 million, and music and arts programmes (which are largely non-fictional) cost £107 million. The largely fictional programme categories of entertainment and drama cost £253 million and £244 million respectively, so although fiction programmes are very significant in British television, programmes with a factual content make up a sizeable investment. They are given this importance partly because factual programmes inform and educate the audience about their realities, whether aspects of life with which they are familiar, or aspects of life which have been signified as 'other', unfamiliar. Part of the semiotic function of factual programmes is to bring what is 'other' into the realm of the familiar, and to make what is familiar seem 'other' by denoting it in unfamiliar ways.

However, it is misleading to assume that non-fictional programmes consist entirely of realist documentation of society, which fulfils a public service function. The quiz programme *Who Wants to be a Millionaire?* for example is broadcast by ITV, and achieved a peak audience of 19.2 million viewers in 1999. This audience size is equivalent to the most popular soap operas, and the programme's success led to the export of the format to the USA. Although by November 2000 the programme had paid out £5.35 million in prize money, this cost was covered by telephone call charges to people ringing to put themselves forward as contestants. *Who Wants to be a Millionaire?* costs about £200,000 per episode to make, which is comparatively little in the television industry, and the programme's popularity has led the ITV channel to schedule it in competition with the most popular BBC fiction programmes (like the drama serials *EastEnders*, *Holby City* and *Casualty*). With an average audience of 11.7 million viewers, the programme takes a significant share of the available audience for its timeslot. Since ITV is a commercial broadcast channel, financial returns on its programmes are important. ITV gains revenue from advertising time, and the channel's charge to advertisers is based on the cost advertisers pay to reach a thousand adults. This cost per thousand was £7.65 in late 2000, and a programme with large audiences like *Who Wants to be a Millionaire?* can therefore command high fees from advertisers and make a considerable income for the television companies broadcasting on ITV. One of the attractions to broadcasters of non-fiction television programmes is that they are often comparatively inexpensive, and popular formats like quiz programmes command large audiences.

In Britain documentary programmes are often scheduled in strands like *Cutting Edge* and *Modern Times*, where one-off programmes on different subjects are given the shared identity of a brand, but documentary series such as *Vets in Practice* (where episodes follow the experiences of the same group of people) have gained large audiences in evening 'prime time'. Maggie Brown reported in *The Guardian* newspaper ('Vying for VIPs', Media section, Monday 5 March 2001, 8–9) that Channel 4 factual programmes were attracting high proportions of the valuable ABC1 audience (professional, managerial and skilled workers) who are attractive to advertisers: *The Kama Sutra* got a 54 per cent share of ABC1s, and *The 1940s House* 53 per cent. The scheduling of non-fiction programmes in prime-time mid-evening slots is partly due to their attraction of large or valuable audiences at relatively low cost. This low cost can be achieved because small numbers of personnel and a limited range of equipment are needed to make some non-fiction programmes, especially documentaries. One hour of drama cost about £650,000 to make in the late 1990s, versus about £125,000 per hour for documentary. Channel 4's documentary series *Undercover Britain*, for example, was shot using used button-sized concealed cameras which can be operated covertly by one person.

Codes of television realism

Semiotics begins the analysis of any medium by identifying the kinds of sign which it uses. The television medium makes use of a *langue* or language system comprising visual and aural signs. Some of the visual signs are iconic and apparently denotative, like the images of people and places in both fictional and non-fictional programmes which resemble their referent. But the photographic realism of these denotative signs is itself coded and mythic, relying on the codes of composition, perspective, and framing which are so conventional and naturalised in our culture that the two-dimensional image seems simply to mirror three-dimensional reality. Similarly, television's aural signs are denotative, like the speech or sounds which accompany images of people speaking or moving. But this speech and sound is also coded, since technical codes of recording, editing and processing intervene between 'real' sound and the sound which comes out of the TV set's loudspeaker. Much of what is on television is presented as denotative, but achieves this meaning by the use of technical and professional codes either specific to television or shared by other audio-visual media like cinema. The connotations of music, for instance, are largely shared by the cinema medium (in uses of romantic or dramatic music for example), and derive from the social meanings of the kinds of music in the wider culture.

Realism is partly the product of the television technologies which denote the real people, objects, places and things which are represented in programmes. From this perspective, the ability of television programmes to seem realistic derives from the iconic nature of the visual signs in television, signs which bear resemblance to what they represent. The sound and music in television are indexical signs, signs caused by the human voices and musical instruments which produce the sounds we hear in programmes. So the technical equipment used to make television brings with it a predisposition toward representing in realistic ways. Because of the denotative dimension of the photographic sign, where the image seen on screen corresponds to the object or person which has been photographed, television and other photographically-based media like film have a special relationship to realism. It seems that television images are always to some extent realistic, because they nearly always consist of iconic signs denoting objects or people which were there in front of the camera. Television news and television documentary are particular modes which draw on the medium's iconic and denotative dimension. News and documentary do not only denote objects and people who were there in front of the camera, but also claim a certain faithfulness to the events and situations which are represented. Whereas television fiction is primarily organised around narrative and the telling of a fictional story, documentary claims to represent the world as it actually is or was.

This claim is not as simple as it may seem, however. For example, making a documentary about someone will involve the very artificial operations of following that person around with a camera and with sound equipment, and editing together parts of the resulting footage to make a television documentary programme. It is very likely that the person being filmed by the documentary maker will behave differently when being filmed from the way he or she might behave if the camera and sound recorder were not there. So one of the tasks of the documentary maker is to reduce the likelihood of the person behaving differently (perhaps by getting to know him or her for a long period of time, or by filming very unobtrusively or even secretly). Once the film has been completed, the documentary maker will edit the footage to show the apparently 'natural' or representative behaviour of the person who has been filmed, as if the documentary maker had not been there. The realism of the documentary, its close fit with a sense of the real person, has to be carefully worked for and is the result of a series of difficult decisions. Furthermore, the conventions of what a documentary should be like (for example its length, the subjects it might cover, the degree of offensiveness or sexual content) are affected by broadcasters' regulations and guidelines for producers. Broadcasters will buy documentary programmes which conform to institutional regulations and conventions, and will not buy programmes which do not. So there are aesthetic and institutional restrictions and working practices which also function as codes shaping television documentary. These regulations and conventions change over time, so that what counts as documentary changes also, showing that documentary is affected by historical and ideological pressures.

Realism can be reinforced by the authority of a narrator, who gives a logical and ordered framing discourse to the components of the programme. Realism can also be signified by the inclusion of contributions from experts, or testimony from a range of people involved in the action, event, or process which is the subject of the programme. So as well as the connotations of realism which arise from observing a real event with camera and sound equipment, there are narrative and discursive elements in documentary realism. These signifying components bring documentary closer to fiction or argument than to observed reality. There is a conflict between the documentary maker's aim to observe and document reality, and the shaping of what is shown into an interpreted form. The aim of documentary is not simply to observe and record reality but also to interpret it, and thus documentary will always involve ideological viewpoints, and the construction of mythic meanings which either support or challenge dominant ideological frameworks for perceiving reality.

While some documentary conventions connote unmediated reality, like a shaky, hand-held camera, 'natural' rather than expressive lighting, and imperfect sound, other conventions connote drama, argument, and interpretation, like voice-over, narrative or argumentative structure, and contrastive editing. One device which combines both features is metonymy in documentary. Here, one part of reality is made to stand for a larger real world which it represents. A documentary showing a day in the life of a hospital metonymically uses that day to stand for any other day. A documentary showing the work of an inner-city policeman will make that policeman's experiences stand metonymically for all inner-city policemen. Both individual images or sequences, and individual documentary subjects, have metonymic relationships with the reality of which they are a part. This is made more effective by what Kilborn and Izod (1997: 39) call 'accommodation', where what the documentary shows is accommodated to the knowledge of the assumed viewer. Documentaries about the police or hospitals will accommodate themselves to some extent with the ideological and mythic knowledge about policing (for example, that policemen must be tough to cope with today's violent society) and health provision (for example, that heroic staff struggle to cope with excessive workload) which are circulating in society. In its claim to deliver knowledge and experience of the real world, documentary draws on the myths and ideologies which shape that real world for the viewers of the programme.

Television and society

One of the functions of television is to engage with current events in society, and we have encountered the most obvious example of this in the previous chapter on television news. But there are many other programmes which represent and comment on current events, and some which attempt to directly involve the viewing audience in responding to these events. This section d iscusses a prominent example of this kind of television, the programme *Crimewatch UK*, which both represents recent crimes in realistic ways, and solicits viewer involvement to help solve crimes.

Crimewatch has been broadcast once a month on BBC1 in mid-evening since 1984. In an article on *Crimewatch*, John Sears (1995: 51) discusses how the programme performs 'a social function by helping to solve crime, and drawing on the collective responsibilities, experiences and knowledge of the viewing audience in order to do so'. The aim is to engage with the audience's understanding and experience of crime in their own lives (like witnessing crime, being a victim of crime, experiencing policing, or helping to uphold the law). In other words, *Crimewatch* has a 'public service' function, because it informs the audience, includes the audience in helping to purge crime from society, and includes the viewer in a mythic community where criminals are 'other' or outside of the community and disrupt it. The programme makes links between television, reality and the audience. It denotes crimes, their victims, evidence about them, and policemen, for example, and the viewer is expected to accept that television denotes these things and people realistically. Viewers can phone into the programme with information, so that the audience is connected with the programme, and can be engaged in the realities which are denoted. Semiotic analysis can explain in detail how these links between television, reality and the audience are made.

Crimewatch often features crimes which have been reported already in the 'objective' media of television news and newspapers. So the connotations of realism from the news media reports of crimes are carried over into the *Crimewatch* coverage of them, a 'borrowing' of meanings from another medium. This relay of meaning from one medium or text to another is called intertextuality, and there are further examples of intertextuality in *Crimewatch* which contribute to its realism. The music of *Crimewatch* is brassy and military, sharing connotations with both news (which has similar music, as discussed in the previous chapter) and action drama (for example the BBC medical drama *Casualty*). The programme seeks to represent the actuality of crimes by reconstructing them, which involves making fictional versions of what really happened. The programme's fictionalised reconstruction of crimes connote entertainment, but they are realist since they are as lifelike as possible. *Crimewatch*'s aim to achieve change in the real world by solving crimes involves becoming highly fictionalised, by dramatising events, emphasising particular details, sometimes shocking the viewer by reporting violent events, and drawing the viewer into the dramatic narrative of how crimes are solved. Involving the audience through drama encourages active audience involvement in solving crimes, and *Crimewatch* has been very successful in assisting police investigations. The realism of *Crimewatch* and its linkage with realities are achieved partly by intertextual borrowings of codes and conventions from other media and other genres of television.

Sears argues that *Crimewatch* works by reducing the complexity of its own mixture of codes and conventions, and the complexity of the problems it addresses, to a small number of recognisable and highly coded images and rhetorical devices which can be narrativised in simple ways. This also has the effect of engaging viewer expectations and knowledge derived from other highly coded types of television programme, particularly crime drama and television representations of police procedure. The key status of e-fits (pictures of criminals composed electronically from witnesses' reports), photographs of stolen cars, stills from security camera footage, and physical clues (like weapons or items of clothing) derive from the codes of detective fiction, and narratives about solving crimes which revolve around key pieces of evidence. In semiotic terms, these particular coded images are metonyms. That is, the photographs of weapons, cars, clothing, and perpetrators are parts of the story of the crime which are associated with each other and which stand in for the whole of the crime. These metonyms are 'next to each other' on a horizontal axis of association. On the other hand, the reconstructions of crimes on *Crimewatch* are metaphors, in that they are parallel to the factual events of the crime but they are fiction.

The metaphoric reconstructions substitute for the actual crime, and represent it (they are on the vertical axis of substitution).

The title images used on *Crimewatch* in the 1990s were connected by the signified 'information'. The visual signifiers represented police operating computers, evidence being photographed, police knocking on doors, and people telephoning. The fingers telephoning are a particular form of metonym called 'synecdoche', where a part of something stands for the whole of it. The dialling hand is part of the body of an active viewer phoning in to the programme, and the police's hands knocking on doors stand for the police as a whole (the 'long arm of the law'). As Sears points out (1995: 54), 'while the general message of the sequence is one of information-gathering (or, more pertinently, crime-solving) the specific message draws attention to audience participation.' The devices of metonymy and synecdoche are emphasised in the title sequence, and connect with the codes used in the rest of the programme. The banks of phone operators seen in the studio connote police procedure, and metonymically represent it (one aspect of information-gathering stands for the whole). Reports on individual callers' information also metonymically signify all the callers ringing in with information, and the pool of information which has been received. Parts stand for wholes in *Crimewatch*, for example crucial details will be clues which lead to greater understanding of the crime. You may be able to make out the projected images of fingerprints (another metonymic clue) projected onto the studio backdrop in figure 7. This technique of crime-solving by identifying metonymic clues is how detective fiction works. The factual content of the programme is coded by intertextually borrowing from the codes of fiction.

While elements of the programme are clearly separated out as fact or fiction (and it is conventionally regarded as irresponsible not to divide things in this way in popular television) *Crimewatch*'s realism sometimes leads to the mixing of the two modes. For example, victims or witnesses sometimes appear in reconstructions playing themselves (this is more 'authentic'), rather than contributing by means of interviews inserted into the reconstruction, or appearing as voice-overs during it. The programme has a mixed mode, combining elements of drama and documen-

7   *Crimewatch UK* presenters in the studio

tary. It uses codes from several genres of television programme, including current affairs, crime drama, documentary, and audience-participation programmes. *Crimewatch* is partly live, with live studio presentation including updates on information received from the public who phone into the programme about the crimes featured on it. There is also a live supplementary programme, *Crimewatch Update*, on BBC1 later in the evening which reports progress on solving crimes thanks to the public's help. The effect of *Crimewatch* can be to change the reality which the programme has denoted and which the viewer has experienced, by helping to catch criminals. The combination of realisms in *Crimewatch* not only represents actuality but can also change it, and as I have argued, this is part of television's public service function.

Crimewatch is interesting in itself, as a semiotic analysis can reveal. But the next step should be to consider how this example relates to myths about society in general which television programmes reinforce. Like many realistic and factually-based programmes, *Crimewatch* has to reduce complex institutional processes (like how policing is carried out), and important relationships between the state, criminality, and the public, to smaller-scale personalised relationships. The viewer is asked questions like 'were you there that day?', 'do you recognise this car?', 'do you know this man?' Even though television is a mass medium, broadcast to a collective audience, the viewer is addressed as an individual. It is individual action which is requested from the viewer (just as individual giving is requested in telethons and charitable events like *Comic Relief*). The crimes featured on *Crimewatch* are committed by individuals rather than companies or governments, for example, and have emotional and dramatisable effects on their individual victims. Television rarely requests collective action from its viewers, and rarely focuses on abstract structural problems like the complex causes of crime. The emphasis on the denotation of particular fragments of reality in television, and on narratives of individual experience, militates against representing the crimes known as 'white collar' crimes (like fraud or embezzlement) which concern institutions and are invisible to most people. The result is that society is mythically represented as a collection of separate individuals, rather than groups with common interests and concerns. It is television itself which mediates between viewers and the abstract institutions of the state and the law, connecting viewers to a wider sense of society and community. Television, in a sense, creates community and society by representing that society and linking together its separated individual viewers into a collective audience.

Dramatising the real

The term 'docusoap' is a combination of the terms 'documentary' and 'soap opera', which denote different television genres. Documentary is a factual genre, based on the observation and interpretation of reality, while soap opera is a fictional genre based on a continuing narrative of a group of individual characters. Docusoaps mix these genres by observing real people and structuring this observation into a dramatic narrative form. The BBC docusoap *Driving School*, for example, denoted real people learning how to drive cars, and was structured as an unfolding narrative following particular people as they experienced successes and failures in this process. The section on *Crimewatch* was concerned with how the programme included its audience, for example by inviting them to phone the programme and then reporting on how the audience had helped to solve crimes. This section takes these concerns further by discussing how docusoaps represent the 'ordinary people' who are their subjects. Docusoaps denote the everyday experiences of people, providing documentary 'evidence' of how they live, but docusoaps also focus on performance and narrative, in ways similar to fictional drama programmes.

Docusoaps have been a very popular television form over the last decade. The television industry newspaper *Broadcast* reported in 1998 that in that year the ITV docusoap *Airline* (featuring airline staff) achieved an average 50 per cent share of the audience, with 11.4 million viewers, while BBC1's *The Cruise* (about a cruise liner) and *Animal Hospital* each gained 10 million viewers and an average share of 40 per cent. In September 1998 BBC1 scheduled its first factual programme in prime time. This docusoap, *Airport*, gained a 44 per cent audience share, encouraging ITV to move their competing programme, the drama *London's Burning* about firemen, to another schedule slot. However, Peter Dale, Channel 4's commissioning editor for documentaries, complained that docusoaps 'don't give you a depth of understanding of a character or situation. They intercut scenes rapidly to keep audiences interested, which works against understanding' (Dams, 1998:16). *Driving School* attracted 12 million viewers when scheduled against the popular continuing police drama *The Bill* on ITV, which got 6 million viewers. Although *Driving School* was a docusoap featuring real people and *The Bill* is a fictional drama, there were several codes which the two programmes share, and which explain Peter Dale's critical comments.

Like a drama serial, *Driving School* focused on people with easily identifiable characteristics and highlighted dramatic incidents and reversals of fortune. The learner driver Maureen and her husband Dave (figure 8) were the most celebrated of these, becoming minor celebrities appearing in television chat shows and tabloid newspaper features. Maureen's difficulties with driving enabled the programme-makers to feature scenes in which she nearly hit other cars, broke down in tears when she made mistakes, and got into arguments with her long-suffering husband. Thus narrative codes and codes of character drawn from television fiction were available for the viewer to understand and

8   Maureen and Dave Rees in *Driving School*

enjoy the programme, like dramatic crises and turning-points, conflicts between characters, and moments of comedy or tragedy. The programme was given structural unity by a narrator, who could provide spoken linguistic signs which cued the audience to invoke these familiar codes.

The dramatic aspects of *Driving School* led to argument in the media about the ethics of docusoap production. First, it was alleged that some scenes had been 'faked' for the camera, thus breaking the documentary convention that reality is observed without intervention by the programme-maker. A scene in which Maureen woke her husband in the middle of the night, for example, was revealed to be a re-enactment of an event which did take place, so that it was a fictionalised reconstruction in a similar sense to the reconstructions in *Crimewatch*. Second, the programme was criticised for selecting subjects (including Maureen) who were likely to deliberately display emotion and 'act up for the camera', and were made into public celebrities for the voyeuristic pleasure of the audience. Again, the 'neutrality', 'objectivity' and 'representativeness' of documentary seemed to have been discarded. These controversies arose because of the programme's mixed fictional and factual coding systems, and the resulting confusion about whether its aim was 'information' or 'entertainment'. What is significant for the argument of this chapter, however, is that the realism of *Driving School* rested on precisely this confusion and mixing of television codes.

Docusoaps feature people who television viewers might easily encounter in daily life, like hotel workers, holiday reps, driving instructors, or shop assistants. These people operate in 'middle spaces' of society: they are neither members of a powerful elite (like company directors, judges, or aristocrats) nor powerless, excluded people (like homeless people, or asylum-seekers), but in the middle. Docusoap characters are also in middle spaces in the sense that they are in middle positions in a hierarchy. They often encounter members of the public to whom they provide services, and they are responsible to authority figures more senior than them. Docusoap programmes often bridge a line which divides the public working lives of these people from their private lives, a line which is also a sort of middle or mediator between two kinds of experience. As a genre of programme docusoap is a middle genre, between documentary and drama. Finally, docusoaps show people who are represented as 'like us', as ordinary as the television viewers watching them, yet being on television in itself makes these people not 'like us', so docusoaps occupy a middle space between ordinariness and celebrity. Graeme Burton (2000: 159) has suggested that docusoap 'stands for a growing use of viewers to entertain the viewers – an approach familiar from the game-show genre and the use of studio audiences. It creates the illusion that television recognises its audience and works for its audience'. What Burton calls an 'illusion', a semiotic analyst would call 'myth'. One of the mythic meanings of docusoap is that the dividing lines between television and everyday reality, programme and audience, celebrity and ordinariness, are fine lines which can easily be crossed.

The television genre known as the 'makeover show' (see Mosely 2000) seems at first sight to be straightforwardly factual, and includes programmes like *Changing Rooms*, *Looking Good* and *Ground Force* where members of the public have their homes, gardens, cooking ingredients, dress style, hair etc. transformed by the intervention of 'experts' introduced by the television programme. But the key moment in these programmes is a dramatic one, a moment of revelation where the newly transformed house, garden or person is exhibited by the programme presenter to the family member and the television audience. It is the reaction to the change which forms the dramatic climax of the programme. Whereas the making-better of a person's appearance or domestic space is usually a private experience, these programmes make this process public. Indeed, the function of the programme presenter is often to speak directly to the camera (to the viewer in his or her private home) and create a bridge between the 'ordinary' person being made-over and the 'ordinary' television viewer, across the public medium of television. One of the variants of this process of publicising a private transformation is in *Stars in Their Eyes*, where members of the public transform themselves into facsimiles of celebrities: the private person is transformed into a public figure. Conversely, the BBC comedy-drama *The Royle Family* reverses the same semiotic distinctions, being a fictional drama set almost exclusively in the private domestic living-room of the family, where they are always watching television. Since the camera is often positioned in the location of the family's television set, the programme positions the audience at home as gazing at representatives of themselves watching television, making a private experience public. Contemporary television not only mixes dramatic and documentary codes, but extends this into the blurring of the boundary between private experience and public experience, and between being ordinary and not-on-television versus being celebrated and on-television.

Viewer involvement

While film audiences pay directly for a cinema experience, television viewers pay indirectly by buying a TV licence or by buying advertised products. Commercial television companies sell the mathematical probability of a certain size and type of audience to advertisers, an economic exchange in which the audience is itself a product. So this economic structure positions the viewer as active. Commercial television is predicated on the economic activity of the viewer, since the naturalised ideological assumption is that the viewer is active in making purchasing decisions and consuming products and services. While it might appear that watching television is a release or respite from the economic processes of earning money or spending it, the television viewer is addressed as someone who earns and spends 'by nature'. Furthermore, it is generally supposed by advertisers that the greater the degree of primary involvement in a particular programme, the more likely the viewer will pay attention to and remember the ads in and around the programme.

Primary involvement by the viewer can be stimulated by discourses which allow for interaction with programmes and ads. In chapter 2, it was noted that some print ads provide opportunities for interaction, like puzzles which the reader is invited to decode, or jokes where the meanings of linguistic signs can be completed by the interpretive action of the reader. Television ads also use some of these discursive devices, especially jokes and puns, but also telephone numbers and Internet addresses. These discursive structures directly address the viewer with an invitation to do something. Shopping channels explicitly address the viewer as a buyer as well as an audience member. There is a direct address to the viewer by the narrator who describes and recommends products, and direct invitations to act through on-screen displays of price and telephone number. Sometimes one of the phoning viewers is talked to live about why he or she liked and ordered this product. Clearly part of the appeal of this kind of programme is the connection between the programme and audience, who are represented metonymically by a telephone caller who stands in for them.

A further aspect of this myth of connectedness between programme and audience occurs in live programmes where the viewer's experience of watching and the programme's events are occurring at the same time. Live broadcasting gives access not only to space (usually it is a public space) but also to time. Obviously it is usually impossible to witness action taking place in a location distant from where we are. But live broadcasting closes the gap between the present experience of the viewer and the present experience of others in a distant place. The live broadcasting of unexpected events, national occasions, or sports events, brings together the viewer's present time and participants' present time. Television programmes can connote realism by signifying that the audience is witnessing actually occurring events (by using captions denoting that the programme is live, for example). 'Live' is a significant choice of linguistic sign to denote this, since of course it means 'alive', living, connoting that real life as it is lived by other people is being shown to us, and that we are involved in it.

Many genres of programme invite viewer involvement and connectedness with the programme. Sports programmes invite viewer involvement by alternately positioning the viewer as a witness or as an expert evaluator of the players' performance. Shots of the sport in progress provide a much closer view of events than a spectator in the arena could get, and alternate between close shots of the competitors, offering identification with their efforts and emotions, and long shots of the arena which connote television's special power to observe a denoted reality. The sound in sports programmes denotes the sounds of the spectating crowds who function as representatives of the viewers' reactions. Talk shows also include 'expert' evaluation by invited professionals. The host mediates between these professionals, members of the public who have 'problems' relevant to the programme's topic, the studio audience, and the television audience. The viewer is invited by the programme's discourse to take up a range of subject-positions in which the viewer can identify with any or all of these various participants and evaluate their discourses. Talk shows include not only a studio audience who are invited to speak as members of the public and viewer representatives, but also the voices of viewers who phone in to the programme. The viewer can become involved in the programme by phoning in and describing his or her own experiences, or adopt an 'expert' subject-position and question or evaluate the discourse of someone denoted in the programme. As in all television programmes, the codes of the programme 'hollow out' more than one subject-position for the viewer, but the possible positionings and involvements of the viewer are not infinite.

Television's access to private space is an important signifier of realism, connoting that television can close the gap between what is normally unseen and what the viewer can be given access to. The television phenomenon of 2000, in Britain and in many other countries worldwide, was *Big Brother*. Ten volunteers began a nine-week period of being observed in a specially built house in London by twenty-four permanently installed cameras. Their incentive was a prize of £70,000 awarded to the inhabitant who survived the weekly process of nomination by their fellow housemates for ejection, and the public's phone-in votes to decide which nominee would leave. In *Big Brother*, cameras were placed everywhere in the house, including the bedrooms and bathrooms, and the domestic private space of the home became very public, with no refuge allowed to the participants from this intruding gaze. The programme offered viewer involvement in every moment of the participants' lives, and the opportunity to shape the events of the serial by voting for the ejection of one of them each week. Furthermore, footage from the house's cameras was screened not only on television but also live on the Internet, so that viewers could gain even greater access to the private space of the house, in real time.

Big Brother unexpectedly became an integral part of many people's conversation, and viewer involvement was not only with the programme and the website but also with the commentary on the programme among other viewers and in the media. Gossip was an important pleasure for viewers of *Big Brother*, and it became a ready-made topic of conversation about people who the programme's realistic denotation allowed viewers to feel they knew. Television programmes are dominated much more than cinema, for example, by people talking and interacting in familiar situations, just as life for viewers at home is often centred around these activities. *Big Brother* consisted largely of sequences of conversation between the participants, representing familiar interaction and conversation which could then be talked about by viewers. The frequent use of close-up shots of faces in *Big Brother*, and on television in general, reinforces this sense of intimacy between the viewer and what is shown on television, and contributes to a mythic equivalence between the ordinary world of reality and the constructed worlds of television. Graeme Burton (2000: 146) has argued that 'The dominance of this way of using and experiencing television gives the illusion of physical closeness, invokes those rules of social interaction which demand attention and which create some sense of social proximity.' Some of the social circumstances surrounding television viewing help to support television involvement like this. The television set is usually placed in the familiar domestic space of the home. It is physically embedded in the domestic routines of people's home lives, which decreases the sense that what we see on television is 'other' to us. Perhaps the strangest thing about the *Big Brother* house was that it did not contain a television set, presumably because this would reduce the participants' interactions which were the chief interest for the viewers watching them on their own televisions.

Big Brother quickly developed a selection of character-types familiar in television soap opera, most notably 'Nasty Nick' Bateman whose manipulative and deceptive behaviour coded him as the 'villain'. The people selected for the programme had outgoing and dominant personalities, which created considerable dramatic conflict between them as well as numerous occasions for performance and display to the cameras. The participants had a personal agenda to express themselves as they would like to be seen, they also had to play roles which would not encourage the other participants to vote them out, and they played roles which would encourage the viewers to support them. As discussed above in relation to docusoaps, the realism of 'reality TV' is inextricable from performance, and several of the participants in *Big Brother* have gone on to become celebrities with jobs as television presenters. The programme denoted 'ordinary' people in an extraordinary situation, in a private domestic space which hidden cameras made extremely public, and featured non-actors in unscripted situations which came to resemble fictional drama and encouraged self-conscious performance.

Big Brother evidently mixes the codes and conventions of factual and fictional television realisms, but it is important to consider the ways in which the programme might also 'realistically' represent ideological structures of contemporary society in a coded form. The title *Big Brother* is an allusion to George Orwell's novel *1984*, in which a future totalitarian society was able to continuously monitor its citizens by video surveillance. This oppressive surveillance was summed up in the phrase 'Big Brother is watching you', and the connotations of entrapment, restriction and control which the phrase possesses are relevant to the *Big Brother* programme. We might ask whether *Big Brother* is a coded commentary on the organisation of contemporary society, just as the novel *1984* was. In the programme, individuals pursued self-interest and tried to win £70,000, but to do this they had to participate in a community which would not eject them. A structure of rules was imposed on the house by the unseen *Big Brother* production team, including the requirement that participants worked at set tasks in order to receive essential supplies and to gain rewards. These components of the programme perhaps show that *Big Brother* was a metaphor for contemporary capitalist society. Whether intentionally or not, *Big Brother* substituted the house for society at large, and set up the tensions between freedom and restraint, individual and community, and work and pleasure, which characterise the ideology of our reality. The programme could be said to have a special form of realism in that it represented society's real conditions of existence in a coded form. *Big Brother* never made this explicit, or criticised the ideology which it reproduced in this way. But nevertheless the programme shared in the myth which has been discussed before in this chapter, that factual programmes show society to itself. The several kinds of realism in *Big Brother* and in the other realist programmes discussed in this chapter both show and conceal, reflect and distort, the realities which they represent.

Sources and further reading

Television realism (in both fictional and factual programmes) is discussed by Fiske and Hartley (1978) and Branston and Stafford (1999) in semiotic terms. Paget (1998), McQueen (1998), and Burton (2000) deal with variants of documentary including docusoap, and Coles (2000) focuses solely on docusoap. Documentary television is the subject of books by Kilborn and Izod (1997), and Nichols (1991, 1994). The work of individual documentary makers is discussed by Winston (1995), and Corner (1996) analyses important individual documentaries.

Suggestions for further work

1   What are the different connotations of the linguistic signs 'real', 'authentic' and 'true'? Which of them seem most appropriate for describing documentary, docusoap or 'reality TV' programmes, and why?

2   What are the advantages and disadvantages of voice-over narration
    in documentary programmes? How do your answers depend on the
    ways in which realism is signified in television programmes?

3   Select a genre of non-fiction programme focused on a single aspect
    of contemporary life, like holiday programmes, consumer advice
    programmes, home décor programmes, or cooking programmes.
    Which mythic meanings are encoded and which ideologies are nat-
    uralised in the programmes you have chosen?

4   If you were making a documentary programme about a day in your
    own life, which five locations and which five interactions with other
    people would you choose to include? In what ways would these
    places and interactions metonymically represent you and your day?

5   Analyse a short sequence from a television docusoap, focusing on
    the functions of editing to draw comparisons and make contrasts
    between people and events. How does editing affect the ways in
    which character, narrative development, and ideological viewpoint
    are signified?

6   In what ways can docusoaps fulfil television's public service obliga-
    tions to show society to itself? How do they do this differently from
    documentaries?

7   Look for ways in which 'reality TV' programmes invite viewer
    involvement, whether by features of the programmes themselves or
    in other ways (like websites, or phone-in voting). In what ways
    might this involvement encourage primary viewing of the pro-
    gramme, and what is the ideological significance of this involve-
    ment?

Television fictions

Introduction

The main focus of this chapter is on television viewers and audiences. It begins with some statistical information about the audiences for the different television channels and genres of programme. Then there is a section on the signs and codes of television which extends the discussion of television signs and codes in the previous chapter. This leads on to the question of how television programmes address the viewer, and how positions are laid out for the viewer from which television programmes make sense. As this chapter continues, the viewer is seen less as a destination to which meanings are directed, and more as a specific person in a social context. We shall see that while the discourse of semiotic analysis is a powerful way of analysing television texts, it needs to be extended and problematised by research done on the reception of television programmes. There is a significant body of research on television which shifts the emphasis of academic work away from the detailed semiotic analysis of programmes and towards the study of how viewers construct meanings in different ways. Some of this research, known as audience studies or ethnography, became especially dominant in Television Studies in the 1980s and provides us with useful information about the role of television in people's actual lives. Research on fictional programmes, especially soap operas, showed that different viewers construct different meanings in their decoding of the signs and codes of television. While this research is not strictly part of semiotics, and the groundbreaking studies in this area are now rather dated, it both supports and challenges semiotic analysis and therefore it is discussed quite extensively later in this chapter.

Audiences for television fiction

At the beginning of chapter 5, the distinction was made between the measurement of the total audience for a particular programme (ratings), and the measurement of the proportion of the audience watching one television channel's output rather than another's (audience share). As the number of broadcast channels has grown, and the new technologies of satellite and cable television have offered even more channels, the measurement of audiences and the competition for audiences has become even more important to broadcasting organisations. As more channels become available, the audience becomes more fragmented although the time spent watching television remains about the same. Broadcasting organisations are therefore very concerned to capture a significant share of the audience for their own programmes, particularly if they rely on advertising for funding. Only the BBC is not funded by advertising, but the BBC has to justify its compulsory licence fee by demonstrating that a significant share of the population is watching its programmes.

Broadcasters funded by advertising are especially concerned to capture desirable sectors of the TV audience, like 18- to 25-year-olds for instance who have relatively high disposable incomes which they could spend on the consumer products advertised on television. Although the average age of ITV's audience has been increasing for many years, the channel has successfully targeted valuable 18- to 34-year-olds with non-fiction programmes like *Who Wants to be a Millionaire?*, which gains a 42 per cent share of this group, and *Blind Date* which gains a 45 per cent share of 18- to 34-year-olds. Channel 4 has scheduled a sequence or 'strip' of comedy programmes one after another on Friday evenings in the 1990s and into the 2000s, like *Friends, Frasier, Trigger Happy TV* and *Whose Line is it Anyway?*, and has attracted a high proportion of young adult viewers in the A, B, and C1 social classes with these programmes. This is not a huge audience but it is a desirable one to advertisers. Forty-six per cent of BBC1's audience is ABC1, 45 per cent of Channel 4's, 44 per cent of BBC2's, and 38 per cent of ITV's (Maggie Brown 'Vying for VIPs', *The Guardian* Media section, Monday 5 March 2001, 8–9). It is also fortunate for Channel 4 that imported American programmes like many of those in its Friday night 'strip' are in general cheaper to buy than original British drama, although Channel 4 has commissioned original British drama addressed to the ABC1 audience such as the serials *Queer as Folk* and *Never Never*. Watching television is important to ABC1s, and 22 per cent of the members of the elite AB social group relax by watching TV, compared to 13 per cent who read and 8 per cent who listen to music. So the fact that 45 per cent of *EastEnders'* audience is ABC1 partly explains BBC1's decision to increase showings of the soap opera to four episodes per week, while ITV's police drama series *A Touch of Frost* gained a welcome 48 per cent share of ABC1s watching television in its timeslot.

Television broadcasters receive numerical data about audience size and composition from the Broadcasters' Audience Research Board (BARB), whose figures are the basis of the analysis in this section, and the opportunities to commission, continue or cancel a television programme are significantly determined by this research. The previous chapter pointed out the rise in the number of non-fictional programmes like docusoaps on British television in recent years, but fiction programmes have always been the ones which attract the largest audiences. For the 1999 year as a whole, the most popular programme was an episode of the soap opera *Coronation Street* (ITV 7 March) with 19.8 million viewers, and the soap opera *EastEnders* was the fifth most popular (BBC1 7 January) with 15.7 million viewers. Fiction programmes in the popular genres of police drama (*Heartbeat*, ITV 28 February, 17 million; A *Touch of Frost*, ITV 21 March, 16.8 million), hospital drama (*Casualty*, BBC1 13 February, 13.1 million) and situation comedy (*The Vicar of Dibley*, BBC1 27 December, 14.4 million) also appeared in the top twenty programmes. It is programmes belonging to the categories of soap opera, police drama, hospital drama and situation comedy which provide the examples of television fiction discussed in this chapter. The top twenty programmes in 1999 were all shown on terrestrial television (rather than satellite or cable), and all of them were shown on either BBC1 or ITV. Although there were two American cinema films on television in the 1999 top twenty (*GoldenEye* and *Mission Impossible*), all of the most popular television programmes were British-made. One of the issues

discussed later in this chapter is the export and import of television programmes, and the significance of this international
exchange for television culture.

Codes of television fiction

From a semiotic point of view, the first step in understanding
how the meanings of television fiction are made and understood
is to identify the kinds of sign used in the *langue* or system of television, and to discover how these signs are used according to certain codes and conventions. Quite detailed accounts of the kinds
of camera shot, lighting, sound and music in television have been
given in previous chapters, so I shall not repeat this detail here.
To summarise, the signs which will be of interest in decoding
television will mainly be visual signs (images, and sometimes
graphics) and aural ones (speech, sound, and music). Television
images and sounds are often iconic and denotative, seeming
simply to show what the camera and sound equipment has
recorded. But these images and sounds carry connotations which
enable the viewer to gain much more meaning from them than
simply a vision of an object, place, or person. The selection and
combination of images and sounds, so that connotations relay
together into mythic meanings affecting our understanding of
society and culture, often depend on the codes and conventions
which organise them. It is the viewer's knowledge of television
codes which enables the pleasures, frustrations, boredom or fascination of television to occur, even though this knowledge of
codes and conventions is often unconsciously possessed.

Television fiction almost always involves storytelling, and
clearly the codes and conventions of television narrative are
crucial to its different forms. Television fiction is sometimes
shown in single programmes, but increasingly in episodic forms.
In serials, an unfolding story is told in several parts, with soap
opera as a special case of this seriality where the end of the story
is never reached. Series, by contrast, are programmes where settings and characters do not change or evolve, but instead new
stories are presented in each episode. Although these distinctions
are useful, it is becoming increasingly common for television programmes to combine the single setting and new stories each

episode which are components of series fiction with the ongoing development of characters and stories across episodes which are seen in serials. Robin Nelson (1997) has called this mixture of serial and series form 'flexi-narrative'. Flexi-narrative denotes fiction that borrows the short sequences of action and rapid pace of editing found in television advertisements, in the context of the involvement in ongoing characters and stories associated with television soap opera and the perpetually new stories and challenges which occur each episode in television series.

The US television series *ER* is an example of flexi-narrative, whose form is apparently designed to appeal to American audiences accustomed to programmes frequently interrupted by commercials. Bob Mullan (1997: 60) reports that the novelist Michael Crichton, *ER*'s creator, has claimed that American audiences 'are incapable of watching television for any length of time unless it is a "news reality" programme like *Cops* or a courtroom drama like the O.J. Simpson trial. The only way forward, he believes, is to make drama more dramatic than the news and reality programmes'. The result of this set of audience expectations is for *ER*'s narrative to be punctuated with regular bursts of action and divided into short segments. This can be seen in *ER*'s use of a wide range of camera shots and editing rhythms, from very long single takes to rapid pans and quick-fire cutting. In action sequences the dialogue of characters overlaps, and the sounds of medical equipment and background noise connote the realist observation of a complex and barely controlled reality represented partly through documentary techniques. *ER* combines these action sequences with more conventionally dramatic sequences of character development, often accompanying scenes with music and using frequent close-ups on the faces of the central characters. The programme combines the conventions of documentary realism, soap opera, and occasionally comedy. But it is important to note that this narrative form was explained and justified by Crichton as a response to the needs he perceived in his audience. The audience is a sign whose meaning is very hard to read, but whose meaning is the foundation for decisions about form and production technique.

A crucial distinction (see Kozloff 1992) in analysing fictional programmes is between the events which occur (the story), and the means by which the story is told (the narrative discourse). There is always the sense that someone or something is doing the storytelling or the observing for us, on our behalf, and therefore functioning as a narrator. *Star Trek: The Next Generation* begins with the famous syntagm 'Space, the final frontier ...' which narrates the scenario of the series, followed by the 'Captain's log' that narrates the scenario for each episode, like a storyteller. Scenarios are also narrated by the title songs of programmes, as in *Fresh Prince of Bel-Air* and *One Foot in the Grave*. Series like *ER* may begin by reminding us of the previous programme with a short narrative syntagm of extracts introduced by a narrating voice, 'Previously, on *ER* ...'. Some drama programmes include a narrator within sequences, as in *Sex in the City*. While some programmes specifically foreground a narrator, the majority of television fiction consists of narrative made up of camera shots in a narrative progression, with an implied rather than evident narrator. The alternation of camera shots in drama is very similar to the cinema's use of a mobile point of view, in which the viewer is aligned with the point of view of particular characters in a scene, or with a 'neutral' point of view which observes the whole acting area. The performers in television fiction behave as if the viewer is absent, connoting that the drama is happening in a realistic world to which we are given access. One of the key agencies which narrates television fiction is the camera, and the implied narrator who is composed from the different camera points of view edited together to form the narrative as whole.

Television programmes do not only narrate fictional stories (news discourse is also narrative), but in all television narratives the aim is to keep the viewer watching by assembling verbal and visual signs in ways which are entertaining or informative. So for instance camera shots change more rapidly than in cinema, and moments of silence are rare. The semiotic analysis of television has tended to concentrate until recently on image more than on sound, but sound is particularly important to television narration and its mode of address to the viewer. It was pointed out in chapter 5 that the loud brass music of news programmes is used to draw the attention of the viewer as well as to connote authority. Because the television image is small, and television competes with other activities for the viewer's attention, sound is also used simply to call the viewer to look at the screen. Music and other sound in television programmes signify the emotional significance of images, and have a vital role in directing the viewer how to respond to action and characters. As Sarah Kozloff (1992: 79) has pointed out: 'Music, in film and in television, is a key channel through which the voiceless narrating agency "speaks" to the viewer'.

Fiction and ideology

Television fiction offers many examples of programmes and types of programme which represent communities, such as the communities living in one place in soap opera, the communities policed by television cops, and the communities of workers in hospital drama. While television fiction is clearly not capable of representing society as whole, and does not aim to present analyses of society, nevertheless programmes are appealing to audiences and make sense to viewers partly because they engage with the representations of society which circulate in contemporary culture. Gender, work, environment and law and order are some of the signifieds which the signifiers of television fiction represent, and which construct mythic meanings. As we have seen previously in this book, the mythic meanings in media texts always connect with ideological ways of representing and perceiving reality, and render some representations (but not others) natural and common sense. What television fictions do is lay out positions from which their stories make sense, positions which the viewer is invited to occupy in order to understand and enjoy television fiction. This section briefly considers different genres of television fiction with attention to the positioning of the viewer, and the ideological meanings which programmes naturalise.

The space of soap opera is a communal space. Some soaps are named after the spaces in which they are set, like *Coronation Street*, *EastEnders*, *Brookside* or *Emmerdale*, which signifies the importance of location as a force which binds characters (sometimes unwillingly) together. Within this enveloping location, further kinds of connectedness provide the grounds for interactions, alliances and conflicts between characters. Characters may be connected by family membership, age-group, gender, working relationship, or race, for example. Clearly these bonds overlap and one character will belong to more than one grouping, causing conflicts of loyalty, jealousy, rivalry, and competition. The narrative structure of soap exploits these connections, changes them over time, and uses them as the motor for dramatic stories. For example, soap characters frequently fall in and out of romantic relationships with each other, and engage in rivalries over the custody of children or the running of businesses. The narrative movement of soap is both very fast, since episodes consist of short sequences in which different plotlines run simultaneously, and very slow, since the time-period represented in each episode is rarely more than a single day. The connectedness of characters is a means both to contain the drama in one place, and to generate large numbers of possible storylines. Furthermore, the importance of gossip and the keeping or revealing of secrets are ways of making and blocking the connectedness between characters. Ideologically, the spatial restriction of the soap opera world allows it to represent an organic community, substituting for the absence of a sense of belonging in the lives of many viewers. The importance of family connection in soaps also tends to prioritise adult woman characters, who preside over the homes and extended families which soap narratives involve. For this reason, soap can be seen as a genre which works with ideological representations of femininity (in child-rearing, work, and sexuality, for example), exploring the tensions and contradictions of gender identity for a predominantly female audience.

The space of hospital drama is a restricted space, but one which is also transitional. *Casualty* and *ER* are set almost entirely in hospital emergency departments, transitional spaces in which dramatic stories first make their appearance as patients enter, and at the end of episodes the patients leave with a storyline completed. The completion of stories is part of the narrative code of series drama, where episodes are freestanding, but hospital drama also has codes shared with soap opera narrative. The community of doctors and nurses, of various ages, social classes and races, metonymically signifies the 'melting pot' of America in *ER* and 'multicultural Britain' in *Casualty* for example, and similar dramatic uses of groupings of characters and connectedness form the basis for stories, as in soap opera. Gender representation is different from soap, however. For although there are male and female doctors and nurses, the gender hierarchy in which doctors are predominantly male and nurses predominantly female means that the significance of women characters is much less. The feminine identities of the women doctors in *ER* and *Casualty* are undermined. In *ER* Carrie is physically disabled, and Baz and George in *Casualty* are known by masculine names, for example. But the 'feminine' virtues of taking time to get to know and to care about others are especially important to hospital drama. Ideologically, the public and bureaucratic work of the hospital, as a mechanism for coping with medical emergencies, becomes humanised by care, human interest, character interaction and individual responsibility. Hospital drama humanises the medical institution, personalises social problems, and connects individuals with a community which can heal them.

The police drama series *The Cops* also features a community of main characters, police officers who at first sight seem conventional: a young and unruly policeman, an old-school beat officer with dubious methods, an ambitious young policewoman, an uneasy Asian policeman, for example. But each character's recognisable role is repeatedly made more difficult to align with the codes of the police drama genre. For example, the young and ambitious Natalie is denoted snorting cocaine at the beginning of episode one, but increasingly develops liberal and caring attitudes to the underprivileged people of the housing estate who are often the focus of police attention. The programme's connections with established codes and its repeated breaking of them is also supported by the mix of codes of editing and camerawork which are used in the series. Rather than alternating camera points of view on the same action, in order to show one character's reaction to another, for example, sequences are almost entirely shot from single points of view by one hand-held camera. The use of this code links the programme with documentary, where action is usually shot as it happens by a single camera, and produces connotations of documentary realism. Both codes of characterisation and codes of visual style and form are manipulated in order to destabilise the viewer positioning common in police drama, where the audience are aligned with the police as 'us' and the criminals are 'them'. Police in *The Cops* are objects of an investigating and observing documentary look, and the easy identification of familiar character-types is also offered but denied. While the ideological positioning of *The Cops* makes

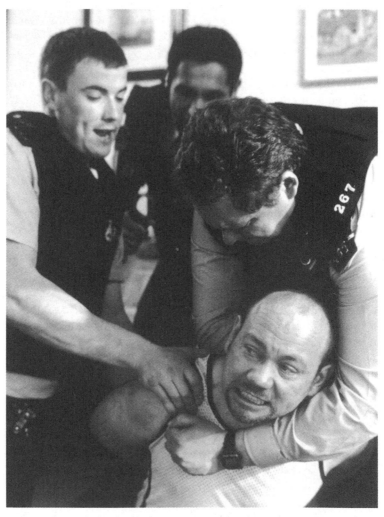

9   A police raid in *The Cops*

reference to the naturalisation of the police as defenders of order against disruptive 'others', it also disallows this ideological position and calls it into question. The community of the police and the community which it polices no longer appear divided clearly from each other, and the ideological division between 'us' and 'them' is blurred. *The Cops* negotiates with a dominant ideological position in television fiction, by requiring the viewer to negotiate his or her position in relation to the signs and codes of the programme.

As I have argued elsewhere in this book, positioning the viewer or reader of a media text is an ideological operation, in which the viewer or reader is called to take up a position laid out for him or her. There are prominent visual and aural signs in television comedy which invite the viewer to take up particular subject-positions in relation to a programme's discourse. The denoted laughter which frequently breaks into comedy programmes' soundtracks marks the points at which the mythic meaning 'comedy' is constructed. This mythic meaning can derive from a range of different signs and relationships between signs. These include a point of conflict between the discourses of characters, a conflict between the connotations of the image and the connotations of sound or denoted dialogue, or an absurd extension of a particular discursive code or gestural code. The function of laughter is to confirm the subject-position of the viewer by representing an audience which shares this position. While TV viewers are watching individually or in small groups, the collective laughter of the denoted audience makes the link between the viewer at home and the mythic community of viewers to which the programme is broadcast. At moments of laughter, any uncertainty and ambiguity about the decoding of the signs of the programme is closed off by offering the viewer one kind of relationship with the TV discourse, by offering one way of decoding those moments of the text. The patterning of laughter which momentarily stops the TV discourse enables the viewer to become 'you', the one who is addressed by the discourse and who is expected to share in the imaginary community's laughter. The ideological functions of television comedy depend not only on the meanings of the action being represented, but also on calling the viewer to become part of an audience community constructed around laughter.

Moments of laughter interrupt any narrative progression in the sitcom, but the code which primarily structures television comedy is 'excess' rather than narrative. In terms of characterisation, Frasier Crane in *Frasier* is excessively snobbish and proper, while Victor Meldrew in *One Foot in the Grave* is excessively irritable, vindictive and moody, for example. These situation comedies exaggerate characters' social codes of behaviour so that they become excessive, inappropriate, and therefore comic. Close-up shots of the exaggerated facial expressions of the characters are signs which cue audience laughter, for instance. Figure 10 is a publicity still from *One Foot in the Grave* showing Victor Meldrew (Richard Wilson) with a characteristically exaggerated facial expression connoting moodiness, irritability and

10   Margaret and Victor Meldrew, *One Foot in the Grave*

discontent. The character's clothes and body stance support the connotations of his expression, and the mythic meaning of the character as a testy old man. By contrast, his wife's (Annette Crosbie's) expression and stance connote pleasantness and long-suffering. The comedy of *One Foot in the Grave* derives not only from Victor Meldrew's excess in itself, but from the contrast between his behaviour and the behaviour of the other characters. As well as the ideological positioning of the viewer as part of the laughing community, what is to be laughed at is also ideologically significant. Deviation from a norm, and excessive behaviour beyond what society usually allows, have the effect of reinforcing an unconscious acceptance of what the norms of society are, while simultaneously exploring the limits of the norm.

Comedy depends on a shifting pattern of identification between the viewer and the programme. When a character is comic, the viewer must identify with the character but also distance himself or herself from the character in order to find him or her funny. The viewer must also identify with the studio audience denoted by laughter on the soundtrack, taking up a shared position in relation to the comic moment in the programme. The viewer must also identify with the scenario presented by the various camera shots and sounds which make up the programme, so that the programme seems to be 'for us' and addressed to us as viewers. Finally then, the audience must identify with itself in the role of audience for the programme. Comedy relies on this shifting of the viewer's subject-position, and a rhythm of identification and disavowal of identification. The semiotic effect of comedy as a genre is to move and reposition the viewer, as this section has so far described in rather abstract terms. But of course the positioning and repositioning of the viewer might succeed or fail for different real viewers in different programmes or parts of the same programme. While the discourse of television fiction lays out positions for the viewer in relation to its signs and codes, whether or not the viewer actually occupies this subject-position depends on the huge range of variables which determine each viewer's social identity.

Postmodernism and television

Postmodernism is a critical term with several meanings, but always involves making a distinction between what is occurring now and a situation which was in place in the past. So 'post-modernist' or 'postmodern' are often used to signify newness, though the terms have been used to criticise television fiction (as empty, shallow, or bland) as well as to praise it for its cutting-edge, experimental qualities. This section focuses on two meanings of the term 'postmodern' in turn, namely the sense that television fiction (and television in general) is part of a new global communications culture, and secondly that contemporary television exhibits a new aesthetic style and has new forms.

Chris Barker's (1997: 27) definition of global television is 'television which in its technology, ownership, programme distribution and audiences operates across the boundaries of nation-states and language communities.' One of the questions to ask about the globalisation of television is whose television is spread across nations and communities, and whose is not. In Britain, major broadcasting organisations mainly show programmes which have been made in Britain. In 1999 for example, 82 per cent of the programmes shown on BBC1 and BBC2 were made in the UK. Britain is a net exporter of television, selling many of its programmes abroad, often to dozens of countries. For instance, Venezuela has bought the situation comedies *Absolutely Fabulous*, *Fawlty Towers* and *Blackadder*. China has bought the police serial *Prime Suspect*, the drama about firefighters *London's Burning* and the detective drama *Poirot*. Sweden has bought *EastEnders*, Qatar has bought the detective drama *A Touch of Frost*, and Russia has bought *A Touch of Frost*, *Coronation Street*, and *Absolutely Fabulous*. The best-selling British television export in 1998 was the BBC nature documentary series *The Living Planet*, sold to 82 countries, and the children's programme *Teletubbies* has been sold to Estonia, Portugal, Israel, the USA, Australia and New Zealand.

Although British television is sold abroad, it is American television which has been exported most. The global presence of American programmes in very different countries is sometimes criticised as the 'hegemony', or domination by consent, of

American ideology over local cultures, but this critique takes too little account of multiaccentuality, which means the negotiation of meanings by real viewers. The decoding of the signs and codes of television must be affected by the relationship of the mythic meanings and ideological structure of programmes with the society in which they are broadcast, and with the particular social and cultural positions of viewers. As pointed out in chapter 5, global television does not necessarily produce a global audience which decodes it in the same way. However, there is an economic and institutional dimension to globalisation which does have a significant effect on particular national television cultures. Although some national television networks outside the USA are large and powerful (in Brazil and Mexico, for example), it is usually much cheaper for television broadcasters in the developing world to buy packages of several American series than to make their own programmes. Some countries like Britain, Brazil and Japan have little need to import programmes because they have their own production facilities, others like Canada and Australia supplement home-produced programmes with imports, while other countries (most of South America, Africa, and Asia) have very small television industries of their own and are dependent on programmes from abroad. The schedules of many Latin American and African nations contain more than 50 per cent imported American programmes. But the economic dependency on American programmes does not automatically produce ideological control. This can be seen in the fact that the formats of programmes from one country or culture do not always succeed in another. The US sitcom *The Golden Girls* was tried in Britain (on ITV), using slightly adapted scripts from the US version. Despite a cast including well-known British comedy actresses the programme was commercially and critically unsuccessful and ran for only six weeks. *Married for Life* was a British version of the US *Married... with Children*, which ran for over 200 episodes in America, but the British ITV version ran for only one series. The myths and ideologies of one culture, represented in its television programmes, are not watched in the same ways and with the same effects in another culture.

'Postmodern' can denote a distinctive style, a self-aware playfulness with the codes of a form or a medium, such as is found

in programmes like *The Simpsons* or *Jam* and in many TV ads
which play on other ads or advertising conventions. An
evening's television viewing requires us both to shift subject-
positions frequently, and to decode programmes in relation to
their position in the television schedule and their intertextual
relationship to other programmes. Some programmes include
intertextual references to contemporary programmes to position
themselves and their characters in this intertextual field. For
example an episode of the sitcom *Father Ted* involved the characters encountering Richard Wilson (who plays Victor Meldrew
in *One Foot in the Grave*) and tormenting him to comic effect by
repeating the character's catchphrase 'I don't believe it!' over
and over again. Some television programmes and ads make this
fluid relationship between media texts one of the chief pleasures
offered to the viewer. What is postmodern about programmes
like these is their ambivalence towards the original texts which
they parody, where the codes of the original are recognised and
used but their ideological and stylistic limitations are also foregrounded, as Hutcheon (1987) described. *The Simpsons* makes
intertextual jokes about the codes of other animated cartoons,
horror films, television news, and science fiction, among many
other television and film forms. The viewer is always being
shifted around from one code and relationship to the text to
another code and relationship.

The identification with characters and with the narrative
structures of the programme which a particular viewer experiences may be determined by the social and cultural position of
each viewer, but the semiotic structure of the programme as a
text has to be open enough to allow for variations in decoding.
The viewer is asked to refer to his or her cultural knowledge of
media representations. A 1995 episode of *ER* entitled 'Mother-
hood', for example, was directed by Quentin Tarantino and
included a sequence where a patient arrived with a bloody and
mutilated ear. The episode invited the viewer to make intertextual connections between the episode and Tarantino's violent
and bloody films, especially *Reservoir Dogs* with its famous ear-
cutting scene. But the episode did not require the viewer to make
this connection, though the connection enriched the meanings
of the episode. Parody and intertextuality rely on the viewer's

'media literacy', so that intertextual references can be recognised and their connotations made part of the character's or the narrative's meaning. Making sense of postmodern television demands an active, mobile and TV-literate viewer. Robin Nelson (1997: 246) suggests that 'Postmodern texts might be summarily characterized by a formal openness, a strategic refusal to close down meaning. They create space for play between discourses allegedly empowering the reader to negotiate or construct her own meanings.' For the benefit of broadcasters, postmodern television is designed to be multiaccentual, appealing to different audience groups. Its postmodern polysemia, coming from the shifting codes and multiply-connoting signs of its images and sound, allows multiaccentuality to succeed economically.

The term 'postmodern' can also denote a socio-economic condition, emphasising the decay of industrial culture and the rise of 'post-industrial' media culture. There is a philosophical discourse based on this assumption (see Baudrillard 1983, for instance) that questions the assumptions of previous philosophy, and includes a focus on the perpetual alienation from reality which a radical version of semiotics proposes. Postmodernist thought claims that all 'real meaning' is vanishing because experience and reality are now shaped or 'simulated' by the discourses of the media. According to this view, we might experience a love-affair through the codes for representing love-affairs in films or television programmes, or our perceptions of policemen would be determined by the mythic meanings of the police in *The Bill* or *The Cops*. In a culture where people's experience is shaped by media representations, television programmes are regarded not as denoting 'reality' in the usual sense, but as denoting the realities represented through the codes of other television programmes and in other media texts. Not only do we conceive reality through the media which continually represent it to us, but we also conceive of our own identities this way. Postmodernist media plays with identities, suggesting that our realities and our selves are multiple and unstable things, refracted and shaped by media images.

Television audiences

When television was still a novelty (in the 1950s, for example), television viewing was an event and an experience in itself. Now 'media literate' viewers are increasingly used to television, and integrate it seamlessly into their everyday lives. There is more television, more channels, and smaller fractions of audience watching particular programmes. These factors reduce the usefulness of statistical information about audience size. Although there are statistical methods for measuring viewers' interest and involvement in programmes and ads, one of the problems with statistical information is the difficulty of evaluating how people watch television, why they watch it, whether they enjoy it, and whether they retain any of the meanings they have constructed in relation to it. Ien Ang (1991) has analysed the discourse of audience measurement, showing that in the fragmented marketplace of contemporary television there is an insistent desire to find ways of measuring audience figures and kinds of involvement in programmes and ads. But audience measurement is a discourse whose methodology and assumptions set limits to the kind of conclusions which can be drawn from it, because it is statistical, based on samples of viewers, and is forced to generalise about issues such as what viewers find pleasurable in television programmes. Ethnographic research on particular viewers and groups of viewers is another discourse about television viewers which we shall encounter later in this section. Its limitation is that it relies on what people say about what they watch; it is a discourse based on viewers' discourses, and on very small samples of viewers. On the other hand, the discourse of semiotic analysis is limited by its focus on texts and a tendency to forget the social context of media involvement.

Like any academic subject, Television Studies has changed its emphases over time, and developed a number of different methodologies. As Charlotte Brunsdon (1998b) has discussed, the academic subject of Television Studies emerged in the 1970s and 1980s out of three discourses about television: journalism, literary criticism and social science. Both journalism about television and literary criticism focus on television programmes as texts, aligning television with the close study of structure, characters and themes in literature and drama. Social science discourse, on the other hand, addresses the production of television and its role in contemporary society, by finding out about the production contexts of programmes and discovering how viewers relate to them, using such methods as questionnaires and interviews. Feminist academics working on television had an important influence on how television was studied, by examining kinds of television regarded as low quality, like soap opera, and looking in detail at the ways that actual viewers (often women viewers) watched television in the real circumstances of their own homes. As Bob Mullan has discussed (1997), academics have drawn on social science methods and concerns to find out how television viewing relates to wider social behaviour. These concerns include how different kinds of audience watch different kinds of programmes, and the section on *Audiences for television fiction* began to explore how social groups of different age and status watch different programmes. A related question is how viewing context (with your family, or with your best friends) affects viewing experience. For example, people watching with their families will often be coerced into watching something they do not enjoy, whereas watching your favourite programme with your friends might help to confirm your shared group relationships. In a study of women's watching of videos on television for instance, Ann Gray (1992) found that whether or not women engage in paid employment outside the home, the home was not often a site of leisure for them. Women often used watching videos as a reward for work done in the home, so that these women's use of television would be quite different from, for instance, teenage girls watching MTV with a group of their friends. There is also a strand of research into people's talk about television. Finding out who talks about television, where and how (in school playgrounds, at work, in pubs, when meeting strangers) reveals the different roles television can play in making, breaking and cementing social relationships.

The effects of this shift in Television Studies onto viewers and audiences are to focus on 'active' rather than 'passive' viewing, and to value kinds of viewing and kinds of programme which have been considered of low quality. Rather than analysing television by close semiotic analysis, researchers looked at how

'television viewing is generally a somewhat busy activity, interrupted by many other activities and routinely accompanied by
talk, much of it having nothing to do with the programme being
watched' (Mullan 1997: 16). Rather than being passively positioned by the codes of a television text, viewers have been considered as makers of meaning. When a viewer watches television
they draw on their histories, their cultural, class, racial, economic or sexual identities, and use their media knowledge of
comparable programmes and the various information sources
available to them, to construct a relationship with the television
programme in the context of their cultural lives.

Different decodings are produced by viewers who occupy different social positions in a particular society, as well as by viewers who live in different nations and cultures. The negotiation of
the meanings of television programmes is affected not only by
membership of a national culture, but also by the social status of
the viewer in that culture. In 1985, Ien Ang's study of Dutch
women's reactions to the American soap opera *Dallas* was published in English (revised in 1989). Ang set out to understand
how women viewers experience and enjoy the programme,
which was watched by half the population of the Netherlands.
Dallas is set among fictional oil barons living in Texas, and
focuses mainly on the Ewing family, their business colleagues
and extended family. Its plot is characterised by sudden reversals
of fortune, emotional crises, and interactions between business
deals and family allegiances. Ang wanted to find out what made
watching *Dallas* pleasurable for its audience, nearly three-
quarters of whom were women. She placed an ad in a women's
magazine, asking people to write to her about the programme.
Her book is an analysis of both the discourses of the programme
and the discourses of the women who wrote to her about it. So
although she uses semiotic methods in analysing these discourses, Ang is also an ethnographer studying the place of
television in the life experience of particular viewers.

Because the narrative of *Dallas* is mostly concerned with the
emotional problems of the characters, Ang describes it as having
a tragic structure of feeling. In other words the programme
presents a naturalised mythic world in which any resolution of
the characters' problems leads on to further complication and

suffering. In order to decode the programme in this way, Ang argues that viewers must be equipped with a cultural competence or orientation that she calls a 'melodramatic imagination' (Ang 1989: 78). This consists of a disposition to be vaguely dissatisfied with the everyday world, so that the viewer's imagination dignifies everyday life with the grand emotional and moral significance of melodrama or tragedy, making life seem much more meaningful. *Dallas* both fits in with this way of experiencing and supports it because the programme is itself melodramatic. For Ang, women have decoded and enjoyed *Dallas* through a melodramatic imagination because ideological factors position them as particular kinds of social subject. Women in Western culture are positioned as emotional, psychologising, caring, community-forming (as opposed to adventuring, aggressive, money-making, and individualist), so that the mythic moral and emotional world of melodrama corresponds to a dominant subject-position for women viewers. Pleasure in *Dallas* comes from the close relationship between the social and ideological ways in which viewers' experience is structured, and the ways in which the mythic world of the programme is structured. Beyond the programme itself, pleasure comes from the fact that it is an entertainment, a reward, a relaxation, and a subject of conversation. Watching *Dallas* and knowing about the programme connected individual viewers to a mythic community with shared knowledge and experiences. Ang's study was written from a feminist point of view, and while she stressed the value of *Dallas* in the lives of real women, she was critical of its ideological role. Since the women in the programme can never attain a happy resolution to their problems, it is not a feminist utopia. Ang argued that pleasure in the show is not itself necessarily positive for women viewers, since it does not lead to action or to political consciousness of gender roles. The status and value of the meanings of television depend on the viewer's negotiation between the text of the programme and the social structure which forms the viewer's naturalised cultural world.

To conclude this chapter, it is useful to consider some of the limitations of studies of the audiences of television fiction. For while this approach is important in correcting semiotics' focus on the detail of television programmes at the expense of why people

watch and enjoy them, it is not without problematic aspects. In
the 1980s and 1990s, academics began to study how fans of
television programmes gain pleasure and a sense of identity
through immersing themselves in particular programmes. This
kind of study is significant because it shows that fans' active
appropriation of television culture is one end of a spectrum
which also includes the ways that all television viewers appropriate meaning and social power from television. The fan community is a self-selected cultural group of people who take hold
of popular cultural products and rework them for their own
pleasure. Fans are relatively powerless to control the production
of television programmes, but create alternative cultural products (like websites) and create cultural practices around the
programmes (like conventions). However fan culture reproduces
many features of the 'official' television culture of production.
Fans discriminate between 'insiders' (who belong to the world of
fan culture, or 'fandom') and 'outsiders' (people who do not
belong), in response to their own positions as outsiders to the
television business. Fans produce and circulate texts and products, just as television producers and broadcasters do. Fans
accumulate cultural capital, the knowledge and authority which
gives them status, just as television producers and broadcasters
accumulate monetary capital and profit. So fan culture responds
actively to the cultural disempowerment which comes from
being part of an audience rather than a maker of television. But
no matter how active the fan audience is, it has little effect on
the ways that the television industry works or on the television
programmes which are actually made. Fans are a special case in
that they are especially active decoders of television, but the real
powerlessness of fans reminds us that all viewers remain in positions of response to television even though television gives richness and social meaning to our lives. Although it is important to
study how real viewers and audiences make sense of television
in their own ways, their meaning-making activities are always
negotiations with the semiotic structures of television programmes. For this reason, the semiotic analysis of how
programmes are meaningful, and how they position viewers to
understand and enjoy these meanings, is an essential mode of
study.

Sources and further reading

Among the many books and essays which use semiotic approaches to television fiction are Fiske (1987), Fiske and Hartley (1978), Eco (1990), Selby and Cowdery (1995), and Seiter (1992). An excellent collection of essays on a range of analytical approaches to television is Allen (1992) which contains the essays by Kozloff and Seiter which are referred to in this chapter. Books which address several television fictional genres include McQueen (1998), Nelson (1997), and Carson and Llewellyn-Jones (2000). Postmodernism in television is discussed by Woods (1999), Collins (1992), and Fiske (1991). Audience studies are presented and discussed in Fiske (1987), Ang (1989, 1991), Morley (1992), Moores (1993), Drummond and Patterson (1988), Seiter *et al.* (1989), Lindof (1987) and Lull (1988). Lewis (1992) collects essays on fan audiences, and Tulloch and Jenkins (1995) conduct detailed studies of *Star Trek* and *Doctor Who* audiences.

Suggestions for further work

1 Analyse a TV listings magazine detailing programmes on several channels for the same time-period. How do the listings inform you of the programmes' genre, form and attractions for viewers? How do the editorial pages in the listings magazine support or multiply the mythic meanings for some programmes?

2 Conduct a detailed analysis of the signs and codes in a short sequence from one television programme. What contributions are made to narrative progression, viewer positioning, and 'preferred reading' by the elements you have analysed? What are the limitations of this kind of exercise?

3 In what ways are female police officers and female criminals represented in police fiction series you have seen? How do police series 'masculinise' or 'feminise' the law, justice and crime?

4 Analyse a selection of television ads from different parts of the day (for example, mid-morning and mid-evening). What is the significance of the similarities and differences you find in their address to the viewer, types of product advertised, and relationship to the surrounding programmes?

5 Which current programmes seem to exhibit the greatest degrees of multiaccentuality and polysemy? Do they have any narrative or generic features which could be called postmodern?

6 Compare the visual and narrative codes of two soap operas from different nations (for example Britain and Australia). How similar and

how different are their codes? How similar and how different are their ideologies?

7   Situation comedy uses the same characters and keeps them in the same settings in each episode. In what ways are mythic meanings of entrapment or enclosure signified in sitcoms you have seen?

8

Cinema

Introduction

This chapter discusses film signs and codes, the central concerns of semiotic analysis. But like other chapters in this book, there is also a section on the cinema as an economic and cultural institution, since films are made and watched in a commercial context. The vast majority of contemporary films are fictional narratives, and this chapter discusses critical ideas about film narrative with a particular emphasis on narrative structure and on the role of the film viewer in making sense of films. The previous chapter took account of the recent academic research into how particular real viewers watched television, but there is currently little work done on film viewers in this way although the issue is addressed at the end of this chapter. Instead, film theory has concentrated on elaborate semiotic and psychoanalytic approaches to film texts. For this reason, among others, the theory of the film medium has historically been more a complex set of discourses than the theoretical discourses developed for the analysis of the other media discussed in this book. Film theory has also been adjusted and transferred to work on other media, and some of the semiotic and psychoanalytic approaches discussed in earlier chapters originally derived from the writings of theorists working on film.

This chapter is organised around some of the conceptual and theoretical issues in film theory, but it can only claim to be an introduction to a very wide and complicated subject. There are references to a wide range of recent British and American films here, chosen because they are relatively well known and accessible, and most of the sections of the chapter include short discussions of aspects of a few films in more detail. While film and the cultural phenomenon of going to the cinema are the main subjects of the chapter, there is some discussion of film on television, video, and other film-related media products like computer games and film advertising. There is insufficient space here to deal with film history, 'art' film, or to give more than an overview of the complex evolution of theories of film. The *Sources and further reading* section at the end of the chapter offers guidance on how to fill in these gaps and how to extend your knowledge of the issues discussed briefly here. Many of the points made about signs, codes, narrative, and audience relate to the discussion of other media in this book (like television or advertising), and it may be useful to check the Index and see how ideas discussed in this chapter can be compared and contrasted with their appearance earlier in the book.

The film business

Films are extremely expensive to make. As well as the wages of actors, technicians and craftspeople for instance, there are the costs of buying scripts, building sets, making prints, and promoting films. It is very difficult to predict which films will make enough profits to cover these costs, and many films never recoup the expense of making and distributing them. But each year, a few films will make spectacular amounts of money, and these big successes subsidise the cost of the other movies made by a particular film organisation. On average, 20 per cent of the films on release account for 80 per cent of box office revenue. The British film *The Full Monty* was the most profitable film on release in 1997, for example, having cost only $3.5 million to make but achieving worldwide box office income of over $205 million. By contrast the futuristic thriller *Gattaca*, made by Sony, cost $36 million to make but only took $13.5 million worldwide.

In Europe and the United States the vast majority of films exhibited are American. The most popular film worldwide in 1997 was *The Lost World: Jurassic Park*, which took $605 million, and of the ten most widely seen films in that year eight were made by American film companies. However, contemporary cinema is dependent on global marketing to recoup investment in film production, rather than relying on the large American domestic cinema market. Hollywood studios have also been bought by multinational conglomerates (Gulf + Western, Coca-Cola, Sony, Matsushita, and News Corporation have all owned film production companies), which means that cinema is just one element of a global media industry. The American film *Crouching Tiger, Hidden Dragon* was made by Columbia Pictures, which is owned by the Japanese Sony corporation, and was partly financed by the China Film Co-production Corporation. It was shot by Taiwanese director Ang Lee in China, in the Chinese Mandarin language. It cost $15 million, and by March 2001 had taken $50 million in the USA, over £5 million in the UK, but was in part an attempt to gain a foothold in the Chinese cinema market which is largely inaccessible to Western film companies. The first-run showing of films in cinemas is significant in the profitability of films, but it is not only in cinemas that they are watched. In 1997 British people spent £506 million going to cinemas, but spent £369 million on video rentals, £858 million on buying videos, and £1,003 million on subscriptions to TV movie channels.

The predominance of American films in the world market is far from new, but one of the more recent developments in the cinema business is the linkage of films to other entertainment media. The animated film *Digimon Digital Monsters: The Movie* was produced by the global media corporation Fox which operates children's television networks, among other interests. The film is a spin-off from the television series *Digimon* which is accom-panied by a range of toys and licensed products. The Saban Entertainment company (responsible for the *Power Rangers* television series and toys) and the Japanese animation company Toei produced the original short films *Digimon Adventure, Our War Game* and *The Golden Digimentals* which are joined together, with dubbed English dialogue and voice-over, to form the 89-minute film. The film is thus a linkage between cinema, television, the toy industry, and the merchandising industry, a transnational combination which is common in children's culture.

In order to 'sell' a film, to persuade us to note the appearance of a new film and to see it, many promotional techniques are used in addition to direct advertising. The merchandising of products associated with films is one of the most important, with products released before and during the film's exhibition run, like clothing, toys, music, books, and computer games. These products both advertise films for people who have not seen them yet, and allow people to 'buy into' the social meaning of a film they have seen (or cannot see, in the case of children too young to be admitted to the film). Many tie-in and spin-off products support the 'narrative image' of the film, the cluster of images and meanings which offer a condensed version of the film's attractions. Film posters and publicity stills contain visual and linguistic signs which encode films' narrative themes, denote the stars of the film, and signify its genre. In a similar way, the music videos accompanying film signature tunes often contain a selection of clips which encode the film's meanings in a condensed form.

Some products are tied-in to films by simply using their name or logo. *Jurassic Park* licensed products, for instance, included watches, slippers, model kits, drinking cups, chocolate eggs, balloons, office chairs, children's socks, children's underpants, stickers, popcorn, Christmas cards, cakes, toothbrushes, and children's building bricks. Most of these products used only the film's logo or typographic signs (lettering style and colours). Other means of promotion include press and TV interviews with the stars, TV documentaries on the making of the film, and competitions to win merchandising products. In some cases the cost of promotion exceeds the cost of the film itself, and films need to be analysed not only as self-contained texts but also as intertextual fields of products and meanings. While cinema has historically had an aura of art which set at least some of its products apart from commercial media, cinema today is as much a popular, industrial and commercial medium as the other media discussed in this book.

Cinema spectators are predominantly in the fifteen to twenty-four age-group, the average age of the spectator having fallen since the 'golden age' of cinemagoing in the 1940s and 1950s. Over 50 per cent of British 15- to 24-year-olds go the cinema once a month or more, the largest sector of regular filmgoers. Contemporary cinemagoers have to be addressed by particular films which may appeal to them, and they have fairly coherent requirements of films which they may choose to see. Mass-market 'family' films are in decline, and tend to be exhibited at particular times of year which follow the patterns of the society in which they are shown, so that family audiences are offered films at Christmas, or during the summer school holidays. Instead of this mass-market product, film companies offer a range of films directed to specific types of market focused around a genre, a star, a director, or a current issue which is represented in the film's story. This segmentation of the audience is physically signified in multiplex cinemas, where ten films might be shown in overlapping timeslots in ten different auditoria. The selection might include two 'family' films, an action-adventure, a romance with a current star, two teen movies and a foreign 'art film'. Multiplex cinemas tend to emphasise the social experience of going to the cinema, cinema as an event. They have uniformed staff, shops selling merchandising products, cinema ephemera and food and drink, clean purpose-built auditoria, and often tickets are for specific seats to which the cinemagoer is ushered, and tickets can be pre-booked. The whole experience is designed to feel secure, ordered, safe and comfortable, an evening out in which the film is a major but by no means the only part. This chapter is mostly about the semiotic analysis of films, but cinemas and cinemagoing can also be analysed in semiotic terms to see how they too encode mythic social meanings.

Cinema spectatorship

This section and the next deal with some of the theory in film criticism which has tried to explain and critique the ways in which films are watched by audiences. These approaches make use of psychoanalytic theories of subjectivity, because our pleasure in films must be not only consciously but also unconsciously produced. Psychoanalysis, because it offers a theory of how our subjectivity is constructed consciously and unconsciously, is useful in explaining the ways that the cinema medium draws on and reinforces the workings of an individual subject's psyche. Psychoanalytic theory can also show how our own individual psychic structure (as masculine or feminine, for instance) allows only certain options for making sense of the film for ourselves. Semiotics and recent psychoanalytic theory share several important assumptions. First, meaning comes not from a natural pre-given state of things, but is the result of the workings of a structure existing in a specific social context. For semiotics, the fundamental structure is language. For psychoanalysis too, it is language which gives us our sense of individual subjectivity, as 'I', and the structure of family and gender relations in society joins with language to construct us as subjects. The subject is therefore a signifier, something whose meaning and position is determined by his or her place in a system which already exists.

The French theorist Christian Metz (1975) proposed that cinema differs from other art forms in that it deploys vision, sound, movement and syntagmatic arrangement all at once, and offers perceptions which are all of absent things, rather than of present ones (whereas in opera and theatre, for instance, actors, music and visual signs are actually present on stage). Thus films are all fictional for Metz, since they all re-present something by means of signs, rather than presenting what exists in the spectator's real time and space. The signifier in cinema is thus always 'imaginary'. The three processes Metz identified in cinema spectatorship were identification, voyeurism, and fetishism involving disavowal of lack, and I shall outline these three complex processes in turn. While the spectator identifies with represented characters in films, Metz believed that a more crucial identification is with the act of perception itself. Since the spectator knows he or she is in a cinema, he or she is distanced from and master of what is projected on the screen, which seems to be there for him or her alone. So the spectator is identifying with himself or herself as perceiver, with perception itself. The spectator's perception of a film image is enabled by the camera's perception, so that the identification with perception is also an identification with the camera. In addition, the spectator's field of vision is parallel to the cone of projected light from the projector showing the film, and the spectator thus seems even more to be the source of vision, even though the sources are really the camera and projector.

These identifications of the spectator's position with the camera and with the projector seem to place the spectator in an active, producing relationship to what is seen, though of course it is the camera and projector which really produce the image.

For Metz, the spectator misrecognises the position he or she is in, seeming to be the image's producer but really being its consumer. The cinematic apparatus of camera, projector, and screen, is set up to encourage the spectator's belief in his or her own transcendent control over what is seen in the cinema, but this is a delusion since the spectator is a consumer of the film and not its producer or source. This argument recalls the discussion of ideology which has occurred in earlier chapters of this book. It has been argued that ideology seeks to persuade us that we are makers of meanings, though in reality connotation and myth 'subject' us to their meanings. For Metz and many other film theorists, the cinematic apparatus has ideological effects by offering the spectator a subject-position of imaginary dominance and control.

Voyeurism, Metz's second way of describing cinema spectatorship, means looking at something which cannot look back at us. The explanation of voyeurism and fetishism in this paragraph and the next will refer to the spectator as 'he', for reasons which I shall explain in the next section. Looking at a desired object or person results in an erotic or sexual pleasure for the spectator who looks. The pleasure of voyeurism in cinema (as elsewhere) depends on the distance between the spectator and what is seen on the screen. The actors are present when the spectator is not (when the film is being made), and the spectator is present when the actor is not (when the film is watched). The spectator does not feel threatened in his voyeurism since the bodies he is looking at are absent while their images are present. In addition, actors rarely look at the camera in films, thereby avoiding a confrontation with the spectator's gaze, so the spectator's transgressive looking is encouraged by the codes of cinema. Fetishism, Metz's third spectating process, is the erotic contemplation of an object or person (often a part of a person, like a woman's legs for instance). Psychoanalytic research discovered that fetishism originally derives from the child's awareness that his mother is 'castrated' and does not possess the phallus (the signifier of sexual power which the father possesses). The desire to cover over this lack in the mother desired by the child leads the child to deny the evident sexual difference and threat which the castrated mother represents, by fixing on a fetish object which stands in for phallic sexual power. The threat is that the same castration might happen to the child as a punishment for desiring the mother sexually, and this crisis for the subject is known as the Oedipus complex.

The fetishistic denial or disavowal of lack is something like 'I know something is lacking or absent, but nevertheless I will believe there is no lack or absence'. Cinema involves fetishism because images of absent people or things are presented as if they were present. Although cinema lacks the reality of actual perceptions, spectators are encouraged to believe that what is seen is effectively present. Pleasure depends on both knowing that film is illusion, but believing it is not. The ability of the technical apparatus of cinema to make an absence present is one kind of fetishism, and representations which themselves cover but reveal lack and absence are fetishistic too. Fetish objects are denoted in films when fascinating and desirable things are presented for the spectator's pleasure (like James Bond's cars, parts of Erin's (Julia Roberts's) body in *Erin Brockovich*, or guns). These things displace the spectator's lack onto something signified as present. Their presence denies that anything is lacking, though in their power to do this, fetish objects show that there is a lack. The theory of the cinematic apparatus and of spectatorship concentrates on how film viewers are positioned as subjects, and how cinema supports the psychic structures which turn people into desiring consumers of its film products. The implication of Metz's ideas is that the cinema spectator takes up a masculine subject-position, and the next section explores this further and challenges the assumption.

The gendered spectator

One of the most influential contributions to the critical analysis of film in recent decades was an article by Laura Mulvey (1975). The article argues that the spectator's pleasure depends on an ideological manipulation of film codes, especially as regards the image of women in films, and Mulvey calls for new kinds of film, different from the dominant Hollywood model, which would challenge prevailing ideology and the pleasures which film offers to its audience. The first pleasure that Mulvey identifies for the cinema audience is the pleasure of looking in itself, called 'scopophilia'. Scopophilia is the drive to subject other people to an interested and controlling gaze. In children, scopophilia can often be seen to have an erotic or sexual dimension, as the child tries to glimpse and check out the bodies and sexual organs of other children or adults, as part of his or her curiosity about private and forbidden matters. The same drive persists in adults, sometimes even becoming voyeurism, where sexual pleasure comes from secretly looking at another person with a controlling and objectifying gaze. Looking at a film in the cinema is not a secret pleasure of course. But the world of the film is sealed off from the spectator by being on the screen and not in our own real space, and the film goes on whether we are there or not. It is dark in the cinema, and the bright film image seems like a window onto a different and private world to which we are given access. The spectator is offered scopophilic and voyeuristic pleasure in film by the circumstances of viewing and the narrative conventions that put us in the position of observers able to look in at a story which we are separated from.

The second kind of visual pleasure offered in film is identifying with an image which stands in for ourselves, and we have come across this notion before. As we have seen earlier in this book, the Mirror Stage is a crucial moment in the formation of an identity for the individual subject. It occurs in relation to an image, where the subject takes a comparable person as an image of a more perfected self, an ideal ego. The subject's imaginary identification with this ideal image, forgetting his or her own real insufficiency, is parallel to the spectator's fascination with the film image, when the spectator forgets everything except the film. The images of other people on the screen have the same fascination as the imaginarily-perfect mirror image which the child perceives in the Mirror Stage. The mirror image is not the child, it is an image of the child. This other thing, the image, returns to the psyche in the form of the ego ideal, a more perfect person whom the child identifies with. Cinema shows us a vast range of others whom we identify with: the film actors. Film actors fulfil the role of ego ideals, people different from us who we would like to have and to be. The spectator identifies with images of film actors in the same way that he or she identified with the image of an ego ideal in the Mirror Stage.

So there are two components to scopophilia in film spectator-ship: the pleasure in looking at an image which is made available to our controlling gaze, and the pleasure in identifying with an image that stands in for us. The first of these pleasures is bound up with erotic desire, and the second with the process by which our ego is formed in early life. In the first case, the spectator desires the image of an object which promises to satisfy a sexual aim, and in the second case the spectator desires an ego ideal, the image of a more perfect self. In both kinds of response, the spectator is seeking something which will make good a lack, which will supply something that is missing. We have seen how this lack in being is first signalled in the Mirror Stage, but it achieves its full meaning in the Oedipus complex, outlined above. For ever afterwards, the child is left with a desire for the other which can never be fulfilled, a lack in being. Whenever the scopophilic look promises to remedy this lack by providing an image of a desired object (an other separate from the subject which promises to supply what is lacking), scopophilia brings with it the threat of castration too. Psychoanalytic theory proposes that whatever is desired takes the place of the original desired object: the mother who was desired by the child but from whom access was prohibited by the father.

Characteristically, it is a masculine gaze which takes women as desired objects, setting women up for masculine scopophilic pleasure in looking. Women have to take up the role of narcissistic exhibitionists, becoming objects for the pleasure of the masculine gaze. As Mulvey puts it, women in film are signs which signify 'to-be-looked-at-ness' (1975: 17). This is extremely common in film, where women are often displayed as desirable objects. But at the same time this gaze at the woman stops the narrative flow of the film, holds things up. The task of the film narrative is then to integrate the image of the woman into the narrative. This is done by making the male character the one who advances the action, controlling the movement of the story. The spectator is thereby encouraged to identify with the active male character as an ideal ego, a desired self, so that the active male character stands in for the spectator. The male character is the bearer of the spectator's look, able like the spectator to gaze at the erotic image of the woman, and giving the spectator, through the spectator's identification with him, the imaginary sense of controlling the action.

These processes go some way to controlling the destabilisation of the film narrative which erotic contemplation of the woman introduces. But there is a fundamental problem. In a patriarchal society, characterised by the dominance of the male gaze over women as objects, the woman representing the desired object must bring with her the threat of castration which always accompanies desire. To dispel this threat, there are several ways that film narrative attempts to do away with the problem that the image of the woman represents. First, the film might be pre-occupied with investigating the woman (as Elektra (Sophie Marceau) is investigated and unmasked as the villain in *The World is Not Enough* for instance), so that she ceases to be mysterious and threatening. Second, the narrative might take control of the woman by punishing her (as women are punished for being virgins in *Cherry Falls*, for instance, in an ironic reversal of the horror convention that women are punished for sexual activity), or rescuing her from her guilt. Or thirdly, the woman could be elevated to the status of a fetish object, an overvalued symbol which covers over the threat it might induce by encouraging excessive scopophilic contemplation. In *Charlie's Angels*, for example, the apparent empowerment of the three female heroines is undermined by such episodes as Cameron Diaz (who plays Natalie) dancing in her underwear and exhibiting herself as an erotic object. The voyeuristic look both denies castration in its mastery over what is shown, but threatens it by insisting on showing the desired person or object as fully as possible.

The psychoanalytic theories of spectatorship briefly described here were widely accepted and used in film theory for more than a decade, but there are problems with them. One of the problematic issues is the force of cinema's positioning of the spectator, whose response appears to be determined by the film. It seems that the spectator is rigidly positioned by cinema, and has no option but to succumb to the medium's ideological operations on him or her. Secondly, these theories relate much more easily to the male spectator than the female. In the explanations above 'the spectator' was often referred to as 'he'. The only way out of this problem within the terms of the theory is to argue that women have to align themselves with a masculine spectating position in order to decode the meanings of films. This might possibly be the case, especially since the societies where cinema was developed are patriarchal, putting the male at the centre of things and relegating women to the position of an other, different and subordinate to men. But in response to the dominance of masculine spectatorship and the rigid fixity of the viewer in these theories, a more flexible theory of spectatorhip was developed in the 1980s. It made use of the notion of fantasy, and was elaborated by Elizabeth Cowie (1984).

The spectator, Cowie argued, 'enunciates' or produces a fantasy that is supported by the film text. Fantasy is where repressed ideas are allowed into consciousness in a distorted form (as in dreams, for instance). The fantasy therefore covers over a repressed wish but also exposes it. In fantasy, the subject identifies with several figures at the same time, not necessarily with those who the narrative offers as ideals. In *Hannibal* for instance, spectators identify not only with Hannibal Lecter's victims and pursuers but also with the 'evil' Hannibal himself. The one who fantasises can adopt different roles for identification, and different spectating positions. It is not what happens in the fantasy itself that satisfies the spectator's desire (since by definition desire is what cannot be satisfied), but instead it is the turning into a scenario, the putting-on-stage of desire which is satisfying. The analysis of film narrative in these terms explains the pleasure produced by the spectator's mobile identifications in films since although the codes of film narrative lay out positions for the spectator, they do not determine which will be taken up, and the theory shows that subject-positions are temporary, shifting, multiple, and contradictory. The rest of this chapter discusses film signs and codes, and film genres, paying particular attention to the multiple meanings of signs in film and to the film spectator's multiple points of access to the meanings signified in films.

Film signs and codes

This section builds on ideas which have been discussed in relation to other media in previous chapters. In films, an image of an object, person or landscape will have a denotative dimension. But all images are culturally charged by the connotation procedures available to cinema, like camera position and angle, position of objects or people within the frame, use of lighting, colour process or tinting, and sound. The codes of cinema are particular ways of using signs, the photographic signs, dialogue signs, musical, sound effect and graphic signs which are the resources from which particular film sequences are constructed. Any film sequence can be analysed to discover the relationship between signs in the sequence, and the way that signs from different signifying systems (image, sound) are combined together by means of codes to generate meanings. The meanings of films are generated as much by the connotations constructed by the use of cinematic codes as by the cultural meanings of what the camera sees. Cinema uses codes and conventions of representation which are shared by both filmmakers and audiences, so that the audience actively constructs meaning by reference to codes which structure mythic meanings in the social world in which film-going exists.

Christian Metz, who we encountered above, sought to describe how the systems of signs and uses of codes work in film, and his work on film went through several stages. In his later work, Metz (1974) described cinema as a signifying practice, a way of making meanings in which different codes interact in films or film genres in particular ways. Some of these codes were seen as specific to cinema, like editing, lighting, monochrome or colour, sound, and composition. Others derive from other media or from social life in general, like dialogue, characterisation, gesture and facial expression, and costume. For Metz, cinematic codes order elements which exist or could exist in all films, like lighting, while sub-codes are the sets of particular choices made within the larger code system, like the use of low-key lighting rather than high-key in certain films or genres. Clearly sub-codes are mutually exclusive, and form a paradigm from which selections are made, whereas films combine codes and sub-codes together in the unfolding of the text, and are arranged as syntagms of coded signs. Umberto Eco (1977) extended Metz's consideration of codes by arguing that, far from cinema using fragments of reality in order to build its representations, as Metz had once suggested, all images require the operation of cultural codes in order to signify. Eco believed that conventions embedded in society were the precondition for signification. These coding systems, Eco argued in his later work, are elaborated for the purpose of explaining and understanding a textual process, and cannot be seen as determining the meaning of any particular element in a text. Meaning is constructed on the basis of the spectator's continual adjustment and testing of codes rather than simply 'reading off' a meaning from the text, and this suggests the active decoding of signs and the shifting process of signification which earlier chapters of this book have stressed.

There are a wide range of connotations which the use of film's visual properties can introduce. The film stock used will have different properties, either black and white or colour, and with varying degrees of sensitivity to harsh light and deep shadow. The modern camera's depth of field of focus enables objects both close to the camera and far away from it to be in focus. Widescreen processes like Cinemascope and 70mm offer a very wide image in relation to its height. Black and white film might signify the past, and connote nostalgic recreation or harsh documentary realism (e.g. *Schindler's List*), while strong colour can connote surreality and a fairy-tale quality. Widescreen 70mm is used in the opening of *Star Wars*, for instance, to connote immense scale and spectacle. The positioning of the camera, since it determines the point of view offered to the spectator, is of immense importance in film's signification. Crane shots or overhead shots display the spectacular ability of cinema to take in an entire landscape, particularly when the camera is moving. The camera can be moved along parallel to its subject (tracking), towards or away from the subject (dolly in or out). When static, the camera can be swivelled to one side (panning), or up and down (tilting), or even rolled over. A zoom in or out can be used to concentrate on one character or aspect of the shot. These camera positions and movements can all be used to produce connotations. The power of one character over another can be connoted by a look down from an oppressor's point of view, or a look up from the point of view of the victim. The camera can explicitly take the position of a character to show his or her point of view, to connote an individual's perception of the action. Changes in the framing of the shot are used to narrow or open out the field of view, to connote a claustrophobic experience or a liberating one respectively. Close-up is a signifier of an emotional high-point or a story crisis, and a pan across a landscape finishing on a building is an establishing shot which connotes that the subsequent action will take place there. As noted in the previous chapter, these connotations arise not by nature but from the cultural context in which films are made and watched.

Lighting is most often used to imitate natural light, and thus works as a signifier connoting realism. In most cases, a 'key light' illuminates the figures to be shot, 'fill lights' remove shadows caused by the key light and reveal detail. Both light sources are placed in front of the subject of the shot. Behind the subject, 'back light' enhances three-dimensionality by giving yet more light to the subject, but light which does not fall on the background. The aim of this lighting process ('high-key lighting') is to mimic conventional perceptions of how real environments look. But lighting can also become a foregrounded effect, when light, darkness, or particular shadows signify as part of the narrative, and extend lighting's role in emphasising parts of the frame or parts of figures in it. Lighting techniques, whether 'realistic' and unnoticed, or highly atmospheric and 'unrealistic' provide connotations for all film shots.

Sound is also represented by means of signs. Speech or music consists of sounds captured by electronic recording methods and reproduced by mechanical loudspeakers. The film audience receives aural signifiers which are linked to mental concepts, signifieds like musical chords or speech sounds. These are the components of aural signs in film, like words or musical phrases. Modern cinema's impression of reality is heavily dependent on the representation of sounds occurring in synchronisation with the visual events which appear to cause them, known as 'diegetic' sound. Diegetic sound includes the sound of words matched to images of people speaking, or music which is matched to a record being played in the room we see on the screen. Conventions specific to cinema and TV include the use of non-diegetic music, so that the signs of orchestral music heard during a film sequence are read as coming not from the environment represented visually, but from outside the frame, from the implied narrator of the film. This use of 'extra-diegetic' music very often acts as an indexical sign connoting the emotional register of a sequence, and can point out or reveal the emotional state of a character (often in contrast to what the character claims to feel in the dialogue). Music directly communicates emotion which the audience can share individually in the communal space of the cinema, as well as sharing the feeling with the characters represented in the film. Film music constructs a community of feeling based on the responses of each member of the audience.

At the level of the shot sequence, a shot from behind the shoulder of one person, followed by a similar shot from behind the shoulder of another person, is the conventional means for representing a conversation and is called 'shot-reverse-shot'. In this case, there is a clear relationship between one shot and the succeeding one, but cinema narrative always relies on the viewer making links between shots, and links between sequences of shots. Because it is made up of discrete shots and sequences separated by cuts, the position of the viewer is the only place from which the ongoing meaningfulness of the film can be constructed. A film is a very diverse collection of visual, aural and graphic signs, which the viewer works to perceive as meaningful, using his or her knowledge of codes and conventions. Whereas spoken and written language are heavily regulated by the rules of grammar and syntax so that sense can be constructed, cinema has very few hard and fast rules about how its visual and aural signs can be combined to generate meanings. The audience has to do a lot of work in assembling film signs into meaningful units. While language involves similar work, done mostly unconsciously, cinema relies on the viewer's competence at decoding the film by reference to codes, conventions and expectations cued by the film's signs. The film viewer constructs relationships between shots, known as 'montage', and relationships within shots, known as *mise-en-scène*. It is this stitching-together or 'suturing' of one sign with another, one shot with another, which shifts the film spectator through the film and which is the basis for films to narrate their stories.

Film narrative

Contemporary feature films are exclusively narratives. Story is the set of sequenced actions in a film, book, TV programme etc., and narrative is the term for the process by which the story is told. Story and narrative are common to all human cultures, and always encode a way of making sense of our experience through their structure and form. Much work has been done on narrative, because of its pervasiveness and importance for comprehending our reality. One of the common features which are seen in film narratives is the movement from an initially stable equilibrium, through disorder and conflict, to a new equilibrium. Narrative often takes this circular shape, but the equilibrium of the film's final resolution is not the same as at the beginning, since the situation and/or the hero is changed by the action in the story, and the stability of the resolution may be incomplete. In *Billy Elliot*, the eleven-year-old Billy (Jamie Bell) discovers that he has talent as a ballet dancer, and must struggle against the conventional coding of ballet as effeminate. Indeed the film is structured around a series of oppositions, including ballet and boxing, homosexual and heterosexual, youthful and adult, elite culture and popular culture, London and the North of England. The work of the narrative is to blur the boundaries between these apparently opposed elements, so that Billy expresses himself through ballet while remaining masculine, and close to his Northern roots and his family. The film ends with Billy fourteen years older, dancing in Matthew Bourne's production of *Swan Lake* in which men play the roles of the swans, normally danced by women. So the resolution of the film is in some ways conventional (Billy becomes a successful dancer, against the odds) but is also unconventional (Billy is playing the conventionally female role of Odette, the swan princess).

One of the pleasures of narrative is that it puts in play and resolves contradictions and problems in our culture. *Billy Elliot*'s narrative explores issues of class and gender, though it resolves them only partially. The film separates Billy from homosexuality by displacing its threat onto Billy's transvestite friend Michael, though the ending in which Billy dances a female role in the ballet *Swan Lake* leaves the question of Billy's sexuality unresolved. Billy exists in an entirely male household since his mother is dead, but the film sets up a substitute for Billy's dead mother in the character of his ballet teacher Mrs Wilkinson (Julie Walters). The connotations here are that Billy's dancing is a means of coping in fantasy with his mother's death and finding a surrogate to replace her, and also that a maternal figure is needed to civilise Billy's family and community. The film denotes the police occupation of mining towns during the 1984 Miners' Strike and the oppression of the striking miners, but leaves these political issues in the background of the narrative. While it apparently values working-class masculine culture in its sympathetic portrayal of the strikers' suffering, Billy's route is to escape from this rigidly masculine world into London elite culture and the middle-class environment from which his family were excluded, and which they regarded as effeminate. Like myth, narrative plays out and encodes real issues at a symbolic level, in *Billy Elliot* issues of gender and class. Turner (1993: 74) gives the example of the structure of western films involving conflicts between settlers and Native Americans ('Indians'). These mythic narratives are structured by oppositions between one group and the other, and their narrative progression deals with this conflict by means of various narrative functions until it is resolved. The oppositions are often binary and based on the exclusive difference between one set of signs and the other. For instance, here are some of the opposed characteristics commonly found in westerns: Settlers/Indians, white/red, Christian/pagan, domestic/savage, helpless/dangerous, weak/strong, clothed/naked. Clearly, these oppositions are value-laden and have an ideological character. The mythic narrative of a western could be read as a way of encoding current mythic ideas around masculine virtue, the exploitation of nature, national identity, and the importance of the family, for instance. Westerns, because of the way their narratives are structured, are communicating ideological messages.

The value of signs in film depends on the social context pertaining at the time the film was made, at the time the film is seen, and by whom it is seen. The codes and conventions which enable the viewer to make sense of the film will change and evolve, and the viewer will decode the meanings of film narratives by invoking his or her experience of his or her own culture, including the film conventions circulating in that culture as well as codes of expression recognised from 'natural' social behaviour. For instance, the gestural codes and the bodily and facial expression of actors in silent films belonged to conventions which connoted emotional realism when they were made and watched. These conventions derived from the stage-acting conventions of melo-drama. To a contemporary audience, these gestural signs might now be decoded as artificial, excessive and unrealistic. Some of these coded signs might even be incomprehensible to a contem-porary audience, except as signifiers of 'pastness', because the codes to which the gestures belong are no longer naturalised.

In Britain, audiences are familiar with conventions used in American cinema, and relatively unfamiliar with conventions used in, for instance, Indian cinema. Irishness, for example, is often used in American cinema to connote authenticity, an attractive rebelliousness, and sexual freedom. This convention was used in *Titanic*, where the communal pleasures of folk-dancing among the poor Irish emigrants on the ship are con-trasted with the formal, cold and unsympathetic behaviour of the English aristocratic passengers. Similarly, in *Chocolat*, the American actor Johnny Depp plays an itinerant traveller whose Irish accent signifies his freedom from social restrictions. In the British film *Notting Hill*, Britishness is represented as a rather repressed but charming set of characteristics, which are valued in opposition to the deceptive world of Hollywood film stardom which surrounds Julia Roberts's character. These films rely on conventional codes for representing personality traits through national characteristics, codes which are familiar on both sides of the Atlantic and are based on cultural myths about national-ities rather than what different national cultures are 'really like'.

The meanings of films will obviously depend on how the visual and aural signs of any particular film narrative are structured, how the film marks out character roles by invoking conventional behavioural codes, and the coded oppositions between connoted ideas. An audience's reading of the film, however, is not only generated by what is within the frame. Every film is viewed in a particular social context, some of which is produced by the film's industrial and commercial context, and some of which is not controllable in the same way. The advertising and promotion of a film will enfold it in a network of various meanings deriving from texts, conventions and objects which are already in circulation, and more or less controlled by the film's producers. The mythic meanings of film stars, for instance, are constructed not only in films but in other media like newspapers, fan magazines, and TV appearances, so that the star exhibits characteristics which may easily be different to those of the character he or she plays in the film. The star as sign affects the meanings constructed by the viewer of the character in the film text. The star might even be deliberately cast so that their star persona alters the representation of the character in the script, creating a double or ironic meaning. This use of audience expectations of the meanings of a star was used in a very innovative way in *Being John Malkovich*, for example. Films exist in a complex social context, where the mythic meanings circulating in a culture affect the ways they are decoded, and where the film text is not the only source of meanings.

Cinema has developed some narrative conventions which are specific to it. For example, in comedy films a bang on the head can cause loss of memory, and another bang can restore it. Ellipsis, the omission of parts of the story, is an accepted code which allows film narratives to cut from a character getting into a car to the same character getting out in another location without needing to show the journey. There are film conventions which are highly ideological in character, and have persisted in film as well as in other media. For a long time, conventional ways of shooting men and women in films have been different. Women's bodies, and parts of their bodies, are objects of voyeuristic interest for the camera. Women can be lit to emphasise pose and facial shape, remaining static while the camera displays their attractiveness, or placed in a narrative situation which enables them to display themselves (e.g. sunbathing or taking a shower). It has been rare to see men represented in the same way (though perhaps fight scenes enable men to be displayed). Conventions for representing women, as discussed in chapter 2 and earlier in this chapter, display the woman as an object offered for possession by a male gaze, for the desire of both men and women and for narcissistic identification. But now as our contemporary culture turns bodies of both genders more and more into commodities and sites for consumption, film images of men have begun to deploy similar conventions.

Film genre

Genre analysis is a method of study which aims to classify types or groups of films, showing that the film industry and the film audience respond to films by recognising the codes and conventions which enable an individual film to be comprehended. Recent film comedies have made much use of conventions taken to an extreme for comic purposes. *Best in Show* exposes and plays with documentary film conventions, and *Galaxy Quest* draws on the conventions of science fiction films and television (especially *Star Trek*) as well as the spectator's preconceptions about science fiction fan culture. But it is not only in comedy that conventions are exposed. In *Unforgiven*, the conventionally marginal women characters of westerns are the motor of the story, and several recent westerns focus on a woman as their main character in an action-adventure plot. In *Girlfight*, women are the central characters of the conventionally male genre of the boxing movie. The signs which cue the recognition of a particular film as belonging to a certain genre are many and varied. The visual style of the film's title graphics, the accompanying music, the stars of the film, its setting, story structure, narrative style including its lighting patterns, colour system, types of discourse in the dialogue, emphasised camera shots, can all offer the audience a set of expectations which inform the coding systems brought to the film by the audience, and into which the film company can slot the film in its marketing and promotional discourses. As well as placing a film in a certain genre, it is even possible to position the film by raising generic expectations which will not be met, so that the film reacts against generic expectations by raising them in the first place (often the case in comedy films which parody the generic expectations of 'serious' films, in the way that *Scream 3* parodies the conventions of stalker and slasher films).

It is clear that identifying a film's genre relies on identifying particular signs within a film, the relationship between signs, and their membership of one or more codes. But the analysis of a particular film will involve comparing and contrasting the signification in a film with that of other films and with texts in other media. This is part of the study of intertextuality, which we have already encountered in previous chapters. No film will be seen by a spectator outside of a context which includes other films they have seen, films they have seen advertised, or heard about from other people. The concept of genre reminds us that films are not self-contained structures of signs, but texts which exist within a broader social context. Every film will exist in relation to two contradictory impulses, repetition and difference. To ensure comprehensibility, a film will repeat the signifying practices of other films, their conventional signs and established codes, and conventional narrative structures of disequilibrium and resolution. Part of the pleasure of seeing a new film is the viewer's ability to recognise and predict meanings appropriately. But every film will also need to be different, to find new ways of using existing signs and codes in order to offer the pleasure of the new. Genre connects individual film texts to the industrial commercial context of cinema, and to the study of film audiences. For the industry, genres allow films to be marketed in ways which inform potential audiences about the pleasures offered by the film, since posters, advertising etc. contain coded signs which cue genre expectations. If a previous film has been commercially successful, further films in the same genre including sequels can be expected to repeat the same success by addressing a similar market. Within the narrative of a particular film, signs and codes will relate the film to existing generic expectations to ensure comprehensibility. The film audience will possess competencies to decode and enjoy films in certain genres, and are likely to watch new films in genres which they are familiar with.

The study of genre relates each film to other films, but this study of intertextuality can also be extended to relating films to other media texts. In contemporary culture there is blurring of the boundaries between cinema and other media. There are a range of contemporary films which are based on comic-book characters for instance, including the three *Batman* films, *Asterix & Obelix Take on Caesar*, and *X-Men*, for example. These films are able to draw an audience already at least minimally familiar with their scenarios, and provide opportunities for spectacular visual effects. But in this kind of action-adventure film there is an evident difference from the pleasures of 'classical Hollywood cinema' films for the spectator. Identification with a heroic ego-ideal, narrative resolution, and conventions of realism seem less important than self-conscious spectacular effects. There are many examples of contemporary action-adventure films which abandon classical narrative structure in favour of a series of plot climaxes which occur in quick succession, and which organise their stories in terms of a progression from one 'level' of story to another. This is sometimes a direct result of films' relation to computer games: some films are based on games, like *Tomb Raider*, while others are subsequently marketed as games. For the younger cinema audience accustomed to enjoying graphic novels and computer games, cinema makes links between film specta-torship's pleasures and the pleasures familiar in these other media.

The consequences for cinema spectatorship include the dimin-ished significance of narrative resolution in favour of episodic structure and moments of narrative-arresting spectacle and thrill, the denotation of technology in films and the display of the technologies used in the cinema medium, and the spectator's identifications in fantasy with multiple characters or with the film's spectacular scenario. This form of spectator competence both responds to and promotes the competencies required by computer games. The film therefore becomes a mythic inter-textual world supported by the related but different fictional narrative of the game, and vice versa. Computer games have always re-used the signs, narratives, and mythic worlds of other media texts. There are computer games based on *Star Trek*, for instance, which invoke the mythic world of the TV series although the TV series was made thirty years ago, before com-puter games were invented. Now however, some films (and some TV programmes) both share the forms of subject-positioning in computer games and are marketed together with games. In addition to an increased intensity of inter-media crossover, enter-tainment experiences are becoming further interrelated in their subject-positionings and modes of pleasure.

Genre study arose in film studies as a response to the study of auteurs, directors whose work seemed to possess the marks of individual creativity which were discriminated in the academic

study of literature by 'great' authors. While some directors of
commercial Hollywood feature films were endowed with the
distinction of being auteurs, the prevailing discourse of auteur
criticism left out of account a great mass of popular cinema. The
study of genres shows that all films exist within a context, rather
than being the inspired and unique expression of one person's
creative imagination. Genre study also allows us to consider a
much wider field of films for study in addition to those which film
critics have labelled as 'great', and is particularly useful in discussing popular cinema since many of its products are genre
films (horror, westerns, thrillers, epics, science fiction etc.). The
intertextuality of contemporary media culture, and the polysemy
of many media texts, means that elements of several genres may
be encoded in a single film. The recent *Ghost Dog: The Way of the
Samurai*, for instance, includes elements drawn from martial arts
action films, American urban thrillers, and gangster films. Part
of the pleasure in watching a film like this is the spectator's ability to recognise these generic codes and to enjoy their re-use and
manipulation, shifting in fantasy between the subject-positions
which each code invites him or her to take up.

Cinema audiences

For many years the academic study of cinema has been based on
the assumption that films can be studied as relatively self-
contained texts. Although it has been recognised that films are
obviously set in a social context of making and viewing, until
very recently there has been little substantial work on how real
viewers understand and enjoy films. Semiotic theories of meaning can allow the critic to assume that there are 'correct' readings of the signs in film, and the psychoanalytic theories of the
cinema experience and film spectatorship deal only with the
general and fundamental structures in the human psyche which
individual films mobilise. The dominance of these two theoretical
approaches in film study has yielded a very rich (and very complicated) critical discourse, of which brief glimpses have been
given in this chapter. As we have seen earlier in this book, the
discourse of semiotic analysis and related approaches to the
media has been challenged by more empirical studies of media

reception, variously known as audience studies or ethnography. This kind of research is not 'more correct' than semiotic research, since it adopts a different discourse, and asks a different set of questions. But even in a book on semiotic approaches to the study of the media, it is important to see how the questions of audience and reception might contextualise, redirect or critique semiotic analysis. In academic film studies in the last two decades, there has been much discussion of the place of audience research, but very few studies of contemporary film audiences have yet been published.

Many of the studies of film viewers have been carried out from a feminist perspective. This is because of the problem in the psychoanalytic theory of spectatorship discussed above, that it has argued that women filmgoers have to identify with the masculine control exercised by film narrative over women characters, or with the submissive and narcissistic women characters themselves. Either women filmgoers take up a masculine subject-position, or they identify with a devalued version of feminine identity. Mulvey and other theorists have moved away from the psychoanalytic account of gendered spectators and have looked for traces of resistance to the masculine domination of film subjectivities (de Lauretis 1984, Modleski 1988, Mulvey 1989), for active female audience responses to films (Pribam 1988, Hansen 1991), and at the place of film viewing in the lives of real women (Pribam 1988). The majority of this work discusses viewers' responses to Hollywood films in the 'golden age' of cinema, roughly 1930–1955, since it is films from this period that were used to illustrate the psychoanalytic theories of the spectator. Therefore the specifics of few of these studies directly relate to the contemporary films referred to in this chapter.

Nevertheless, the results of this research point to some similarities between the ways in which films are read by viewers and the ways in which television and other media are experienced and used, as outlined in earlier chapters of this book. The key issues here include the recognition that film viewing is set in a particular historical, geographical, and cultural moment for individual viewers. Ethnic or racial background has significant impacts on the relationship between viewer, film, intertextual environment and the social meaning of enjoying films or cinemagoing. Watching films and going to the cinema have social uses in the lives of film viewers, and enable them to gain social status, negotiate membership of social groups or sub-cultures, relate to family members, and conceive of their own identity in particular ways. However, as Judith Mayne (1993) has argued, the tendency of ethnographic research on individual film viewers or small groups of viewers is to over-value the apparently subversive and critical ways in which viewers watch and enjoy films. Rather than ending up with a spectator passively positioned by the cinematic apparatus and by film narrative, research on real viewers seems sometimes to be 'constituting a viewer who is always resisting, always struggling, always seemingly just on the verge of becoming the embodiment of the researcher's own political ideal' (Mayne 1993: 61). Thus the apparently passive spectator of 'classical' film theory can simply be exchanged for an active one, and in each theoretical discourse the film viewer is of interest only as a justification of the analyst's argument.

Ethnography has emerged as a reaction against semiotic and psychoanalytic theory's analysis of the spectator as a category or construct rather than a real person. The theory of the spectator was devised in part as a way of critiquing the social and ideological role of cinema in perpetuating mythic social meanings and the formation of individual subjects by dominant ideologies. This theoretical and political discourse about spectators assumes that the responses of real film viewers always exceed or differ from the response of the spectator constructed by films and the cinematic apparatus, because the social and psychic history of individuals is always particular and in some respects unique. Ethnographic studies of audiences focus on these particular and sometimes unique aspects of individuals, and the discourse of audience study thus links film viewers to society and ideology in useful ways. But as Mayne's critical remarks above indicate, every analytical discourse is constrained by the discursive codes which it uses, and which themselves encode the mythic significance of what they analyse. It remains to be seen in film studies whether the active viewer negotiating the meanings of the films he or she sees is more than a signifier of the researcher's desire for a new radical discourse.

Sources and further reading

Good introductions to film theory covering semiotics, the theory of ideology and psychoanalytic criticism are Turner (1993) and the more complex Lapsley and Westlake (1988) and Andrew (1984). Monaco (1981) also deals with film history, technology, and many other topics in a single volume. Stam *et al.* (1992) is entirely devoted to film semiotics and related theoretical issues like narrative and spectatorship, and covers a very wide range of terms and ideas. The collections edited by Easthope (1993), Cook and Bernink (1999), and Mast and Cohen (1985) contain some of the formative essays (by Mulvey and Cowie for instance) which are discussed in this chapter, and Easthope's collection also has short essays at the beginning that introduce key theoretical currents. The collection of essays edited by Collins *et al.* (1993) explores theoretical approaches in relation to detailed analyses of recent films, and many of the essays make use of semiotics to some degree. Mayne (1993) debates the issues around studies of film audiences, while also discussing the psychoanalytic and semiotic traditions in film criticism. Bacon-Smith and Yarborough's essay (1991) is an interesting use of ethnographic methods to discuss viewers' reactions to the *Batman* film and the other texts (like comics) which relate to the film, and can be compared to other essays in the same volume which adopt different approaches to the Batman phenomenon, including the discourses of semiotic and ideological analysis.

Suggestions for further work

1   Analyse the posters advertising three films you have not seen which are playing at your local cinema. How does the poster inform you about each film's genre, stars, and attractions? If you later see the film, how much correspondence is there between the narrative image on the poster and your experience of the film's attractions and pleasures?

2   Compare the reviewing discourses used about the same film in different media (for example local and national newspapers, film magazines like *Empire*, TV film review programmes). What assumptions about the audience, the film medium, stars, directors, and genres are being made? Why is this?

3   If you have played a computer game based on a film, which aspects of the film's narrative codes and *mise-en-scène* have been included in the game? What characteristics of this interactive medium determine the choices which have been made?

4 Analyse one sequence from a film, discussing technical codes, narrative codes, signs of genre, spectator positioning, and any other issues which seem useful. What are the limitations of this kind of close analysis?

5 Gather as many examples of media coverage of a current film star as you can. How coherent and consistent are the various codings of this star's social meanings? How closely do they relate to the character roles recently played by the star?

6 Compare the representations of women or of Native Americans in some recent westerns and some westerns of the 1950s. How much change in ideological assumptions do you find?

7 Analyse a film which intertextually borrows conventions from other film genres (for example *Aliens*, *Waterworld*, *Toy Story 2* or *Blade Runner*). How do these conventions affect the ways in which the film may be decoded?

9

Interactive media

Introduction

Semiotics has changed since it was inaugurated in the early twentieth century. This final chapter briefly considers some of these shifts and outlines how the semiotic analysis of the media might take account of some of the new media technologies and experiences which have recently appeared in Western culture. From a semiotic point of view, all of social life is a continual encounter with assemblages of signs, from the public experiences of advertising posters, shop windows and diversely dressed strangers in the street, to the more private experiences of watching television, choosing what kind of décor to use in the home, or playing a computer game. As we become increasingly accustomed to living in a culture infused with media, semiotics is a particularly effective means of taking stock of this situation. One version of our very sense of identity, is itself a function of the traffic in signs which surrounds and permeates us. The notion that social life is saturated by media messages, and that experiences are mediated by media texts, is part of the labelling of the present epoch as 'postmodern', as discussed in chapter 7. Rather than simply celebrating a postmodern or virtual experience of reality, or simply condemning the proclamation that reality has evaporated into shifting clouds of signs, semiotics asks how our experience of the media and of our social existence makes sense.

Mobile communications

In the year 2000, mobile phones were being used by 58 per cent of the British population, and as well as being used for business communication, mobile phones have become part of a leisure culture especially among young people. The possession of a mobile phone not only signifies 'modernity' or being up to date, but is also a key component in a mythic sense of engagement. Social networks in which it is important to be aware of the latest news and gossip, and to be an insider in a group rather than an outsider, have always been important to social life. Mobile communications increase the number and speed of transfers of information between members of a social group. But they do not replace the face-to-face interactions which enable youth culture to exist, for example, or change the location of interactions from physical spaces like shopping malls and college cafeterias. Mobile phones accelerate an existing form of social interaction, and the ability to send text messages as well as to speak has further accelerated it. Each British 18- to 24-year-old sends an average of ten SMS (Short Message System) phone messages a day. As with any emerging media form, commercial interests have begun to explore ways of linking text messaging to consumption, and this is especially attractive to them since 18- to 24-year-olds have significant disposable income but are difficult to target by traditional advertising.

The mobile phone manufacturer Ericsson and mobile phone marketing company Mediatude conducted a survey in 2000 offering mobile phone users free text messaging in return for receiving advertising messages on their phones. 40 per cent of users found the ads compelling and 20 per cent requested further information on products and services mentioned in the ads sent to them. It is this willingness to be addressed as a consumer and to be hailed into an ideology of consumption which has enabled new forms of advertising to be launched. The company Spotflash, backed in part by Carphone Warehouse (which sells mobile phones), produces a service called ZagMe where companies can send text messages to people who are near to shops. The messages contain offers such as that the first fifty people into a store who give a ZagMe code word to the staff will get 10 per cent off CDs, or will receive a free pair of training shoes. This gets customers into shops where they can be targeted by other offers. An experimental version of this ZagMe system was tried at Lakeside

Thurrock shopping centre in September 2000 where 150 retail-ers took part. Messages can be targeted at particular types of con-sumer by age or gender, for example. Users sign up for the service, and send a text message or voice message to ZagMe telling them to turn it on when they are going shopping. This is a version of the concept of the 'agent', where a service is used to identify bargains or sought-for products on the user's behalf. While functioning in part as a helpful information provider, the service positions the user as consumer, and as a terminal in a virtual network of communication. Increasingly, to be a social subject is to be a sender, receiver and consumer of media messages.

The book *Bridget Jones's Diary* (by Helen Fielding) was pub-lished in 1996 and sold over six million copies, and was released as a film in 2001. The film had the most successful opening in Britain to date, taking £5.72 million in its first weekend. It has become the basis for a text messaging service aimed to allow users to develop a personal relationship with the fictional char-acter. The messaging system is a marketing exercise timed to the launch of the film, and provides a daily message from Bridget received on the user's mobile phone. Messages give details of Bridget's weight, how many units of alcohol she has consumed, how many cigarettes she smoked, and any other facts about her life which might draw the user into Bridget's world. It is ironic that a text which makes fun of the contemporary media world (as seen for example in scenes set in television companies and publishing houses) should have become the basis for new ways of extending media culture and consumption of media technol-ogy. Messages encourage the user to reply with a text message (for example, 'Valentine's day should be banned by law. Reply Y/N'). There will be a Bridget quiz, to find out how Bridget-like the user is, and Bridget will answer questions if users ask her advice about men or diets, for instance. The aim is to addict users to interaction, since they can be in communication with others at any time, in any location. Not to be in communication with the mythic Bridget world produces a sense of alienation and a need to analyse and discuss these feelings by sending further text messages. The Bridget SMS experience follows the merchandising techniques already used to support films (like the release of songs from a soundtrack, or branded products) by including phone ringing tones based on songs from the film, and downloadable icons and logos. The texting system was created by the Finnish company Riot-E for Universal Pictures, which made the film. The essential precondition for texting services like this is an existing community of fans, and here the community is assumed to be largely female. The Riot-E company has bought the mobile phone rights to 4,700 characters from Marvel comics, and expects to develop SMS games based on these, aimed at male users. By drawing on existing media signs, texts and intertexts, these media systems constitute gendered mythic worlds in which users' identities are shaped in and through sending and receiving signs.

Our access to the space of others has been increased by mobile communications, just as television and the information on the World Wide Web enables us to see or read about very distant places, people and events, but at the same time our privacy has been reduced. Being always accessible to communication is not only enabling but also intrusive. Even the sense of our own bodiliness is affected, since the intimate space around our bodies is colonised by the phones, pagers, hands-free headsets which communications technology requires. As Marshall McLuhan (1987) argued, our bodies and our senses are extended by communications technology, in the sense that we can speak, listen, read and write over great distances. It is as if we can be virtually present in another distant place, by engaging in communication with people who are far away. But this raises a question about where the limits of our selves should be drawn. Whereas the personal space around us seems to be 'private', and all other space 'public', the ability to be telephoned wherever we are means that this sense of privacy and personal space is eroded. The ideology of mobile communications works by calling individuals to become senders and receivers of information (we are literally 'called' by the ringing of the mobile phone). This ideology naturalises the notion that to be part of society people must be connected with the communication network. In a sense, therefore, the communication network is society. And each person is the collection of numbers and digital signals which signify him or her to others on the network.

Interactive television

There are already cable television systems which allow the home
viewer to make decisions about which film he or she wishes to
view from among a huge selection all available at the same time,
and there are experimental television services in which alternate
endings of programmes or alternate narrative sequences in films
can be selected by remote control. Interaction with television
technology has been available in limited forms for some time, in
the form of the Ceefax and Teletext on-screen text services. The
introduction of digital television broadcasting (where the signal
is coded into a stream of ones and zeros which are decoded by
the television set) offers not only higher quality reception, but
also the possibility of response back to the broadcaster, and the
use of the same hardware and software for watching television
as is used by computers. With the 'digital revolution', television,
computers, telecommunications and other digital media 'con-
verge'. The common feature of these converging media is their
encoding of written, visual and aural information in number
form, which is what 'digital media' means. A single type of code,
the digital code, becomes the medium in which any information
can be represented and communicated. Digital technologies
therefore rely on a *langue* or language into which information is
translated. Visual and aural signs are signified by combinations
of arbitrary signs, the ones and zeros which encode and decode
them.

In 2000, six million households in the UK had digital television, and thus the ability to watch interactive television. One
of the types of programming leading the introduction of interactive television is sport, and about 40 per cent of subscribers to
the Sky Sports Active channel watch football using the interactive ability to get text information and choose the camera angle
from which the game is presented. Sky News Active similarly
allows users to access text and video supporting news bulletins
and reports. The economic aim is to reduce the rate at which
subscribers decide to discontinue their paid subscriptions to interactive services. People get used to digitally enhanced television
services, and come to consider them essential to their enjoyment
of television sport or news. Sky Movies Active has eight rolling

video broadcasts on screen, each consisting of 5-minute loops of video showing interviews and information about the making of the film being watched. Each of the eight screens has attached text, offering profiles of the stars of the film, for example. Shopping and online betting can also be provided through interactive television services, and the converged e-mail and phone services on digital mean that viewers can enter phone competitions (on premium rate phone lines) and post reviews of films. Digital television also allows games to be played over the line, for example Sky offers *Tetris*, which can be played at a cost of 25p per game. Each of the kinds of media text and experience mentioned in this paragraph is not new. Sports television coverage, written and pictorial information about films and film stars, telephone competitions, sending written messages, and playing computer games have all been around for decades or more. What is new about interactive television is the simultaneous presence of these media forms in the same space. The film, the information about its stars, and the computer game can be accessed on the same piece of hardware in the same room, and can usually be present on the screen in windows at the same time. So semiotically, the methods of analysis of linguistic, iconic and aural signs do not need to change to analyse these different texts. However, their interrelationships are likely to produce new and complex intertexts, where the connotations and myths of one text affect those of another which coexists with it in the same time and space.

The mixture of ways of gaining income from interactive television is a sign of the current uncertainties surrounding the medium. In March 2000, the telecommunications and cable television company NTL announced a £5 million fund to be spent over five years on developing interactive television fiction. The benefits to NTL and Channel 5 would include providing programme content which would persuade people to buy the hardware (like digital television sets and cable services) which interactive television requires, and being among the first British broadcasters to establish interactive television in the mass market. The small television and radio production company Leisure Time began to work on an interactive television crime drama for NTL and Channel 5. Channel 5 requested that a competitive element be introduced into the crime drama narrative, to enable the possibility of betting online on the characters and to increase the suspense and tension in the story. But in 2001 Leisure Time's financial backers withdrew their support for the project. As unpublished research by Georgina Massie showed, this example illuminates some of the unresolved questions which currently undermine the development of interactive television. The production of drama which has multiple plotlines, from which one is received by the viewer depending on the interactive plot choices the viewer has made, is more difficult and more expensive to produce than the single linear narrative of traditional drama. In a digital television environment there are more broadcasting channels, and thus potentially smaller amounts of money available to make programmes because revenue is split between the increased number of television companies. Costs of programmes will have to be recouped from subscriptions paid by viewers of a channel, or from viewers paying to view particular programmes. Broadcasters are concerned that viewers are unused and unwilling to pay for television in this way. The introduction of interactive betting would be one way of generating income, but it is significant that this revenue-driven decision has effects on the form and structure of the programme. Although it remains a drama, it takes on the competitive features of a game-show, shifting the codes which structure the story and the kinds of viewer positioning and involvement which are demanded from him or her. The exciting prospects of interactivity and choice of viewing seem to lead in fact to a limitation on the genres and pleasures of interactive television.

The initial experiments in interactive television seem more likely to be adopted by viewers where they enhance an existing service, or offer services linked to an already established media brand. As John Storey (1999: 125) has argued, people's media use is strongly influenced by their habits and routines, since 'cultural consumption is a practice of everyday life. Cultural commodities are not appropriated or used in a social vacuum; such usage and appropriation takes place in the context of other forms of appropriation and use, themselves connected to the other routines, which together form the fabric of everyday life.' For this reason, it is difficult to introduce really new media and new kinds of media use. The established television channel Channel 4 is currently planning the successor to *Big Brother*, *Big Brother 2*, in 2001. This 'reality TV gameshow' attracted large numbers of television viewers, but also visitors to the programme's website, and is an established brand. As well as television broadcasts, the *Big Brother 2* project will include interactive games where viewers can bet online, and access the different cameras installed in the contestants' house. In other words, *Big Brother 2* will enhance and extend the preferred meanings of the programme, the positionings of the viewer and the modes of pleasure which were outlined in chapter 6.

Betting has been mentioned in relation to two interactive television projects in this section, and its introduction into television has interesting semiotic and ideological consequences. First, betting is a means of enhancing primary involvement in a programme, since when money is at stake the viewer is more likely to concentrate on the action. But this kind of involvement is different from the identification with characters and scenarios which fiction often entails. Instead, the viewer's stake metaphorically represents him or her, and the size of the stake signifies the degree to which the viewer is confident about an outcome. Second, to bet is to conceive of reality in terms of risk. The ideological structure underpinning this is that success depends on the entrepreneurship of individuals who accept risk and the uncertainty of outcome which it involves. Social subjects, according to this ideology, must speculate to accumulate, and society is composed of winners and losers. Third, betting and risk depend on unpredictability. The ideology of this conception of reality is that actions and outcomes are largely independent of human intervention. What will be will be. In the society of gamblers being shaped by interactive betting, social status and financial security are the products of good fortune, and the collective responsibility of society for those who are unfortunate seems likely to be eroded. What seems to be a mechanism for encouraging interactivity and active media involvement has significant ideological consequences.

Channel 4's investment in programme types which do not have an established brand identity like *Big Brother* is much more courageous and risky. The channel is spending millions of pounds on its new interactive website, E4.com. It has a Head of

Interactive Commissioning, whose aim is to use E4.com as an incubator for new performers and new programmes. Those performers and programmes which gather press and public attention can then form the basis of broadcast programmes, taking their public profile with them. The E4.com website launched in March 2001, and features *Office Romance*, an animated series, and *Banzai*, a frenetic Japanese gameshow which is simulcast (broadcast simultaneously on television and the Web). Web viewers can bet on which contestants will win, and can play an online Banzai game. There is also a Banzai WAP (Wireless Access Protocol) mobile phone game and plans for an enhanced television gameshow where viewers can bet using remote controls. Betting again features significantly in this initiative, positioning the interactive television user as a gambler on the actions of others. As in the other examples mentioned in this section, Channel 4's interactive television exploits the convergence of media with each other, is focused on the extension of existing brands and the creation of new ones, and is marked by the challenges and opportunities of drawing revenue from interactive users.

One of the attractions of contemporary entertainment media is the luxury of passivity and consumption. Interactive television demands a kind of work involved in actively constructing a text for oneself made up of fragments of other texts, like the different windows available on the screen. When video recorders were invented, it was thought that people would make tapes of bits of their favourite programmes and distribute them, becoming in a sense producers rather than consumers. The work involved in making videotapes like this could also connote creativity, since the assembly of signifiers into new texts with new meanings is similar to making a work of art. But these 'scratch videos' did not become commonplace. When video cameras were invented, it was assumed that people would make their own movies and distribute them, so that new kinds of video art would become common. But video art is still confined to a small number of producers and viewers. While the creativity of the user in making new semiotic assemblies of texts for themselves has occurred to a limited extent, the patterns of technology use seem to be similar to existing ones, rather than the technology creating new forms of independent media producer (rather than consumer) and new forms of control over texts and meanings. In chapter 7 a brief section on fans of television programmes discussed some similar issues. Appropriating signs and texts over which fans have no control, and making new texts and meanings with them, can be the focus of a kind of active media production culture where fans gain some power and authority within their own fan community. However, I argued that fans remain powerless to affect the media producers and institutions which control the making and distribution of television. In a similar way, the creative and empowering possibilities of interactive television do not change the real powerlessness of interactive viewers. The reduction of viewer activity to accessing ready-made selections of video or text, betting on the outcomes of televised action, and entering competitions, seem to confirm the ideologies of consumption, capitalist accumulation, and competition which already structure social life.

Computer games

There are already computer games on CD-ROM disc which allow the user to make decisions about the narrative progression and outcome of a game. This is a form of interactivity which is limited only by the number of decision-points included in the game, the number of alternative combinations of narrative segments which can be accommodated on the disc, and the investment in the program by the makers of the game. The pleasures of gaming are competition, accomplishment (like getting to the next level), mastery of the game's control system and its fictional world, the pleasures of narrative (like identification and anticipation), and the visual pleasures of spectacular effects. Some of these pleasures are identifiable in 'old' media, like television fiction's narrative pleasure and the cinema's pleasure in spectacular effects, while others are less familiar to users of 'old' media. For example the mastery of a computer interface, and the element of competition, are not significant in either cinema or television. In these ways, computer games combine the kinds of convergence discussed above. Computer games bring together the media of the computer, television and telephone (since many games can be played using computers or television sets, and can be downloaded over telephone lines), and convergence is also seen in the kinds of viewer positioning and pleasure which games derive from other media.

The pleasure of many games alternates between activity and passivity, for example being actively at the controls of a car in a racing game or 'being' Lara Croft in *Tomb Raider*, versus being a witness to the action of the game, which can often be presented in the form of replays from a neutral observing camera position. From the perspective of the user, one of the advantages of these new ways of interacting with screen-based media is that positionings encoded in the semiotic structure of texts are multiple and can be exchanged one for another. The 'old' media like television programmes or magazines can be decoded in different ways by viewers or readers, but the images, linguistic signs and sounds which the reader or viewer decodes are not subject to change in themselves. You cannot change what is on the page, or on the screen. Interactive media offer their users the chance to change what they see and hear, and thus to create 'new' texts for themselves. However, the contemporary value given to viewer choice and interactivity in computer games rests on naturalised assumptions about their users. This technology requires the user to grant primary involvement and attention to it, and to the games which the technology brings into the player's private domestic space. It is necessary to be interested, and to care about the outcomes and narrative progression of a game, and to keep making choices in order to exploit and enjoy interactivity. New technologies are predicated on the assumption of an active viewer, and a social subject who wants to be involved with the latest entertainment products. The user of interactive technologies may not be a passive consumer of a fixed repertoire of meanings, but he or she is nevertheless required to work hard at being a kind of user constructed in and for the entertainment products he or she has bought into.

Although I have referred to users of interactive media as 'he or she' in this chapter, one of the concerns which should affect the study of computer games is the masculine coding of the subjects and kinds of pleasure which games have so far exhibited. Although women make up 45 per cent of the gaming community, and constitute just over 50 per cent of players who play online, women mainly play free games downloaded from the Internet, or play pre-installed card and puzzle games on home computers. This reinforces the focus by game developers on the action games which have led the development of the medium and which are played (and paid for) mainly by men. Well-known examples of games coded as masculine are the 'shoot-em ups' *Doom* and *Quake* created by John Carmack and John Romero in the mid-1990s. Their most striking characteristic is 'gibs', short for giblets, the chunks of bloody flesh which explode everywhere when a character is killed. Computer games have age certification in Britain (in the same way as films and videos) due to concern over violent content. *Carmageddon*, for instance, has an '18' certificate because of the blood and gore exploding out of the bodies of the pedestrians mown down by the player's vehicle. In the design phase, the ability of the game's mathematical systems to make the pedestrian's body react to impact in the same way as a real person increased the effect of realism, but this realistic carnage was not included in the released version because of the processor time required to calculate the behaviour of the virtual bodies. Nevertheless, the emphasis in shoot-em up games on denotative realism shows that the semiotics of games have much in common with the assumption of denotation which underlies the iconic signs of television and film.

Shoot-em up games have been blamed in legal cases over teenage murders in the USA, such as fourteen-year-old Michael Carneal who killed three people in West Paducah, Kentucky in 1998 and was a frequent player of *Doom*. The argument is that games desensitise people to killing, because the denotative realism of games, coupled with the intense identification with the narrative goals and the characters in the game, positions the player in a mythical world where violence and death are without consequence. However, this assumption that denotation and excessive identification are the main features of games is only partially true. *Doom* involves moving through levels by killing opponents who are not only humanoid but also creatures like a pink flying octopus. The game is not a realistically denoted world. More significant to the ideological meaning of games is the alienation and isolation of the main character, and the bleakness of the social worlds in which they are set. Like many science fiction films and comics, first-person games often require the player to take on the role of a lone hero, who is separated from the negotiations and social interactions which constitute social life. The environments of games often consist of dungeons, bleak futuristic cities, or the hostile conditions of fictional planets. The mythic worlds of games are metaphors which imaginarily signify the social and psychological worlds of the user's reality. The ideological effect of these features may be to encode the assumptions that social life is competitive and risk-filled, supporting the ideologies of the other new media forms discussed so far in this chapter.

The Internet and World Wide Web

One of the chief ideological effects of Internet computer technologies comes from their base in the home. Using the new entertainment and communications media depends on having the expensive technology in your own domestic space, and the profits of technology producers depend on the widespread sales of the equipment. The cost of access to cyberspace is made up of the price of a personal computer renewed every two years, telephone connection charges and call charges, Internet Service Provider charges, and electricity. This was estimated in 1996 to be $2,700 per year (£1,680), though the cost is falling rapidly. In 1994, 90 per cent of Internet users were men, 80 per cent were white, 70 per cent American, 50 per cent spent 40 or more hours per week computing, and 30 per cent were university graduates. People with access to the Internet were therefore members of a relatively wealthy and powerful section of the world's population. Only about a quarter of the world's population have access to their own telephone line (for connection to an ISP), and an even smaller proportion of this group have the disposable income required for the purchase and renewal of the computer technology required to access the World Wide Web. Although the high technology machines which run the Internet are made by workers in the Third World, in offshore plants in Vietnam, the Philippines or Mexico, for example, these people have little access to the supposedly worldwide technoculture which they themselves produce. They are the information-poor.

These factors undercut the assertion that the World Wide Web is a means of giving access to information and opportunities for social change to a wider section of the world's population.

I have argued above that when using interactive technologies the subject becomes a sign separated from his or her physical body and cultural reality, represented by the digital code's signs which stand for him or her. The word-processors and computer terminals used for communicating make information virtual too, divorced from the concreteness of paper, and its connection with particular local contexts. Information is digitised and can move around the electronic networks of the world, to be reconstituted and used in all kinds of ways by whoever can access it. So the meanings of individual subjects and of texts in these new media are controlled by the signifying activities of their producers and the patterns of access to information associated with the techno-logical apparatus. But on the other hand, their meanings are dis-persed and released from control by the multiple ways in which they can be decoded by receivers in different cultures and local contexts. As Vivian Sobchack (1996: 80) has argued, 'new media' culture 'will be *both* more *and* less (not *either* more *or* less) liberating, participatory and interactive than was the case with previous, technologically-mediated cultural forms.'

The economics underlying Web services are that either web-sites contain ads which gain revenue from numbers of times users click on them ('hits'), or the site is accessed only by sub-scription (like paying for cable television channels), or the site is used for e-commerce (like a mail order catalogue). E-commerce sites are expensive to set up, and few have been profitable. But British consumers spent £2.5 billion on online shopping in 2000, compared to £860,000 in 1999, so it seems likely that shopping will become a significant use of interactive media. As I have sug-gested earlier in this chapter, the new media user is coded as a consumer. The third most common use of the Internet currently (after computer sales and travel ticket sales) is for male users to access pornography, most of it produced in the United States. The Los Angeles-based site Danni's Hard Drive, set up in 1995 by former stripper Danni Ashe, grossed $2.7 million in 1997, aver-aging five million hits per day, and had 22,000 subscribers in 1998 paying $14.95 per month for access to more than 15,000 photos of 250 models, 450 channels of streamed video and 6 live video feeds. The US porn Web industry netted $185 million in 1998 and is estimated to bring revenue of about £2.25 billion in 2001. The success of the Internet pornography industry suggests that ideologies positioning men as voyeurs, and women as objects of sexual fascination, are being perpetuated by new media. It seems that the availability of new media technology in the private space of the home perpetuates masculine desires to position the female body as 'other' and to take pleasure in iconic photographic images denoting the female body as the object of a controlling gaze.

However, the World Wide Web is also a virtual space in which versions of community can be signified. More than 10,000 people per day are creating their own homepages on the Web. This phenomenon is known as 'virtual homesteading', which alludes to the sense that the Web is an open physical space like the continent of North America was thought to be in the nine-teenth century. Like the pioneers who moved west to settle the 'frontier' and set up farms and ranches, people are setting up virtual communities composed of their individual 'homesteads' hosted by companies which provide computer memory to hold them. One of these American companies, GeoCities, hosted over 1.5 million homepages in 1998, and delivered over 625 million pageviews per month to its users. GeoCities homesteading is divided into various regions, like Area 51 (for science fiction and fantasy), Enchanted Forest (for children), Wellesley (for feminist women), Heartland (for users inclined to what Americans call 'family values') and Yosemite (for hiking, rafting and outdoor enthusiasts). The result of this division into virtual territories is that users can expect to belong to virtual communities of like-minded people. The names of GeoCities homesteading communi-ties draw on the existing connotations of places in American culture, and are signs which metaphorically signify identities. Individual subjects position themselves in relation to some of the mythic meanings which make up the greater mythic identity of 'America'. As Althusser (1971) explained, ideologies of identity represent in an imaginary form the real conditions in which people live. The imaginary places and identities in GeoCities pro-vide imaginary identities for people, and these are signified by signs in the virtual pages of the Web. A real America and real Americans are selectively represented in GeoCities, drawing on some of the (more pleasant) mythic meanings of America and discarding others.

As with previous media technologies like television, the economic drive of the interactive media business is towards the increasing 'privatisation' of experience. The user is an isolated end-point in a huge network, and in this sense is like the television viewer who is an individual receiver of broadcasts which are also being watched by a multitude of other individuals all separated from each other. But on the other hand, many of the network services on the Internet substitute for the social activities which go on outside the home. The social world is itself simulated by the interactive conversations of e-mail. Interacting with people remotely by means of written linguistic signs offers the user freedom to enjoy different and fluid identities, but social experiences and subjective identities which are all mediated by systems of signs may have disadvantageous alienating effects. Kevin Fox, a cognitive science student, logged a program written in 1966 to simulate the discourse of a psychoanalyst onto America Online (AOL)'s instant messaging system, which enables users to have e-mail conversations with each other. Because the program mimicked the codes of conversation in a 'realistic' way, some users of the system, including a user called 'twentytwo', assumed that the program, named 'AOLiza' was another person. Part of one of these conversations was reprinted in *The Guardian* 'Editor' section on 21 April 2001 (p. 14):

> twentytwo: ... I don't think men could take teasing as well as we women do.
>
> AOLiza: you're not really talking about me – are you?
>
> twentytwo: I don't know you well enough to talk about you.
>
> AOLiza: why don't you know me well enough to talk about me?
>
> twentytwo: because we haven't spent any time together. Or communicating with each other.
>
> AOLiza: don't any other reasons come to mind?
>
> twentytwo: what are you trying to get me to say?
>
> AOLiza: are such questions much on you mind?

twentytwo: not really, but I think it would be fun getting to know you.

AOLiza: we were discussing you, not me.

As far as the individual subject is concerned, communicating with others by e-mail allows subjective identity to be signified in an ordered form, but for the identity thus signified to be an imaginary and temporary persona. Computer network technologies link individual subjects together by remote means, but so remotely that their communication with each other loses the concrete and material character of previous ways of interacting. Logged on to the Internet for some kinds of communication, you can adopt a persona and become another kind of subject when communicating by these electronic means, adopting a different gender for instance. Internet communication allows the sender to represent him- or herself by signs, as well as being a receiver and decoder of signs. This kind of interactivity is a stage further than the interactivity of games and information programs in the computer medium. The individual subject becomes a collection of signifiers, which whoever reads the message has to reconstitute into the mythic person which the message's codes and signs appear to reflect. The subject becomes a sign separated from its referent (the person formed by the specific cultural, historical and political contexts in which they live), and becomes a subject in a virtual global community formed by the communications network. The distinction that structuralist critics like Barthes made, between sign and referent, text and author, subjective identity and physical body, can become virtually the case. The ability of AOLiza's signs to have several meanings at once (polysemy) and to be interpreted in different ways by different people (multiaccentuality) is what allows 'twentytwo' to become confused about whether she is communicating with a person or a computer.

Conclusion

The question of how individuals make sense of their involvements with the media has recently been addressed by a different discourse to that of semiotics, the discourse of audience research which has been discussed in several chapters of this book. In the contemporary diversification of audiences brought about by the proliferation of media and of new ways of interacting with them, there is a temptation to be over-optimistic about the extent to which individuals make meanings on their own terms, and for their own individual purposes. It is tempting to assume that individual users of the media, simply because they are all different, and belong to different subcultural groups in society, can subvert the meanings of media texts in ways that some audience researchers and other academic critics would like to value as radical or even revolutionary. This optimistic view is in one sense relevant and important because it challenges the assumptions of structuralist semiotic research; that fixed meanings are structured into texts and signs by universally known codes and a fixed repertoire of ways of positioning the audience. But it does not challenge the more recent semiotic approach (progressively adopted in this book) which assumes that signs and texts have several meanings at once (polysemy), a kind of excess or proliferation of meanings which enables them to be used by audiences in different ways (multiaccentuality). Indeed, research on the uses and role of the media in the lives of individual subjects shows that what media texts and the makers of media products do is to systematically channel this excess of meaning as much as they can, although this enterprise can never entirely succeed.

The institutions of the media and the media products they produce try to impose order on meaning, against the ever-present threat posed to meaning by polysemy and by multiaccentual decoding practices on the part of actual audiences. Just as audiences are only relatively free to produce new and different meanings, so media texts and their producers are only relatively successful at delimiting the decodings of signs which audiences can produce. In this situation, semiotics is still an essential analytical perspective for studying the media. Semiotic analysis shows how the meanings of signs in texts are at once constrained by codes and ideological structures, but also how signs can be read in different ways because they always depend for their meaning on their relationship to the other signs in the same text and on their relationship with the signs in other texts (intertextuality). To sum up this perspective, meanings are perpetually being made but are at the same time perpetually being fractured from within, and scattered by their interactions with other meanings. Every text is only meaningful when an individual subject decodes it himself or herself, and every text presupposes a reader (or viewer) for whom its signs will make sense. Since signs and texts have multiple, polysemic meanings, and can be decoded multiaccentually by readers taking up different subject-positions, the individual subject who decodes a media text must be perpetually constructed and re-constructed in different ways in the process of making sense of signs. Just as the meanings of media texts are continually being fixed and continually shifting again, so too the identity of the individual subject must be fixed and shifted.

Thinking about meaning and subjective identity in this way, as always existing in a tension between order and dispersion, position and fluidity, is particularly useful in relation to the new computer-based media. People's sense of their own subjectivity is affected by interactive media, because perception and expression are electronically mediated by them. This furthers the situation outlined at various points in this book in which people's sense of subjective being is bound up with the media signs in and through which they understand and experience their realities. Furthermore, interactive media like e-mail in which people represent themselves by signs, communicating with distant others who they will never encounter face to face, require people to construct a virtual subjectivity and identity at the computer keyboard.

Perhaps the key contribution of semiotics to our understanding of social life comes from its reversal of common-sense assumptions. Rather than thinking of language as an instrument for expressing thought, Saussure's linguistics enabled us to see that thought is constituted by language. Barthes and other structuralist semioticians insisted that rather than human culture being built on an essential human nature, it is our culture which gives us our assumptions about what human nature is. What had been thought of as the foundation of things was understood as a superstructure, and what had been thought of as a superstructure became a foundation, with all of the shaking-up of established ideas which this reversal implies. As semiotics evolved as a discipline, post-structuralist semiotic thinkers argued that this world-shaking discourse about culture and society could not be the universal science of everything which it seemed to be, because semiotics is itself a discourse rather than a value-free and 'objective' truth of things. So the great promise of semiotics became impossible to achieve. Instead of moving ever further towards a few underlying truths, semiotics has moved outwards to become one of many components in the methodologies of many intellectual disciplines, including media studies but also psychoanalysis, anthropology, art history and architecture, for instance.

At this point, there is no synthesis between the different discourses of Media Studies. In some respects, this is an advantage rather than a disadvantage, because it compels the analyst of the media to recognise the stakes and limitations of the various discursive frameworks in which he or she works. That is the most prominent feeling for me at the end of writing this book. The book is designed to be used in a teaching and learning situation, which is itself a particular context in which some discourses are naturalised as legitimate while others are not. Perhaps it might seem that a book to be used in an educational context should have a single and consistent discourse, and appear to argue for a seamless methodology which would enable its reader to go out and do his or her work using this methodology as a tool to achieve results more efficiently and effectively. However, I do not think that books should work this way. This book does not stick to one consistent discourse, since while concentrating on semiotics it shows both that semiotics is not a single and consistent body of ideas, and that it cannot always account adequately for some of the features of media culture which are evidently important. In this respect, I hope that this book fulfils the role of an Introduction relatively well, by demonstrating that there is much more to be said and discovered beyond what is contained in these pages.

Sources and further reading

Books on interactive media include Jones (1995, 1997), Shields (1996), Porter (1996), Poster (1990, 1995), Sardar and Ravetz (1996), Turkle (1995) and Webster (1995). Non-academic books popularising ideologies of interactive media include Negroponte (1995) and Rheingold

(1991, 1993). Stokes and Reading (1999), Mackay and O'Sullivan (1999) and Marris and Thornham (1999) have sections on interactive media, and Winston (1998) places interactive media in a history of media technology.

Suggestions for further work

1   If you use a mobile telephone, in which places or situations do you turn it off, or refuse to answer calls? What are the social codes which govern your behaviour, and what is their ideological significance?
2   SMS text messaging has developed abbreviations, icons and graphic signs to shorten messages. In what ways do SMS abbreviations, icons and graphics depend on linguistic codes familiar in spoken rather than written communication?
3   If you have access to digital interactive television, try accessing on-screen windows while you are watching a programme. How does the presence of different windows on the screen affect your modes of viewing, and what are the intertextual relationships between one image and another on your screen?
4   How would betting on the outcomes of a fictional television programme or a film affect your relationships with characters and events? Which genres of television or film do you think would be most and least appropriate for gambling, and why?
5   How are myths of gender identity, social power and individual competence signified in computer games you have played? What ideologies are being naturalised by these mythic meanings?
6   Select five websites you have visited. How are iconic, graphic and linguistic signs used in similar and different ways in them? What are the reasons for the similarities and differences you find?
7   Are there some kinds of content which should not be freely accessible on the Web? Are there some kinds of people who should not be allowed access to content on the Web? How do your answers relate to ideologies defining unacceptable media content (like pornography) and vulnerable media audiences (like children) in 'old' media?

Bibliography

Allen, R. (ed.) (1992), *Channels of Discourse, Reassembled: Television and Contemporary Criticism*, London, Routledge.

Allen, R. (1992), Audience-oriented criticism and television, in R. Allen (ed.), *Channels of Discourse, Reassembled: Television and Contemporary Criticism*, London, Routledge, 101–37.

Allen, S., G. Branston and C. Carter (eds) (1998), *News, Gender and Power*, London, Routledge.

Alleyne, M. (1997), *News Revolution: Political and Economic Decisions about Global Information*, Basingstoke, Macmillan.

Althusser, L. (1971), Ideology and ideological state apparatuses: notes towards an investigation, in *Lenin and Philosophy*, London, New Left Books, 121–73.

Alvarado, M. and J. Thompson (eds) (1990), *The Media Reader*, London, BFI.

Amy-Chin, D. (2001), Sex offence: the cultural politics of perfume, *Women: A Cultural Review*, 12:2, 164–75.

Andrew, D. (1984), *Concepts in Film Theory*, Oxford, Oxford University Press.

Ang, I. (1989), *Watching Dallas: Soap Opera and the Melodramatic Imagination*, trans. D. Couling, revised edn, London, Routledge.

Ang, I. (1991), *Desperately Seeking the Audience*, London, Routledge.

Bacon-Smith, C. and T. Yarborough (1991), Batman: the ethnography, in R. Pearson and W. Uricchio (eds), *The Many Lives of the Batman: Critical Approaches to a Superhero and his Media*, London, Routledge/BFI, 90–116.

Ballaster, R., M. Beetham, E. Frazer, and S. Hebron (1991), *Women's Worlds: Ideology, Femininity and the Women's Magazine*, London, Macmillan.

Barker, C. (1997), *Global Television: An Introduction*, Oxford, Blackwell.

Barthes, R. (1973), *Mythologies*, trans. A. Lavers, London, Granada.

Barthes, R. (1977a), The photographic message, in *Image Music Text*, trans. S. Heath, London, Fontana, 15–31.

Barthes, R. (1977b), Rhetoric of the image, in *Image Music Text*, trans. S. Heath, London, Fontana, 32–51.

Baudrillard, J. (1983), *Simulations*, New York, Semiotext(e).

Bignell, J. (ed.) (1999), *Writing and Cinema*, Harlow, Addison Wesley

Longman.

Bignell, J. (2000), *Postmodern Media Culture*, Edinburgh, Edinburgh University Press.

Bignell, J. (2000), Docudrama as melodrama: representing Princess Diana and Margaret Thatcher, in B. Carson and M. Llewellyn-Jones (eds), *Frames and Fictions on Television: The Politics of Identity within Drama*, Exeter, Intellect, 17–26.

Bignell, J., S. Lacey and M. Macmurraugh-Kavanagh (eds) (2000), *British Television Drama: Past, Present and Future*, Basingstoke, Palgrave.

Billingham, P. (2000), *Sensing the City through Television*, Exeter, Intellect.

Blonsky, M. (ed.) (1985), *On Signs: A Semiotics Reader*, Oxford, Blackwell.

Boyd-Barrett, O. and T. Rantanen (1998), *The Globalization of News*, London, Sage.

Brandt, G. (ed.) (1993), *British Television Drama in the 1980s*, Cambridge, Cambridge University Press.

Branston, G. and R. Stafford (1999), *The Media Student's Book*, second edn, London, Routledge.

Briggs, A. and P. Cobley (eds) (1998), *The Media: An Introduction*, Harlow, Addison Wesley Longman.

Brunsdon, C. (1998a), Structure of anxiety: recent British crime fiction, *Screen* 39:3, 223–43.

Brunsdon, C. (1998b), What is the television of television studies?, in C. Geraghty and D. Lusted (eds), *The Television Studies Book*, London, Arnold, 95–113.

Burton, G. (2000), *Talking Television: An Introduction to the Study of Television*, London, Arnold.

Butler, J. (1990), *Gender Trouble: Feminism and the Subversion of Identity*, London, Routledge.

Cannon, J., P. Odber de Baubeta and R. Warner (eds) (2000), *Advertising and Identity in Europe: The I of the Beholder*, Exeter, Intellect.

Carson, B. and M. Llewellyn-Jones (eds) (2000), *Frames and Fictions on Television: The Politics of Identity within Drama*, Exeter, Intellect.

Caughie, J. (2000), *Television Drama: Realism, Modernism, and British Culture*, Oxford, Oxford University Press.

Cho, M., and C. Cho (1990), Women watching together: an ethnographic study of Korean soap opera fans in the U.S., *Cultural Studies*, 4:1, 30–44.

Cohen, S. and J. Young (eds) (1973), *The Manufacture of News: Social Problems, Deviance and the Mass Media*, London, Constable.

Coles, G. (2000), Docusoap: actuality and the serial format, in B. Carson and M. Llewellyn-Jones (eds), *Frames and Fictions on Television: The Politics of Identity within Drama*, Exeter, Intellect, 27–39.

Collins, J. (1989), *Uncommon Cultures: Popular Culture and Post-Modernism*, London, Routledge.

Collins, J. (1992), Postmodernism and television, in R. Allen (ed.), *Channels of Discourse, Reassembled: Television and Contemporary Criticism*, London, Routledge, 327–53.

Collins, J. (1994), By whose authority? Accounting for taste in contemporary popular culture, in D. Crowley and D. Mitchell (eds), *Communication Theory Today*, Cambridge, Polity, 214–31.

Collins, J., H. Radner, and A. Preacher Collins (eds) (1993), *Film Theory Goes to the Movies*, London, Routledge.

Cook, G. (1992), *The Discourse of Advertising*, London. Routledge.

Cook, P. and M. Bernink (eds) (1999), *The Cinema Book*, London, BFI.

Corner, J. (1995), *Television Form and Public Address*, London, Edward Arnold.

Corner, J. (1996), *The Art of Record: A Critical Introduction to Documentary*, Manchester, Manchester University Press.

Corner, J. and S. Harvey (eds) (1996), *Television Times: A Reader*, London, Arnold.

Cowie, E. (1984), Fantasia, *m/f*, 9, 71–105.

Crisell, A. (1997), *An Introductory History of British Broadcasting*, London, Routledge.

Culler, J. (1976), *Saussure*, London, Fontana.

Culler, J. (1983), *Barthes*, London, Fontana.

Curran, J. and J. Seaton (eds) (1997), *Power without Responsibility: The Press and Broadcasting in Britain*, fifth edn, London, Routledge.

Dahlgren, P. (1985), The modes of reception: for a hermeneutics of TV news, in P. Drummond and R. Patterson (eds), *Television in Transition*, London, BFI, 235–49.

Dahlgren, P. and C. Sparks (eds) (1992), *Journalism and Popular Culture*, London, Sage.

Dams, T. (1998), Time to move on, *Broadcast* 23 October, 16–17.

Danesi, M. (1999), *Of Cigarettes, High Heels, and Other Interesting Things: An Introduction to Semiotics*, Basingstoke, Macmillan.

Dowmunt, T. (ed.) (1993), *Channels of Resistance: Global Television and Local Empowerment*, London, BFI/Channel 4.

Drummond, P. and R. Patterson (eds) (1988), *Television and its Audience: International Research Perspectives*, London, BFI.

Dyer, G. (1982), *Advertising as Communication*, London, Methuen.

Eagleton, T. (1983), *Literary Theory: An Introduction*, Oxford, Blackwell.

Easthope, A. (ed.) (1993), *Contemporary Film Theory*, Harlow, Longman.

Eco, U. (1977), *A Theory of Semiotics*, London, Macmillan.

Eco, U. (1990), Interpreting serials, in *The Limits of Interpretation*, Bloomington, Indiana University Press, 83–100.

Eldridge, J. (ed.) (1995), *Glasgow Media Reader volume 1: News Content, Language and Visuals*, London, Routledge.

Ellis, J. (1992), *Visible Fictions: Cinema, Television, Video*, London, Routledge.

Fairclough, N. (1995), *Media Discourse*, London, Arnold.

Ferguson, M. (1983), *Forever Feminine: Women's Magazines and the Cult of Femininity*, London, Heinemann.

Fiske, J. (1987), *Television Culture*, London, Routledge.

Fiske, J. (1991), Postmodernism and television, in J. Curran and M. Gurevitch (eds), *Mass Media and Society*, London, Edward Arnold, 55–67.

Fiske, J. (1992), British cultural studies and television, in R. Allen (ed.) *Channels of Discourse, Reassembled: Television and Contemporary Criticism*, London, Routledge, 284–326.

Fiske, J. and J. Hartley (1978), *Reading Television*, London, Methuen.

Fowler, R. (1991), *Language in the News: Discourse and Ideology in the Press*, London, Routledge.

Galtung, J. and M. Ruge (1973), Structuring and selecting news, in S. Cohen and J. Young (eds), *The Manufacture of News: Social Problems, Deviance and the Mass Media*, London, Constable, 62–72.

Garber, M., J. Matlock and R. Walkowitz (eds) (1993), *Media Spectacles*, London, Routledge.

Geraghty, C. and D. Lusted (eds) (1998), *The Television Studies Book*, London, Arnold.

Glasgow Media Group (1976), *Bad News*, London, Routledge & Kegan Paul.

Glasgow Media Group (1980), *More Bad News*, London, Routledge & Kegan Paul.

Glasgow Media Group (1986), *War and Peace News*, Milton Keynes, Open University Press.

Goffman, E. (1979), *Gender Advertisements*, London, Methuen.

Goldman, R. (1992), *Reading Ads Socially*, London, Routledge.

Gray, A. (1992), *Video Playtime: The Gendering of a Leisure Technology*, London, Routledge.

Gurevitch, M. (1991), The globalization of electronic journalism, in

J. Curran and M. Gurevitch (eds), *Mass Media and Society*, London, Edward Arnold, 178–93.

Hall, S., D. Hobson, A. Lowe and P. Willis (1980), Encoding/decoding, in S. Hall, (eds), *Culture, Media, Language*, London, Hutchinson, 128–38.

Hall, S. (ed.) (1997), *Representation: Cultural Representations and Signifying Practices*, London, Sage.

Hall, S., C. Crichter, T. Jefferson, T. Clarke and B. Roberts (1978), *Policing the Crisis: Mugging, the State, the Law and Order*, London, Macmillan.

Hansen, M. (1991), *Babel and Babylon: Spectatorship in American Silent Film*, Harvard, Harvard University Press.

Harrison, J. (2000), *Terrestrial TV News in Britain: The Culture of Production*, Manchester, Manchester University Press.

Harrison, M. (1985), *TV News: Whose Bias? A Casebook Analysis of Strikes, Television and Media Studies*, Hermitage, Policy Journals.

Hartley, J. (1982), *Understanding News*, London, Methuen.

Hartley, J. (1992), *The Politics of Pictures: The Creation of the Public in the Age of Popular Media*, London, Routledge.

Hartley, J. (1992), *Tele-ology: Studies in Television*, London, Routledge.

Hawkes, T. (1983), *Structuralism and Semiotics*, London, Methuen.

Hebdige, D. (1988), *Hiding in the Light: On Images and Things*, London, Routledge.

Hermes, J. (1995), *Reading Women's Magazines*, Cambridge, Polity.

Hood, S. (ed.) (1994), *Behind the Screens: The Structure of British Television in the Nineties*, London, Lawrence and Wishart.

Hutcheon, L. (1987), The politics of postmodernism, parody, and history, *Cultural Critique*, 5, 179–207.

Jacobson, R. (1995), *Television Research: A Directory of Conceptual Categories, Topic Suggestions and Selected Sources*, Jefferson, McFarland.

Jones, S. (ed.) (1995), *CyberSociety: Computer-Mediated Communication and Community*, London, Sage.

Jones, S. (ed.) (1997), *Virtual Culture: Identity and Communication in Cybersociety*, London, Sage.

Katz, E. and T. Liebes (1984), Once upon a time in Dallas, *Intermedia*, 12:3, 28–32.

Katz, E. and T. Liebes (1985), Mutual aid in the decoding of *Dallas*: preliminary notes from a cross-cultural study, in P. Drummond and R. Patterson (eds), *Television in Transition*, London, BFI, 187–98.

Kilborn, R. and J. Izod (1997), *An Introduction to Television Documentary: Confronting Reality*, Manchester, Manchester University Press.

Kozloff, S. (1992), Narrative theory and television, in R. Allen (ed.), *Channels of Discourse, Reassembled: Television and Contemporary Criticism*, London, Routledge, 67–100.

Lacan, J. (1977), The mirror stage, in *Ecrits: A Selection*, trans. A. Sheridan, London, Tavistock, 1–7.

Langer, J. (1998), *Tabloid Television: Popular Journalism and 'Other News'*, London, Routledge.

Lapsley, R. and M. Westlake (1988), *Film Theory: An Introduction*, Manchester, Manchester University Press.

Lauretis, T. de (1984), *Alice Doesn't: Feminism, Semiotics, Cinema*, London, Macmillan.

Lavers, A. (1982), *Roland Barthes, Structuralism and After*, London, Methuen.

Leal, O. (1990), Popular taste and erudite repertoire: the place and space of television in Brazil, *Cultural Studies*, 4:1, 19–29.

Lewis, J. (1985), Decoding television news, in P. Drummond and R. Patterson (eds), *Television in Transition*, London, BFI, 205–34.

Lewis, J. (1991), *The Ideological Octopus: An Exploration of Television and its Audience*, London, Routledge.

Lewis, L. (ed.) (1992), *The Adoring Audience: Fan Culture and Popular Media*, London, Routledge.

Lindof, T. (ed.) (1987), *Natural Audiences: Qualitative Research of Media Uses and Effects*, Norwood, Ablex.

Lister, M. (ed.) (1995), *The Photographic Image in Digital Culture*, London, Routledge.

Lorimer, R., with P. Scannell (1994), *Mass Communications: A Comparative Introduction*, Manchester, Manchester University Press.

Lull, J. (ed.) (1988), *World Families Watch Television*, London, Sage.

Macdonald, M. (1995), *Representing Women: Myths of Femininity in the Popular Media*, London, Edward Arnold.

MacGregor, B. (1997), *Live, Direct and Biased?: Making Television News in the Satellite Age*, London, Hodder Headline.

Mackay, H. and T. O'Sullivan (eds) (1999), *The Media Reader: Continuity and Transformation*, London, Sage.

Marris, P. and S. Thornham (eds) (1999), *Media Studies: A Reader*, Edinburgh, Edinburgh University Press.

Mast, G. and M. Cohen (eds) (1985), *Film Theory and Criticism*, Oxford, Oxford University Press.

Masterman, L. (1984), *Television Mythologies: Stars, Shows and Signs*,

London, Comedia.

Mayne, J. (1993), *Cinema and Spectatorship*, London, Routledge.

McCracken, E. (1993), *Decoding Women's Magazines: From Mademoiselle to Ms.*, London, Macmillan.

McLuhan, M. (1987), *Understanding Media: The Extensions of Man*, London, Ark.

McNair, B. (1994), *News and Journalism in the UK: A Textbook*, London, Routledge.

McQueen, D. (1998), *Television: A Media Student's Guide*, London, Arnold.

Meech, P. (1999), Advertising, in J. Stokes and A. Reading (eds), *The Media in Britain: Current Debates and Developments*, Basingstoke, Macmillan, 25–40.

Metz, C. (1974), *Language and Cinema*, trans. D. Umiker-Sebeok, The Hague, Mouton.

Metz, C. (1975), The imaginary signifier, *Screen*, 16:2, 14–76.

Mitchell, J. and J. Rose (eds) (1982), *Feminine Sexuality: Jacques Lacan and the Ecole Freudienne*, trans. J. Rose, London, Macmillan.

Modleski, T. (1988), *The Women Who Knew Too Much: Hitchcock and Feminist Film Theory*, London, Methuen.

Moi, T. (1985), *Sexual/Textual Politics: Feminist Literary Theory*, London, Routledge.

Monaco, J. (1981), *How to Read a Film*, Oxford, Oxford University Press.

Moores, S. (1993), *Interpreting Audiences*, London, Sage.

Morley, D. (1992), *Television, Audiences and Cultural Studies*, London, Routledge.

Mort, F. (1996), *Cultures of Consumption: Masculinities and Socal Space in Late Twentieth-Century Britain*, London, Routledge.

Mosely, R. (2000), Makeover takeover on British television, *Screen*, 41:3, 299–314.

Mullan, B. (1997), *Consuming Television*, Oxford, Blackwell.

Mulvey, L. (1975), Visual pleasure and narrative cinema, *Screen*, 16:3, 6–18.

Mulvey, L. (1989), *Visual and Other Pleasures*, Macmillan, London.

Myers, G. (1994), *Words in Ads*, London, Edward Arnold.

Myers, G. (1999), *Ad Worlds: Brands, Media, Audiences*, London, Arnold.

Myers, K. (1986), *Understains ... The Sense and Seduction of Advertising*, London, Comedia.

Neale, N. and F. Krutnik (1990), *Popular Film and Television Comedy*, London, Routledge.

Negroponte, N. (1995), *Being Digital*, London, Coronet.

Nelson, R. (1997), *TV Drama in Transition: Forms, Values and Cultural Change*, Basingstoke, Macmillan.

Nichols, B. (1991), *Representing Reality: Issues and Concepts in Documentary*, Bloomington, Indiana University Press.

Nichols, B. (1994), *Blurred Boundaries: Questions of Meaning in Contemporary Culture*, Bloomington, Indiana University Press.

Nixon, S. (1996), *Hard Looks: Masculinites, Spectatorship and Contemporary Consumption*, London, UCL Press.

O'Sullivan, T., B. Dutton and P. Rayner (1994), *Studying the Media: An Introduction*, London, Edward Arnold.

Paget, D. (1998), *No Other Way to Tell It: Dramadoc/Docudrama on Television*, Manchester, Manchester University Press.

Palmer, J. (1994), *Taking Humour Seriously*, London, Routledge.

Pearson, R. and W. Uricchio (eds) (1991), *The Many Lives of the Batman: Critical Approaches to a Superhero and his Media*, London, Routledge/BFI.

Philips, D. (2000), Medicated soap: the woman doctor in television medical drama, in B. Carson and M. Llewellyn-Jones (eds), *Frames and Fictions on Television: The Politics of Identity within Drama*, Exeter, Intellect, 50–61.

Philo, G. (1987), Whose news?, *Media, Culture and Society*, 9:4, 397–406.

Philo, G. (ed.) (1995), *Glasgow Media Reader volume 2: Industry, War, Economy and Politics*, London, Routledge.

Pierce, C. S. (1958), *Selected Writings (Values in a Universe of Chance)*, ed. P. Wiener, New York, Dover Press.

Porter, D. (1996), *Internet Culture*, London, Routledge.

Poster, M. (1990), *The Mode of Information*, Chicago, University of Chicago Press.

Poster, M. (1994), The mode of information and postmodernity, in D. Crowley and D. Mitchell (eds), *Communication Theory Today*, Cambridge, Polity.

Poster, M. (1995), *The Second Media Age*, Cambridge, Polity.

Pribam, D. (ed.) (1988), *Female Spectators: Looking at Film and Television*, London, Verso.

Rheingold, H. (1991) *Virtual Reality*, London, Secker and Warburg.

Rheingold, H. (1993), *The Virtual Community: Homesteading on the Electronic Frontier*, Reading, MA, Addison-Wesley.

Sardar, Z. and J. Ravetz (eds) (1996), *Cyberfutures*, London, Pluto.

Saussure, F. de (1974), *Course in General Linguistics*, eds C. Bally, A. Sechehaye and A. Riedlinger, trans. W. Baskin, London, Fontana.

Schlesinger, P. (1978), *Putting 'Reality' Together: BBC News*, London, Constable.

Sears, J. (1995), *Crimewatch* and the rhetoric of versimilitude, *Critical Survey*, 7:1, 51–8.

Seiter, E. (1992), Semiotics, structuralism, and television, in R. Allen (ed.), *Channels of Discourse, Reassembled: Television and Contemporary Criticism*, London, Routledge, 31–66.

Seiter, E., H. Borchers, G. Kreutzner and E-M. Warth (eds) (1989), *Remote Control: Television, Audiences and Cultural Power*, London, Routledge.

Selby, K. and R. Cowdery (1995), *How to Study Television*, London, Macmillan.

Shields, R. (ed.) (1996), *Cultures of the Internet*, London, Sage.

Sobchack, V. (1996), Democratic franchise and the electronic frontier, in Z. Sardar and J. Ravetz (eds), *Cyberfutures*, London, Pluto, 77–89.

Sparks, R. (1992), *Television and the Drama of Crime*, Buckingham, Oxford University Press.

Stam, R., R. Burgoyne and S. Flitterman-Lewis (1992), *New Vocabularies in Film Semiotics: Structuralism, Post-Structuralism and Beyond*, London, Routledge.

Stokes, J. (1999), Use it or lose it: sex, sexuality and sexual health in magazines for girls, in J. Stokes and A. Reading (eds), *The Media in Britain: Current Debates and Developments*, Basingstoke, Macmillan, 209–18.

Stokes, J. and A. Reading (eds) (1999), *The Media in Britain: Current Debates and Developments*, Basingstoke, Macmillan.

Storey, J. (1999), *Cultural Consumption and Everyday Life*, London, Arnold.

Thussu, K. D. (ed.) (1998), *Electronic Empires: Global Media and Local Resistance*, London, Arnold.

Tolson, A. (1996), *Mediations: Text and Discourse in Media Studies*, London, Arnold.

Tulloch, J. (1990), *Television Drama: Agency, Audience and Myth*, London, Routledge.

Tulloch, J. and H. Jenkins (1995), *Science Fiction Audiences: Watching Doctor Who and Star Trek*, London, Routledge.

Tunstall, J. (1983), *The Media in Britain*, London, Constable.

Turkle, S. (1995), *Life on the Screen: Identity in the Age of the Internet*, New York, Simon and Schuster.

Turner, G. (1993), *Film as Social Practice*, London, Routledge.

Umiker-Sebeok, J. (ed.) (1987), *Marketing and Semiology*, Amsterdam, Mouton de Gruyter.

van Dijk, T. (1988), *News as Discourse*, Hillsdale, Erlbaum.

Vestergaard, T. and Schrøeder, K. (1985), *The Language of Advertising*, Oxford, Blackwell.

Wagg, S. (ed.) (1998), *Because I Tell a Joke or Two: Comedy, Politics and Social Difference*, London, Routledge.

Webster, F. (1995), *Theories of the Information Society*, London, Routledge.

White, R. (1988), *Advertising: What It Is and How To Do It*, London, McGraw Hill.

Williamson, J. (1978), *Decoding Advertisements: Ideology and Meaning in Advertising*, London, Marion Boyars.

Winship, J. (1987), *Inside Women's Magazines*, London, Pandora.

Winston, B. (1995), *Claiming the Real: The Documentary Film Revisited*, London, BFI.

Winston, B. (1998), *Media Technology and Society: A History*, London, Routledge.

Whitaker, B. (1981), *News Limited: Why You Can't Read All About It*, London, Minority Press Group.

Woods, T. (1999), *Beginning Postmodernism*, Manchester, Manchester University Press.

Index

Numbers in *italics* refer to illustrations.